PRAISE FOR
THE FLAVOUR P(

'*The Flavour Point Diet* provides a sensible weight-management programme that is good for the whole family.'

James O. Hill, PhD, professor of paediatrics at the University
of Colorado and author of *The Step Diet Book*

'David Katz has a unique gift. He translates scientific knowledge about nutrition and weight loss into practical advice and day-by-day menus that help us reprogramme how to shop, eat and live. And he does it using good humour and real-life stories of success. A must-read for all, but particularly those frustrated by "breakthrough" and "fad" diets.'

Michael Parkinson, MD, MPH, president-elect of the
American College of Preventive Medicine

'*The Flavour Point Diet* is a science-based real-life (and real simple) programme written with the consumer in mind. It makes sense that our sensory overload extends from video and television screens to the table, but when people perceive weight loss as work, it's difficult to achieve. Dr Katz respects the temptations that surround us, but he shows you how to "get your house in order" and get on the weight-loss track.

'Allow yourself to be guided by the caring Dr Katz. *The Flavour Point Diet* is nutritionally balanced, full of ideas for easy meals and snacks, with great recipes, plus information about shopping, reading food labels, dining out in restaurants, plus good advice for making healthy choices wherever you go. This is a fun programme to follow . . . you can achieve your weight goal without dieting or deprivation.'

Susan Burke, MS, RD, LD/N, CDE, vice president of
nutrition services at eDiets.com

'Written by one of the most knowledgeable nutrition experts I know, this book uses the science on the biology and psychology of flavours to offer up one good idea after another for optimal eating.'

Kelly D. Brownell, PhD, chair and professor of psychology,
professor of epidemiology and public health, and director of
the Rudd Center for Food Policy & Obesity at Yale University

THE FLAVOUR POINT DIET

USE GREAT FLAVOURS TO CONTROL YOUR APPETITE
AND REDUCE YOUR WEIGHT – PERMANENTLY

DR DAVID L. KATZ

WITH

CATHERINE S. KATZ PHD

RODALE

This edition first published in the UK in 2006 by
Rodale International Ltd
7–10 Chandos Street
London W1G 9AD
www.rodalebooks.co.uk

Printed and bound in the UK by CPI Bath using acid-free paper from sustainable sources.

1 3 5 7 9 8 6 4 2

A CIP record for this book is available from the British Library

ISBN-13: 978-1-4050-9326-2
ISBN-10: 1-4050-9326-9

This paperback edition distributed to the book trade by Pan Macmillan Ltd

Notice
This book is intended as a reference volume only, not as a medical manual. The information given here is designed to help you make informed decisions about your health. It is not intended as a substitute for any treatment that you may have been prescribed by your doctor. If you suspect that you have a medical problem, we urge you to seek competent medical help.

Mention of specific companies, organizations or authorities in this book does not imply endorsement by the publisher, nor does mention of specific companies, organizations or authorities in the book imply that they endorse the book.

Addresses, websites and telephone numbers given in this book were accurate at the time the book went to press.

On behalf of my family – Rebecca, Corinda, Valerie, Natalia and Gabriel; Catherine and myself – I dedicate *The Flavour Point Diet* to your family. Because in unity there is strength. Because weight loss and lasting weight control should come about through the pursuit of health – and health should be a family affair. So here's to you, your success and good health – and the same for those who love you and share your journey.

CONTENTS

ACKNOWLEDGEMENTS

While two people can conceive a baby, and one person alone can bear and deliver that baby, it has been said it takes a village to enable that baby to develop, mature and thrive. This is true of books as well.

I may take much personal credit (or blame, should any see it that way) for the concept of *The Flavour Point Diet*. And certainly, I have laboured over its embryonic development for years. (The gestational period of books is longer than that of people!) But for inspiring the concept in the first place, refining it, maturing it and taking something as ephemeral as an idea and turning it into something as tangible as a book, I have depended on, and owe thanks to, a veritable village full of colleagues.

The first of these I want to acknowledge is my literary agent, Rick Broadhead. Rick is thoughtful and wise, careful and meticulous, enthusiastic and supportive, practical and candid. He has been the ideal agent and has become a friend. I am very pleased to have found him (or vice versa) before he becomes too busy and successful to have time for me. To any aspiring authors out there – this guy's the best.

I am grateful to Mariska van Aalst, my editor at Rodale, for seeing more in my book proposal than was actually there; for helping me identify the book I was looking to write; and for her faith that I could then write it! Mariska really has been more than the book's editor – she has been a confidante, friend and trusted advisor at every step of its development. All this while having a baby (of the human variety). So my heartfelt thanks to Mariska for her vision and support, along with my congratulations to her and her family.

I owe special thanks to Alisa Bauman, who stepped in while Mariska was out on maternity leave. If I and my book were a baton, Alisa took hold in a smooth pass and then went on to run a magnificent leg of this relay race. A great deal that is good in the book is directly thanks to Alisa, who edited every line with a masterful eye for clarity. Any line or passage that is less good or unclear than it should be is doubtless something Alisa tried unsuccessfully to talk me out of!

I am grateful to Sumiya Khan, MS, RD, and Dina Aronson, MS, RD, for their invaluable contribution of nutritional analyses. I am proud that *The Flavour Point Diet* conforms to the very highest standards of nutrition throughout, and it's thanks to Sumiya and Dina that I can say that with confidence and back it up with data. To Dina, I add thanks, on behalf of Catherine especially, for becoming a genuine and much-relied-upon partner in this venture. We simply couldn't have done it without you. Thanks.

I am indebted to the many nutrition professionals from whom I have learned so much throughout my career and who conducted the research upon which *The Flavour Point Diet* is based. First and foremost, I thank Barbara Rolls, PhD, of Penn State University. Professor Rolls is a true luminary in the fields of appetite and weight regulation. Her research over years and decades is an eloquent and elegant demonstration of the power of science to confront and overcome challenges in human health. Much of what we all know about appetite and its control is thanks to the prolific work of Professor Rolls.

I thank Professor Linda Bartoshuk, my Yale colleague and one of the world's leading authorities on taste perception, for inspiring my interest in the power of food flavour over appetite – and for directing me to the work of Professor Rolls many years ago. I acknowledge, as well, but will not name for fear of unpardonable omissions, the many colleagues, mentors, teachers, friends and predecessors who have enriched the field of nutrition and weight control with their contributions. In any effort to reach a new height or attain a new vista, we stand on the shoulders of others. I thank you all for holding me up.

Special thanks to the 20 participants in our pilot test of the Flavour Point Diet. You'll hear from them throughout the book – but here, I want them to hear from me. I am indebted to you all. I extend my appreciation to Michelle Larovera and Dr Zubaida Faridi, of the Yale Prevention Research Center, who managed the pilot test with such grace, good cheer and professionalism.

My wife, Catherine, ever my partner, best friend, best editor, harshest critic and staunchest supporter, is my collaborating author. I cannot hope to thank her as she deserves. She has taken my theories of nutrition and translated them into a delightful, delicious, real-world practicality. She did that first for the fortunate members of the Katz household. She does that now for you. We can both be grateful to her for that. I, of course, owe her far more, for she fills my life with joy and love and meaning every day.

On behalf of Catherine, as well as myself, I offer thanks to our children: Rebecca, Corinda, Valerie, Natalia and Gabriel. They helped in the kitchen and taste-tested the many Flavour Point trials – and occasional Flavour Point errors! And they did it all with good cheer, esprit de corps and enthusiasm. But more importantly, these terrific kids turned over both of their parents to the care and nurturing of a book for many months. While this didn't quite turn them into orphans, it certainly did come at a cost to them. If they ever complained about that cost, I can't recall. So thanks, gang – we love you. And we have some together time to make up to you!

Thanks as well to my parents, Susan and Don Katz, for their never-wavering faith and support – and their timely attention to our children! They are the likely reason *Flavour Point* did not induce more disgruntlement among the Katz kids.

On behalf of this collaborating village, I am proud to present *The Flavour Point Diet*. All members deserve credit for its merits and whatever good it accomplishes. But should any omissions, deficiencies, errors or mis-statements be discerned, responsibility for them resides with me.

INTRODUCTION

MIND OVER APPETITE

Tapping into the Flavour Point will revolutionize the way you think about eating

At some point during every eating experience, we all begin to feel full and *fulfilled*. When you reach that point of fulfilment – what I call the *Flavour Point* – you stop eating. If you reach the Flavour Point early enough, you will feel full and fulfilled on fewer calories. If you reach the Flavour Point too late, you overeat.

How do you reach the Flavour Point more quickly and fill up on fewer calories?

That's what the Flavour Point Diet is all about. This revolutionary diet taps into this little-known but scientifically proven fact: flavour variety stimulates the appetite centre in your brain, while flavour repetition soothes it. You can eat a variety of flavours over time, but eating too many flavours at any *one* time puts your brain's appetite centre into overdrive.

Let that sink in for a minute. It's every bit as profound, powerful and life changing as it is simple. To safely and permanently lose weight without being hungry, you need only organize the flavours in your meals and snacks. Don't misunderstand me, though. You don't need to give up flavours. You don't need to give up specific foods or entire categories of foods. You don't need to give up the joy of eating delicious food, and you certainly don't need to give up the convenience of easy-to-prepare foods.

THE POWER OF FLAVOUR ORGANIZATION

From breakfast cereals to snack foods to fast foods, our culinary land-scape has become crowded with an overabundance of conflicting flavours that overstimulate important appetite-controlling cells in our brains, making us need more and more food to reach the Flavour Point. For example, many sweet breakfast cereals contain as much salt as potato crisps. Yes, salt! Conversely, salty snack foods often include lots of sugar. You don't always notice all of these flavours when you eat, but your brain registers their presence, triggering hunger and overeating.

When you taste too many flavours at once – whether from too many different foods or too many flavours processed into one food – you overeat before feeling full. On the other hand, when you organize flavours in your diet, you feel full and satisfied on fewer calories and lose weight *without feeling hungry*. Quite simply, you will *want* to eat less!

The Flavour Point Diet subdues appetite on two levels. First, it uses the powerful benefits of flavour themes to subtly organize your eating. These themes infuse your meals with a specific flavour, such as orange or choco-late or pineapple. When you taste this flavour repeatedly throughout your day, you more quickly satisfy your brain's appetite centre so you're able to fill up on fewer calories. Second, you'll shift to a new way of eating – to the Flavour Point way of eating. You'll learn how to choose and cook deli-cious meals using relatively simple, wholesome, minimally processed foods that don't contain an overabundance of extraneous flavours.

Over the next 6 weeks and beyond, the Flavour Point Diet will change your appetite, your weight, your appearance, your health, your relation-ship with food and your life – for good. The plan comprises three phases.

Phase 1. During the first 4 weeks of the meal plan, you'll drape a del-icate flavour theme over your meals for an entire day, with every meal and snack sharing a common ingredient. On Cranberry Day, for example, you'll eat delicious cranberry-banana muffins for breakfast, a salad with cranberries for lunch, cranberry and onion turkey breast for dinner, and Cranberry-Vanilla Soft Ice Cream for dessert. On Pineapple Day, you'll have a pineapple smoothie for breakfast, Pineapple-Walnut Chicken Salad for lunch and Pineapple Prawns for dinner. On Lemon Day, you'll have lemon-poppy muffins for breakfast, Lemon Tabbouleh Salad for lunch, and lemon-flavoured fish for dinner.

FLAVOUR FLUENCY

SENSORY-SPECIFIC SATIETY: The tendency to feel full and stop eating when flavours are limited and to stay hungry and keep eating when flavours are diverse.

This subtle yet repeated exposure to the same flavours will subdue your appetite centre in a delicious and powerful way. But you won't eat enough of the flavour of the day for it to feel monotonous. Instead, your appetite centre will merely register the flavour and, as a result, feel soothed and contented.

Phase 2. As you get into the habit of choosing and preparing foods according to Flavour Point principles, you won't need to depend on the daily flavour themes as much to control your appetite. In other words, as your mastery increases, you'll need fewer rules. This is why, during weeks 5 and 6, the meal plan includes a greater variety of daily flavours. In this phase, each meal or snack has a theme, but there's no single theme throughout the day. Thus, the flavour theme for your breakfast will not be the same as the one for your lunch, and each of those will differ from dinner. For instance, breakfast might have a lemon theme, lunch a basil theme and dinner a tomato theme. In each meal, the flavours are subtle but effective, harmonizing the food – and your appetite.

Phase 3. The Flavour Point Meal Plan guides you through 6 weeks of weight loss by using flavour themes for each day during the first 4 weeks and then for each meal during weeks 5 and 6. After that, you'll be ready for Phase 3 – the beginning of the rest of your life! Phase 3 is permanent, using flavour management at the level of individual foods. We provide examples to get you launched, but then, with the habits you've acquired, the knowledge you've gained and the principles you've mastered, you'll be ready for lifelong Flavour Point success. During Phase 3, you'll continue to lose weight until you reach your goal, and then you'll keep it off.

In Chapter 6, you'll find lots of tips to help you adhere to the Flavour Point principles once you've graduated from the school of flavour themes.

From the first day to the last on the meal plan, you will consume a perfectly balanced, healthy diet. You could stay on any phase of the meal plan forever – it's that good for you. As a doctor, preventive medicine specialist and parent, I wouldn't have it any other way. I am not a 'diet doctor'; I am a doctor who happens to be an expert on diet and nutrition. No matter how important weight loss may be to you, your overall health – and that of your family – is what matters most to me.

DOES THIS REALLY WORK?

As I was putting the finishing touches to this book, many people asked me, somewhat sceptically, 'Can flavour themes really subdue appetite?' Am I proposing something radical? Inventing a theory? Going out on a limb? Defying my academic colleagues? Not at all.

Under the scientific-sounding name *sensory-specific satiety*, the Flavour Point's main concept has been appearing in the scientific literature for nearly 3 decades. It has been percolating near the surface of dietary guidance, but its full potential for weight control simply wasn't recognized – until now. Although this meal plan is unique, the science is tried and true.

In Chapter 1, you'll learn how millions of years of evolution have hardwired this trait into the appetite centre of the brain of every human on the planet. If you've ever overeaten, however, you may already understand how it works. Have you ever enjoyed a delicious holiday feast and eaten until you felt stuffed? Did each bite taste slightly less delicious than the bite before, especially as you became more and more full? Did the main course eventually completely lose its appeal? At some point, did you put your hand on your stomach and groan, 'I'm so full I couldn't eat another bite!' And in the next breath ask, 'What's for dessert?'

Yep, you found room for dessert, didn't you? Me, too! It wasn't because of that hollow leg or extra stomach that some wisecracking relative referred to. It was because of sensory-specific satiety. You had filled up on the savoury flavours provided by the main dishes but not on the sweet flavour of dessert.

As you'll soon learn, each flavour we eat stimulates a different set of cells in the brain. Sweet flavours stimulate one area of the brain's appetite centre, salty another and sour yet another. Once you turn on an area of the appetite centre, you must eat until those cells register fullness. If you turn on many areas at once, you must eat much more food before you feel full. Turn on just one or two areas, and you'll eat less but feel just as satisfied.

I owe a lot to the scientists who have studied sensory-specific satiety during the past several decades. As soon as I learned about it, the power of it was immediately obvious, and I began applying it to my diet and those of my patients. Although many scientists have documented this phenomenon over the years, the Flavour Point Diet is the first to use sensory-specific satiety to enable long-term weight control without hunger.

In my work at Yale, as well as in my private practice, I've now counselled hundreds of patients who desperately wanted to lose weight. When they came to me, most of them knew what they needed to do to shed weight. They knew they should eat less and exercise more, but they couldn't figure out how to do it. Each time they went on a diet, they lost some weight. Eventually, though, their cravings and hunger would win out, they'd break the diet, and they'd gain the weight back – and usually more.

When I taught these patients about sensory-specific satiety and how to use Flavour Point principles to subdue appetite, weight management without hunger suddenly became feasible for them. They would tell me that for the first time in their lives, they had no difficulty holding themselves to reasonable portions. They finally were able to enjoy eating without guilt. It changed their lives and those of their families. I observed this over and over, using each experience to refine the Flavour Point plan – and here you have the culmination of that work.

Recently, I asked 20 men and women to test the meal plan you'll find in this book. Some wanted to lose just a few pounds or a kilogram or two; others wanted to lose much more. They came from all walks of life and included stay-at-home mums, working mothers and fathers, and singles. Most shared one trait: they were busy and didn't have time for complicated meal preparation.

Their results, after 12 weeks on the plan, just blew me away. On average, they lost over 7.2 kg/16 lb. (One gentleman lost 14 kg/31 lb!) Their blood cholesterol levels dropped an average of 0.36 points. Blood pressure, blood sugar and other health indicators also improved. They lost an average of 9 cm/3½ in off their waists. Not only did their clothes fit better but they also felt more energetic, slept better at night and experienced fewer cravings. Most important, they *loved* the food – and so did their spouses and children, who in many cases also lost weight and improved their health. Officially, they weren't even on the diet.

The study participants told me that their cravings for certain foods changed, too. After 12 weeks, even the most hard-core junk-food junkies among them preferred this new way of eating. Take a look at some of their comments.

- 'I'm full and definitely satisfied on this programme. I had a little bit of dessert the other night – and that's all I wanted. It actually tasted too sweet!'
- 'Not only are the foods delicious, but I don't have heartburn any more!'
- 'I actually look forward to eating dinner every night. The food is excellent. I love this programme, and I think I could eat like this forever.'

FLAVOUR FLUENCY

THE FLAVOUR POINT: The point when the flavours in your food fill up the appetite centre in your brain, subduing hunger and appetite. In the part of the brain called the hypothalamus, each of us has a number of specialized cells that respond to flavour. Think of those cells as a series of meters, measuring from empty to full. Each meter responds to a particular taste, from sweet to sour, salty to savoury, and everything in between. Whenever you turn on an appetite meter, it must register fullness before it switches off again. The fewer meters you turn on, the less you will eat before you feel full and satisfied – and the sooner you will reach the Flavour Point.

Those study participants followed an extended 12-week version of the Flavour Point plan. I've streamlined it for you. In this book, you'll find 6 weeks' worth of mouthwatering, simple, convenient, appetite-subduing meals. These meals have helped me, my family, my friends and my patients fill up on fewer calories – enjoying food as well as the satisfaction of lasting weight control. Now they will do the same for you!

Results from the Flavour Point

Our group of testers, 20 in all, tried the Flavour Point Diet for 12 weeks, and their results were amazing. Not only did they lose weight, feel more energetic and experience fewer cravings, several key measures of their health improved dramatically. Check out some stats from the Flavour Point.

	AVERAGE	MOST CHANGED
Kg/lb lost:	7.6/16.7	14/31
Change in BMI:	−2.7	−4.2
Cm/in off of waist:	9/3.5	18/7
Percentage body fat lost:	4.82	8
Blood pressure points dropped:	11.4	28
Reduction in resting heart rate (beats per minute):	4.86	12
Total points cholesterol lowered (mmol/L):	0.36	1.87
Fasting blood glucose lowered (mmol/L):	0.062	0.825

Satisfaction at the Flavour Point

> **THE FLAVOUR FACTS**
>
> Name: Debbie Vashlishan
>
> Age: 50
>
> Family status: Married with two children, aged 24 and 25
>
> Occupation: Registered nurse
>
> Starting weight: 91 kg/14 st 5 lb
>
> Weight lost: 7.7 kg/17 lb in 12 weeks
>
> Health stats: Blood pressure dropped 16 points; resting heart rate improved; waist measurement shrank 9 cm/$3^1/_2$ in; 5 per cent decline in body fat

'I gained weight slowly and steadily over the years. It eventually crept up to about 14 st [90 kg]. I knew I needed to make a lifestyle change, so when I heard a few women discussing Dr Katz's new programme, I was intrigued and decided to go for it. I was thrilled when I heard I'd been chosen.

'My husband has been doing the programme with me, and he actually lost more weight than I did in the first 12 weeks – $1^3/_4$ st [11.3 kg]. More important, he's been able to cut his blood pressure medication dosage in half.

'Health improvements aside, we're eating good, healthy foods – and they taste great! I'm discovering many new seasonings, like curry, that I really enjoy. Also, many of the vinegars and oils included in the plan add wonderful flavour to the recipes. I don't feel hungry on this programme, and my cravings are gone. When I first heard about the flavour themes, I thought, "We're going to eat apples for a whole day? No way!" Eventually, I realized the other foods mixed in with the theme of the day, like nuts and chicken, keep you from getting sick of it. The concept really works.

'Both my husband and I love the recipes. I have actually served some of the dishes to guests because they're so tasty. On my days off, I make the French toast or muffins for breakfast. The Pumpkin and Chocolate Grilled Panini is one of my favourite lunch recipes, as well as the peanut butter and peach jam sandwich. I had the sandwich on Easter Sunday – I made it and took it to work, and I couldn't wait to go to lunch to have that sandwich.

'For dinner, the pastas are great, and my daughter loves the chicken in Dijon "creamy" mushroom sauce. My husband and I aren't big fish eaters, but we like cod, so we substitute that for tuna and salmon, and it works just fine.

'For a snack, the fruit smoothies are both refreshing and filling. I also like the muesli. We went hiking with another couple the other day, and I made individual baggies of a muesli mix with nuts and apricots. It was plenty to get us all through the hike.

'The main dishes and snacks are satisfying enough, but there are also a bunch of good desserts on the programme. We love Baked Bananas with Rum-Pecan Topping, amaretto strawberry salad, Brownies, and Peach Flat Cake. And who ever heard of indulgence days on a diet? I've done the chocolate day twice, and I plan to try the coconut day in the future.

'I've also learned some handy tricks I'll take with me forever. I now use olive oil on veggies instead of butter or cheese. Instead of spreading mayonnaise on a sandwich, I use hummus. I also carry a container of powdered milk in my handbag wherever I go to use in my coffee.

'It feels wonderful to have so many people tell me I look good and that my face looks thinner. My clothes fit much better, I have much more energy, and it's a little weird, but I've also noticed that my fingernails are stronger. Both my husband and I love Dr Katz's programme and are going to stick with it indefinitely.' ■

DELICIOUS AND EFFECTIVE

In this diet, the pleasures of eating food that's good and food that's good for you can – and do – come together. The joys of food and of lasting weight control and good health are not mutually exclusive! When you commit to the Flavour Point Diet, you commit to a diet that:

Delivers lasting weight loss. Based on the results of the people who tested the Flavour Point Diet before this book went to press, you can expect to lose 4 to 7.2 kg/9 to 16 lb in 6 weeks and continue losing weight until you reach your goal. The Flavour Point Diet isn't one that you go on and off of. Rather, it provides a simple and easy transition to a new way of choosing and organizing foods – forever.

Not only helps you shed fat but also improves your health. Every step of the way, the pattern of foods and nutrients you will consume is as good or better than government recommendations and the advice of leading experts in the treatment of cancer, diabetes and heart disease.

Liberates you from the bondage of shunning certain so-called fattening foods. At no point does this diet restrict any foods. At no point does it place a whole nutrient category off-limits. Because the Flavour Point Diet is not based on food exclusions – that's right, there are *none* – each phase of the plan is balanced, sane, delicious, healthy and in step with the very best of modern nutrition science.

Allows you and your entire family to lose weight together. Unlike so many diets out there, the Flavour Point Diet is safe for your whole family. Yes, your kids can follow it with you. Yes, it's safe during pregnancy. Yes, it's fine while breastfeeding. Yes, it's appropriate if you have diabetes. Yes, anyone can follow this diet at any time. It is safe for life.

Makes healthy eating quick and easy. The Flavour Point Diet replaces the convenient processed and fast foods that trigger overeating with foods that trigger fullness and are just as convenient and delicious. Many breakfasts and lunches in the Flavour Point Meal Plan take 5 minutes or less to prepare. Many dinners take 15 minutes or less.

Puts the joy back into eating. The Flavour Point Meal Plan includes incredibly delicious meals, snacks and desserts. In fact, you can eat dessert every night if you are so inclined!

Flavour management makes all this possible. You're about to embark on an exciting journey to a slimmer, healthier you. In Chapters 1 and 2, you'll discover the science behind the meal plan. In Chapter 3, you'll find out how the meal plan works. Chapters 4 and 5 bring you the Flavour Point Meal Plan and corresponding recipes. Finally, in Chapter 6, you'll find out how to move on to Phase 3 and maintain the Flavour Point way of eating for life.

Since the food is delicious and the nutrition stellar every step of the way, why would you ever go off this plan? If, after 6 weeks, you find that you have lost a lot of weight (you will), are feeling great (you'll see) and are loving the food (just wait) – why on Earth would you ever look back? You won't. The next 6 weeks and beyond will change your whole relationship with food, and your body, forever.

PART 1

THE SCIENCE

1

MEET YOUR
APPETITE CENTRE

Until now, your brain has controlled
your food choices. Soon, your food
choices will control your brain!

Study after study points to this indisputable but little-known fact: the more foods and flavours we humans taste, the more we must eat to feel satisfied. The fewer foods and flavours we taste, the less we eat and the more satisfied we feel on fewer calories.

We are, quite simply, hardwired to want variety in our diets. We're hardwired to get fed up with eating the same food again and again. We're hardwired to rediscover hunger when some new flavour opportunity comes along.

This hardwiring, however, doesn't require that we all suffer a boring culinary existence in order to remain slim. No, you don't need to eat the same food over and over again – although that tactic certainly would work. Rather, by using the science of sensory-specific satiety to your advantage, you can enjoy delicious meals and still lose weight without hunger. The Flavour Point Diet will show you how. You will consume a variety of flavours over time, just not an excessive variety all at one time.

Once you understand how to use this concept to your advantage, you can lower your Flavour Point – the point at which you feel satisfied and stop eating – and automatically eat less and lose weight. Once you do, you'll never again find yourself out of control, mindlessly shovelling forkful after forkful of food into your mouth.

WHY WE OVEREAT

The most important, prevalent and powerful reason we eat and overeat is sensory delight: we do it because we see, smell and taste food. You, along with every other human, have a sensory relay system that connects your mouth to your brain, your brain to your stomach, and your stomach back to your brain. Ultimately, your brain is in charge of your eating behaviour. It controls what you eat and what you like to eat. As soon as you taste food, the sensory information registers in the hypothalamus in the brain, which, depending on the flavour of the food, sends out signals to eat more or eat less. Because of this sensory relay system, the appetite centre in your hypothalamus can become aroused – and in some cases overly aroused – by how a food tastes.

If you can reach the Flavour Point with fewer calories, you can feel just as full and satisfied but also be thinner. Getting your brain to tell your mind, and your mouth, 'That will do; I'm satisfied' with fewer calories is what the Flavour Point Diet is all about.

To learn how to work with your appetite centre, you must first understand it. It's time for you and your brain to become better acquainted.

As soon as you bite into any food, sensory stimulation of nerve endings on the tongue leads to the release of a number of chemicals, including opioids, into the bloodstream. You release more opioids – the body's natural versions of drugs like morphine – when you consume foods high in sugar and fat, creating a powerful, neurochemical drive to overeat those foods. These opioids and other chemicals enter the bloodstream and carry their messages to the hypothalamus, which sends out yet another set of chemicals to regulate appetite. The more flavours your taste buds register, the more stimulated the hypothalamus becomes, releasing the hunger promoting hormone neuropeptide Y. When you taste a lot of flavours at once, the brain releases a lot of neuropeptide Y.

Meanwhile, in response to the smell and taste of food, your stomach produces the hormone ghrelin, which also stimulates appetite. It continues to produce this hormone until you eat enough food to literally fill your stomach and stretch the stomach wall. Further down the line, in your intestines, levels of several hormones rise to varying degrees – depending on the nature of your meal – either inducing more hunger or turning off hunger.

To understand how your food choices can influence this complex chain of events, let's take a closer look at how this all works by comparing the neurochemical response to two foods you might eat for breakfast: a sausage, egg and cheese muffin sandwich and a bowl of porridge.

FLAVOUR FLUENCY

SATIATION: The point at which you feel full, stop eating and push back from the table. *Satiety* is the state of feeling full and satisfied.

In the mouth: The mix of sugar, fat and salt in the egg sandwich triggers the release of more opioids than the porridge does. These opioids create a powerful, neurochemical drive to eat more sandwich.

In the brain: The sandwich's sausage, egg, cheese and muffin offer many varied tastes, causing neuropeptide Y – and hunger – to surge. The simple flavours of the porridge result in the release of much less neuropeptide Y.

In the stomach: The sandwich delivers a lot of calories in a small package. It doesn't stimulate the stomach's stretch receptors nearly as quickly as the porridge, allowing ghrelin levels to remain high long after you've overeaten. You must eat many more egg sandwich calories than porridge calories before the stomach wall registers fullness.

In the intestines: The highly processed sandwich bread less effectively suppresses hunger-producing hormones than does the porridge, again leaving you feeling hungry despite the abundance of calories.

(continued on page 8)

Satisfaction at the Flavour Point

THE FLAVOUR FACTS

Name: Lisa Seaberg

Age: 30

Family status: Single

Occupation: Communication specialist

Starting weight: 74 kg/11 st 9 lb

Weight lost: 5.4 kg/12 lb in 12 weeks

Health stats: Blood pressure dropped 15 points; waist measurement shrank 5 cm/2 in; 8 per cent decline in body fat

'I was never obese, but I come from a family of fat people, and I was well on my way to becoming heavy myself. During the past 3 to 4 years, I gained 20 lb [9 kg]. I had already read Dr Katz's first book and found it offered some great advice, so I decided to try his programme.

'Before I started, my diet wasn't terrible, but it was unbalanced. I usually ate a decent breakfast (porridge and coffee). For lunch, however, I ate whatever the cafeteria was serving, whether it was chicken or macaroni cheese. Sometimes I would skip dinner and just have a bowl of cereal or an egg, or I would buy dinner out. I live by myself, so it didn't seem worthwhile for me to cook a whole meal. Being a big chocoholic, I ate a chocolate bar every day after lunch.

'Dr Katz's programme has not only taught me how to cook well for myself, it has also taught me to enjoy doing it. I actually shocked all my friends because I was notorious for not cooking (I actually used my oven for a storage space for a while). Now I'm totally comfortable with cooking. I actually find it fun!

'On most days, I stick to the meal plan for breakfast, lunch and dinner because I really like trying the new dishes. I try to swap the days so I can have the omelettes on the weekend (they are my favourites for breakfast). For lunch, I love the different variations of the spinach-lentil salads, but my favourite is the dill chicken salad. For dinner, the

Prawn Pasta Primavera is the one I keep going back to the most.

'Snack-wise, I tend to go for the fresh fruit most often. I never cared much for fruit before, but now I enjoy it.

'One of the best parts is that even though I'm losing weight, I feel like I'm eating more food than ever before. I always liked healthy foods (for instance, I was already eating wholewheat pasta), but I didn't know how to incorporate them into my diet in a realistic way. Now I do.

'The most surprising change? I haven't craved the chocolate after lunch. I have to admit I was happy to see the chocolate day on the menu, but I haven't had the urge to break down and have a chocolate bar.

'Not only have I changed my eating habits with this programme, I've also made a concerted effort to become more active. I joined the YMCA for the fitness facilities, and I go skating and take karate classes. I also rescued my bike from beneath a pile of wood in my mum's garage.

I feel like it doesn't make sense to change the way I eat without changing my activity level as well.

'And it's all paying off. I feel so much better physically and mentally. I have more energy and a greater sense of wellbeing, and I'm no longer falling asleep at my desk at 3 or 4 in the afternoon. Other people have noticed the change in me. One of my colleagues said my face was getting thinner, and I guess it inspired her. She came in to work the next day and said she had exercised after work because she was motivated by how good I look.

'Even though I've finished my initial 12 weeks, I've been sticking with the programme and planning what I'm going to eat every day (so I don't get hungry and decide to order a pizza). The structure is a good thing for me, especially because I love the foods! And because Dr Katz's programme is working so well, I've been talking it up a lot. I would recommend it to anyone. Thanks, Dr Katz!' ■

┌─ **Flavour Pointer** ─┐

TASTE TRIGGERS AND THE FOOD INDUSTRY'S SMOKING GUN

The food industry puts sugar, salt and fat – all potent appetite stimulators – to very good use.

Humans prefer sweet tastes from birth, which is why the industry processes sugar, with a variety of often misleading names (such as high-fructose corn syrup), into most packaged foods. Don't expect a food with added sugar to taste sweet, though. Just enough sugar is added to trigger your appetite but not quite enough for you to notice that your potato crisps are sweet as well as salty.

You'll also find salt in most processed foods. Sweet foods, such as desserts and breakfast cereals, have just enough salt to taunt your appetite centre but not quite enough for you to notice it.

Fat, or oil, doesn't add taste directly, but it enhances the delivery of other tastes, so foods that don't really need to have sugar or added fat generally have both, delivering a large blow to your hapless hypothalamus!

Whenever you see these taste triggers in places they really don't need to be, you are staring at the food industry's smoking gun: wilful manipulation of the food supply to encourage, and even coerce, you to eat more than you should!

In the bloodstream: The stomach and intestines quickly convert the simple starch and sugar in the white bread into glucose, or blood sugar. The glucose seeps through the intestinal wall and into the bloodstream, sending blood sugar levels up. In response, the pancreas overproduces insulin, which moves glucose from the blood into muscles and other tissues. The insulin quickly drives down blood sugar, leading to more hunger.

On the other hand, the fibre in the porridge dissolves in water inside the intestines, where it creates a barrier through which nutrients must pass to get into the bloodstream, thus slowing the entrance of glucose into the blood. The result is a slower, lower rise in blood sugar; a slower release of insulin; no rapid surge and dip in blood sugar levels; and lasting fullness.

As you can see, what you eat has a powerful ability to influence how much you must eat to feel full and satisfied. You can't think yourself thin, as some books in the past have claimed. But by organizing the flavours in your foods, you *can* manipulate this complex series of chemicals and subdue the appetite centre in your brain sooner, before you've overeaten.

THE EVOLUTION OF APPETITE

The secret behind the Flavour Point Diet is this simple fact: our appetites are stimulated by flavour variety and lulled by flavour consistency. Why do we eat more when flavours are diverse? The answer to that question can be found deep in human history and dates back to our hunting and gathering days.

The sweetness of chocolate, the saltiness of a pickle, the sourness of a lemon and the bitterness of broccoli all affect the brain differently. Exactly how the human brain responds to these flavours is a product of millions of years of evolution. Our taste buds developed and evolved not to keep us happy but to keep us alive. They perform a vital function by assessing flavour, indicating what we should and shouldn't eat.

Over millions of years, our evolutionary biology has trained us to enjoy foods that keep us alive and abhor foods that don't. Most humans love sweet tastes, for example, and generally don't like bitter ones; one reason for this is that nature's poisons often come in bitter packages, while sweet foods are rarely if ever toxic.

We've also learned to delight in sweet tastes because sweet foods provided the calories our early ancestors needed to stay alive. The best source of fuel they could burn quickly to chase down an antelope or flee from a sabre-toothed tiger was sugar, found in nature in fruit and honey. The survival advantage of eating foods containing sugar has translated over the eons of natural selection into a strong preference for foods that taste sweet.

A Proclivity for Salt

Most of us prefer salty foods. In fact, without salt, food is often unpalatably bland. Why? Sodium was abundantly available in the oceans of our earliest origins and is thus a resource readily made use of in our physiology. A vital constituent of blood, sodium regulates the trans-membrane electrical potential that makes the nervous system work. This isn't because sodium is unique in its ability to perform these functions. Rather, it was an expedient choice as natural selection meandered haphazardly along, exploiting what was at hand.

When some distant cousin of ours grew tired of the incessant wet and decided land was the way to go, salt took on new significance. Because that expatriate from the briny deep didn't leave his or her metabolism in the sea, sodium remained a key constituent of animal physiology, even though it was suddenly and drastically less abundant. That, among other things, was the cost of drying out: salt was essential but hard to find.

So we can thank our earliest land-dwelling ancestors for our proclivity for potato crisps, pretzels and pickles. We like salt. We seek salt. We always have.

Accounts from ancient Rome, for example, tell of nobles who were kidnapped and held for a ransom of salt and spices. The word *salary* comes from the Latin word for salt – *salarium* – because Roman soldiers were paid partly with this rare and precious commodity. Salzburg, Austria, may evoke scenes from *The Sound of Music*, but the name means 'Salt City', attesting to a historically vital resource the region happens to provide.

Much as we might think there is something intrinsically delicious about sugar, it's not really so. 'Delicious' is simply how our brains interpret certain specific sensations our taste buds register as they interact with the chemical properties of food in our mouths. We learned to think of sugar as delicious because it helped our ancestors survive. Those of our ancestors who liked the tastes linked to survival – foods generally rich in sugar, salt and/or fat and free of toxins – lived into adulthood and made babies. Those who didn't like such foods generally did neither.

Not only specific flavours but also a variety of flavours helped us survive. No one food houses all of the vitamins, minerals and phytochemicals the human body needs to survive. Our early ancestors who got bored with berries – even if they were plentiful – and foraged for seeds and other foods consumed the variety of nutrients they needed to reproduce and pass on their genes to future generations. The early humans who ate berry after berry after berry – and nothing else – tended not to reproduce and pass on their genes. In this way, the traits and tendencies conducive to survival, favoured by natural selection and encoded in our genes, have been passed down through the generations.

THE SCIENCE OF APPETITE

Sensory-specific satiety has been under study for decades; it's amazing, really, that hardly anyone has even heard of it. In fact, when I lecture to my fellow physicians and academic colleagues, I routinely ask who in the audience has heard of this critically important trait. If one hand out of hundreds ever goes up, it's generally someone who has heard me lecture before.

Yet sensory-specific satiety is nothing new. As I was writing this book, I searched the medical literature for every mention of every study done on the topic. I found hundreds. The earliest mention that I could find dates from 1981, the very early days of the current obesity epidemic. Articles on closely related topics date back even further, to the mid-1970s.

I won't overwhelm you by listing all of the studies I found. I do, however, want to share four of the more compelling ones with you.

Satisfaction at the Flavour Point

THE FLAVOUR FACTS

Name: Maureen McGowan

Age: 33

Family status: Recently married

Occupation: Multiskilled technician

Starting weight: 95 kg/14 st 13 lb

Weight lost: 7.6 kg/17 lb in 12 weeks

Health stats: Energy level increased;
    waist measurement shrank
    12 cm/4½ in

'I found out about Dr Katz's programme at the perfect time – about 6 months before my wedding.

'My problem was not overeating; I just used to eat all the wrong foods. Pizza, cheese, steaks, hamburgers and hot dogs were all regular staples of my diet.

'I was at my thinnest when I was in the army. Then, I only ate three meals a day and exercised constantly. When I got out of the military in 1995, I put on 40 lb [18 kg] pretty fast.

'I tried many different programmes in attempts to lose weight, but I always felt like I was starving. I'm not hungry at all on this programme. It always seems like it's time to eat again – you have your breakfast, then a snack like fruit, then your lunch, then a snack like a fruit smoothie, and then it's time for dinner. 'A lot of times, I'm not even hungry for my night-time

- In the mid-1980s, Barbara Rolls, PhD, then at Johns Hopkins University in Baltimore, and some colleagues gave 24 women a test meal of either soup or jelly. Some of the meals were high in calories, while others were low in calories. They all, however, tasted the same. An hour after the test meal, the researchers offered cheese and crackers to the study participants. They all ate roughly the same amount of cheese and crackers regardless of how many calories of soup or jelly they had eaten just an hour before. Why? Sensory-specific satiety. The cheese and snack. I don't feel like I'm depriving myself at all, and I see the weight dropping off, which is motivating.

'On Dr Katz's programme, not only do I feel like I'm eating a lot, but I'm eating much better than I used to, and I really do enjoy these recipes. I enjoy the chicken dinners, and even though I'm not a fish eater, I really like the prawn dishes. And I *love* the Pineapple Prawns.

'One of the best things about Dr Katz's programme is that I'm changing my overall eating habits. It's not a diet; it's a lifestyle change. Instead of butter, I'm using a healthy spread. Instead of vegetable oil, I'm using olive oil. I'm eating wholewheat pasta instead of regular pasta (and I don't even notice a difference!). I'm also eating a ton of vegetables – fresh asparagus, broccoli, cauliflower, you name it. And I know these are all things I'll be able to do continuously.

'People have definitely noticed my weight loss, particularly at work. Personally, I can see that my face and bum are thinner. Luckily, I carry my weight pretty evenly, so it's coming off all over my body. I just got into a pair of jeans I haven't been able to wear in 3 years.

'I still need to lose another 20 to 30 lb [9 to 13.5 kg], so I'm going to keep up with Dr Katz's programme. I love the results I've got so far, and I'm looking forward to seeing more.' ■

crackers provided a new taste, stimulating another appetite meter in the brain that had to register 'full' before being turned off (see 'Flavour Fluency' on page 5).

- In another interesting study completed around the same time, researchers fed 16 men and 16 women meals that varied in taste and texture. The participants found sweet foods less pleasurable when they had recently eaten sweet foods and salty foods less pleasurable when they had recently eaten salty foods.

- In 2001, researchers studied six lean and six overweight men on a metabolic ward. They varied the foods the men could eat each day and then let the participants eat as much as they wanted. The greater the variety of foods the researchers provided on any given day, the more total calories the men consumed and the greater their weight the next day. In fact, the men ate as much as 25 per cent more calories when they had access to more foods. That's the equivalent of consuming 2,000 calories in a given day when you would normally eat only 1,600. Assuming you needed only 1,600 calories a day to maintain your weight, this type of daily excess would result in a gain of 16.5 kg/36½ lb a year.
- Most recently, in 2004, researchers studied the effects of sensory-specific satiety in 21 overweight and 23 lean women. The investigators offered the women lunch, followed about 90 minutes later by a snack. The researchers varied the flavours and fat content of the foods for each meal and found that flavour had a far greater effect on appetite than fat content did. When the flavours in the lunch and snack were similar, the women ate less. When the flavours varied more between the lunch and snack, the women ate more!

As you can see, variety is indeed the spice of life – and our nutritional lives are becoming way too spicy! We now have easy access to a far greater variety of foods and flavours every day than ever before in history. This flavour variety is a cause of obesity, including your personal struggles with weight control.

FROM PREHISTORIC TIMES TO A WORLD OF PLENTY

Originally, hunger was about survival. Hunger motivates us to eat because eating is essential. Sensations of fullness told our ancestors that they could stop risking their lives to find more food. Our brains evolved to deal with appetite in a world in which getting enough nutrients and calories was a constant challenge.

Today, that's no longer the case. Getting enough nutrients and calories is as easy as stopping at any takeaway restaurant in the shopping plaza. Yet, even though the modern world has changed, our brains have not. Our brains respond to this constant barrage of calories by telling us to eat more. Nothing in all of our historical experience has prepared us to resist food, because there has never, until now, been a reason to do so.

FLAVOUR FLUENCY

HUNGER: The various sensations you feel when you confront a deficit in the fuel you need to keep yourself running.

Here's what we're up against. In his excellent exposé, *Fast Food Nation*, investigative journalist Eric Schlosser describes in considerable detail how fast-food companies have engineered fast food to exploit every vulnerability of human taste and preference. These companies systematically test flavour additives with focus groups, tweaking foods until they become maximally pleasurable or, more likely, maximally addictive.

This problem goes well beyond fast food. Along with my Yale colleague and friend, Kelly Brownell, PhD, I have long referred to the modern food environment as toxic.

The food industry bombards our taste buds with a staggering variety of flavours. These companies have processed sugar, salt and harmful fats into foods that no longer bear any discernible resemblance to their origins. They've added flavour-enhancing chemicals. They've engineered salt into sweet foods, sugar into salty foods, and an intoxicating combination of flavours into the contents of every bag, box, meal and snack.

From potato crisps and chips to biscuits and ice cream, many foods have become arguably as addictive – and, in the long run, nearly as bad

How Flavours Affect Eating

Many years ago, scientists identified only four major taste categories: sweet, sour, salty and bitter. Now, science tells us there are at least six distinct taste categories, the two additions being savoury (also called umami) and astringent. Perhaps someday, we'll know of even more. Our ability to appreciate the many subtle variations in the flavours of foods results from our perception of these categories of taste, combined with our interpretation of aromas. Smell contributes a lot to our sense of taste, which is why eating with a stuffy nose tends to be so unsatisfying.

Although sensory-specific satiety drives us to prefer a variety of tastes, not all tastes are created equal. Sweet stimulates our appetites the most. This makes perfect sense. Breast milk is sweet. In nature, sweet foods are scarce and include excellent sources of quick energy, such as ripe fruits and wild honey. Few toxic substances in nature taste sweet, so there are many good reasons for us to be born with a sweet tooth (or gums, as the case may be).

Salt also stimulates appetite. Although humans aren't born with a predilection for salty food, we readily acquire it. The same appears to be true for the savoury quality of protein sources such as meat and cheese. In contrast, bitter and astringent tastes tend to suppress appetite, at least until we acquire a preference for them. For example, coffee and beer are acquired tastes for many people, but once we learn to like them, we may like them quite a lot!

for you – as cigarettes. This type of processing raises the Flavour Point. With so much flavour variety, it's almost impossible not to overeat.

Is this intentional? Probably. The connection between flavour variety and overeating has appeared in medical studies for more than 20 years. Have the smart and well-paid nutritional biochemists working for the food industry failed to appreciate its significance? That would be hard for me to believe.

Is the modern food industry actually involved in some kind of conspiracy? Do executives meet in boardrooms and exchange dark secrets about how to addict people to their foods? No one knows, but it would require a good deal of vacuous inattention on the part of a food company executive not to appreciate the potential utility of sensory-specific satiety in the effective peddling of an excess of wares. Because vacuous inattention is not a trait common among successful business executives, I'm guessing that the food industry quickly figured out what sensory-specific satiety could mean to their bottom line.

An investigative journalist – perhaps Eric Schlosser, if he's inclined to write the sequel to *Fast Food Nation* – might find what I don't have the time, skills or inclination to look for: long-hidden documents lurking in a drawer at some large food or restaurant company that signify the wilful processing of hidden flavours into foods to stimulate overconsumption.

I don't need these documents to know that the practice is widespread. I just need the nutrition facts and ingredient labels that appear on packaged foods. I can see right there that processing has crossed over to the dark side. When breakfast cereals are salty, and savoury snacks provide sugar in doses suitable for dessert, I can see the smoke from the gun, whether or not I can find the bullet or have the evidence needed to indict the person who pulled the trigger.

Take monosodium glutamate, for example. This ingredient does more than make foods taste salty. Glutamate, an amino acid, is responsible for a unique flavour category all its own, known as umami, which signifies the kind of savoury flavour we taste in cheese and meat. It's hard to define, but you know it when you taste it. Because most people like it, it's being processed into ever more foods.

Some of these flavours aren't really intended to be tasted at all. Some so-called flavour enhancers are hidden. They stimulate additional appetite meters in our brains, and stimulate us to eat more, but we don't actually taste them.

For example, many breakfast cereals taste sweet, but they actually contain quite a bit of salt, almost as much as potato crisps. Even though you don't notice a salty flavour (after all, who wants a breakfast cereal to taste salty?), it doesn't escape your appetite centre. We taste the sugar in breakfast cereal, and that activates one appetite meter. Although the sweetness of sugar masks the saltiness of the salt, the salt activates another appetite meter. The activation of two distinct appetite meters by two distinct flavours adds up to a bigger appetite. You'll consume more cereal before both of the meters register fullness.

A large percentage of the shrink-wrapped, boxed or bagged food you find on supermarket shelves contains this enticing sugar-salt combination. Foods that taste sweet contain salt. Foods that taste salty contain sugar.

A Short History of Food Processing

Even in prehistory, food was processed. Humans may have frozen and smoke-cured their food as far back as the last Ice Age. They at times ground wild plants into flour, cooked meat and smoked and dried foods to preserve them. All of this was a departure from eating totally unprocessed food as it was found.

Processing throughout most of history was about making enough food available to forestall genuine hunger. It was about preventing spoilage. It was about making food safer.

That changed in the latter half of the 20th century. The United States now produces, after accounting for export, roughly 3,800 calories each day for every man, woman and child in the country, a calorie load that grossly exceeds the needs of most people. The British throw out 30–40 per cent of all the produce they buy and grow each year. The primary incentive for the processing of food seems to have changed from making enough food safely available to making unsafe amounts of food all but irresistible.

┌─────────────────────────────── **Flavour Pointer** ┐

GETTING ADDICTED TO HEALTH

Even the most powerful habit-forming substances do their damage only when you use them frequently and at fairly high doses. In this way, the need for the substance goes up and up and up. As need rises, however, satisfaction falls.

The same is true of flavours. Most of us have so much sugar and salt in our diets that we don't even notice them in moderate amounts; we taste them only when the dose is quite high. As a result, we need more and more and more added sugar and salt to reach our flavour thresholds, the point at which we feel satisfied with these flavours. Eating ever-higher doses of sugar and salt simply propagates their addictive influence, making us turn to less wholesome, more processed, higher-calorie foods.

Here's the good news: health can be just as habit forming. The Flavour Point Diet leads you steadily to foods that are less processed and have less added sugar, salt and harmful fats. As you acclimatize to these lower flavour thresholds, not only will you completely recover from your flavour addictions, you will also find that it takes less and less and less of these ingredients to satisfy you. You will start to find that the sweets you used to enjoy now taste too sweet and the salty snacks too salty. As you choose and acclimatize to more wholesome foods, you will rehabilitate your taste buds. You don't need to give up the foods you prefer. You will instead come to prefer the more wholesome foods that now, along with better health, are your new habit. Once this habit is formed, you won't need to follow the flavour themes consciously – you'll begin to choose Flavour Point-friendly foods automatically, for life.

Most of these foods also contain an array of artificial flavours. Added together, this flavour excess stimulates a number of appetite meters in the brain, all of which must register fullness before you feel satisfied. Under these conditions, no amount of willpower will hold you to a small serving of potato crisps or cheese puffs.

OVERCOMING MODERN TEMPTATIONS

I have long used the image of polar bears in the Sahara to help my patients understand why weight control is so difficult and frustrating. So let's consider polar bears for a moment. These marvels of survival flourish in one of Earth's harshest climates. They are made for the cold. They have double-layer coats, insulating inner hairs and hollow outer hairs that funnel solar radiation to their skin. Their black skin absorbs all wavelengths of sunlight. Polar bears soak up and retain heat with extraordinary efficiency.

Imagine what would happen if polar bears suddenly found themselves in the Sahara on a summer's day. In a world of abundant heat, they would quickly find that the tendency to absorb and retain heat would be their undoing. They would overheat, not for lack of willpower or because of greed, gluttony or laziness. No, they would soak up heat because that's what polar bears do.

People overeat for all the same reasons that polar bears overheat. Just as polar bears conserve heat, our ancestors conserved food energy. Polar bears have physiologies designed to thrive when available heat is limited; they soak up and conserve warmth. Humans have physiologies designed to thrive when calories are scarce; we soak up and conserve calories, running quite well on relatively few and storing the rest as body fat to use when needed. Just as polar bears are undone by their ability to store heat when heat is suddenly abundant, humans don't cope well when food is suddenly available in excess. We tend to overeat.

One of two solutions can fix the mismatch between human metabolism and the modern environment. The first and most fundamental is to restore the environment to its former state. Many of my most esteemed colleagues are completely devoted to this cause, working to change food industry practices, urban planning and government policy (see, for example, *Food Fight* by Dr Brownell and *Food Politics* by New York University professor Marion Nestle, PhD).

Despite the best efforts of some of the best people in science and public health, I have this advice for you: don't hold your breath. Changing the world is neither quick nor easy, and sometimes it may be nearly impossible. It seems rather unlikely, for example, that we humans will ever abandon time- and labour-saving devices, such as leaf-blowers and e-mail, that contribute to our obesity.

So that leaves us with the other way: adapting to live successfully in our new environment. Most diets do not empower you to out-think the many forces and sources of weight gain. Most diets offer only short-term solutions to a profound and permanent problem. Think of yourself as a polar bear in the Sahara and the typical diet as a big block of ice. You're given the block of ice and invited to climb on. It's cool, comfortable and instantly rewarding.

But what happens to a block of ice under the relentless Sahara sun? It melts. You haven't really fallen off the diets you've tried before; instead, they've disappeared out from under you, never offering anything meaningful and permanent in the first place.

The Flavour Point Diet is not a block of ice. Rather, it provides an exit strategy from the desert heat. Using the power of your brain, the Flavour Point Diet lets you turn the very forces that conspired to produce epidemic obesity – and your own struggle with weight – to your advantage.

WHY WILLPOWER DOESN'T WORK

I'm willing to bet that you have plenty of willpower. You probably have at least the average endowment of discipline and motivation. You're not lazy. You are not the problem. The problem lies in the foods that surround – and tempt – you day in and day out. As you now understand, however, you need more than willpower to overcome the addictiveness of the modern food supply. You need flavour organization.

In this modern environment, there are powerful forces working against your best efforts at weight control. You can't just make up your mind to overcome this genetic wiring. Willpower might work for a day or a week or even a month. Over time, however, your genetics will overpower your willpower, causing you to backslide.

That's where the Flavour Point Diet comes in. You can eat less but feel just as full and satisfied. Indeed, there's only one way to overcome evolutionary biology: you must eat in a way that triggers that appetite centre in your brain to tell the rest of your body that you're satisfied with less. To eat less, you need more than your willpower and determination on your side. You need your brain.

The Flavour Point Meal Plan teaches you to choose foods free of superfluous flavour enhancers, foods that don't overstimulate your appetite centre and lead to excessive eating. It teaches you how to choose foods based on flavour themes that tame your appetite and then make the transition from those themes to a basic pattern of foods and flavours you can sustain forever. By focusing on organizing the flavours in your diet, you wind up improving everything about the foods you buy, stock, prepare and order. More important, you can follow the Flavour Point Diet for life.

That's the power of neuroscience. That's the power of using the hardwiring of your brain, rather than just making up your mind, to lose weight and keep it off. That's the power of lowering your Flavour Point. Let's turn to Chapter 2 to learn more about how you can use your brain to turn down your appetite.

2

OTHER APPETITE TRIGGERS

Although many variables influence how much you eat, flavour matters most

Because my wife, Catherine, is French, our family meals all begin with a hearty '*Bon appétit*', which means 'Good appetite'. As you've learned, however, not everything about appetite is good. A great many pressures cause our appetites to behave badly.

Among those pressures, flavour variety ranks as the most important, but I'd be oversimplifying things if I told you it was the only one. Social, environmental, psychological, economic and biological factors all influence how much humans eat – and overeat. In addition to flavour, the volume of a food, the number of calories it contains and its nutrient content all influence the Flavour Point. The good news: when you organize the flavours in your diet, all of these other appetite-stimulating variables fall into place. Let's take a closer look.

THE VOLUME CONNECTION

The volume of a food refers to how much space a fairly typical serving of the food takes up. A low-volume food would be something like cheese, which packs lots of calories into a small space. A high-volume food would be lettuce, which takes up lots of space but provides very few calories. High-volume foods are generally also referred to as energy dilute, meaning that they have relatively few calories for any given unit of volume; low-volume foods tend to be energy dense. Volume can be altered by adding water, so, for example, chicken soup is a higher-volume and less energy-dense food than chicken.

I mentioned the stomach hormone ghrelin in Chapter 1. Levels of this appetite-stimulating hormone remain high until food stretches the wall of your stomach, making you feel full. This stretch reflex helps explain why Barbara Rolls, PhD, and her colleagues at Pennsylvania State University have linked high-volume, low-calorie foods with reduced appetite and increased satiety. These foods take up a lot of room in your stomach, triggering the stretch reflex in the stomach wall long before you've overeaten. On the other hand, the same researchers have found that low-volume, high-calorie foods, such as potato crisps and chips, encourage overeating, probably because you must eat a lot more of them to trigger the same reflex.

In one study published in 2003, Dr Rolls and her colleagues offered various types of soup to 36 women over several days. When the researchers doubled the volume of the soup but kept calories constant, the women felt full faster and stopped eating after consuming fewer calories. When the researchers doubled the calories in the soup but kept the volume the same, the women consumed more calories.

In a related study, the researchers offered 20 men a milk-based drink, followed by lunch and then dinner. When the milk drink was relatively low in volume, the men ate more for lunch and dinner that day, consuming more calories than usual. When the men had shakes that were higher in volume but had the same number of calories, they subsequently ate less for lunch and dinner.

In yet another study, with 28 men, the investigators varied the volume of a yoghurt drink by putting air into it, keeping everything else constant. Even when they changed only the air content, the higher-volume drink caused the subjects to eat less during that day.

These and other studies clearly demonstrate the powerful effect that food volume has on appetite. High-volume foods can certainly help you in your quest to fill up on fewer calories, but is volume more important than flavour? I don't think so. If I did, I wouldn't have written this book. By controlling the variety of flavours in your meals and snacks, you avoid stimulating multiple appetite meters at any one time (see 'Flavour Fluency'). Then, by incorporating high-volume foods into your diet, you satisfy the meters that are turned on with fewer calories. By activating fewer meters and turning off your activated meters sooner, you will create a shortcut to the Flavour Point.

Luckily, you don't need to earn a degree in biochemistry to use volume to your advantage. Foods with simple, wholesome ingredients and simple flavours tend to be high in volume. You can trick your brain (and stomach) by adding water and air to certain foods, increasing volume without adding calories. So make your soups soupier and your smoothies bubblier.

FLAVOUR FLUENCY

APPETITE: A desire for a particular food or a craving for a particular taste. Many circumstances influence appetite, including exposure to certain foods, timing of the meal or snack, and tradition or convention. The familiarity of food, its palatability (which incorporates taste and texture, appearance and aroma), its convenience and cost, and its place in our culture also influence appetite. Of all of these variables, flavour exerts the strongest influence on appetite.

THE CALORIE CONNECTION

We all have a tendency to eat more than we should when the foods we choose are energy dense, meaning that they pack a lot of calories into a relatively small serving.

To understand why, imagine for a moment that it's 3.00 pm. You're ready to take a break and are in the mood for a snack. You have a simple choice: an apple or a slice of Cheddar cheese. Both provide 100 calories,

(continued on page 29)

Satisfaction at the Flavour Point

THE FLAVOUR FACTS

Name: Nancy Schebell

Age: 36

Family status: Divorced with three children, aged 3, 7 and 11

Occupation: X-ray technician

Starting weight: 108 kg/17 st

Weight lost: 7.2 kg/16 lb in 12 weeks

Health stats: Blood pressure dropped 5 points; waist measurement shrank 18 cm/7 in; 4 per cent decline in body fat

---

'The last time I was thin, I was a teenager. After having three kids and eating junk regularly over the years, the weight just came on. I had tried Atkins in the past and I was a freak on it; after 2 weeks without carbs, I was miserable and I gave up.

'Dr Katz told us in the beginning that this is a way of life and not simply a short-term diet. He was right.

I really love this programme, and I think it's something I'll be able to stick with for life.

'I now love grocery shopping. When I go, I spend a lot of time browsing, and I'm always looking for something different to try in the health food section. I *want* to find new foods that are good for me.

'Not only are the recipes really tasty, they're doable for a family. My kids are aged 3, 7 and 11 and they love the foods, especially the fish. We had never eaten tuna before, but when I made it for the plan, my kids loved it.

'As far as the ease of the meals, I was never big on cooking, and these recipes are pretty simple for me. My mum is impressed that I'm cooking! Overall, I think my favourite flavour themes were the vegetable ones – the tomato and mushroom.

'For breakfast, I make an omelette or a smoothie and take it to work. For lunch, I usually choose one of the flavour-friendly options and have a salad with grilled chicken or tuna. I sometimes eat the hummus sandwiches for lunch. Then I make the recipes specified on the meal plan for dinner.

'I used to crave chocolate a lot. Since I started the programme, my cravings have stopped. Instead of sweets, I now opt for a cracker with some hummus on it or a handful of carrots or cherry tomatoes. I always drink green tea because Dr Katz told us it helps make you feel full, and it really works.

'Dr Katz taught me to honour the flavour that I crave. He says if you want something salty, eat something salty, but don't eat something sweet right after it. The same thing goes for craving sweets – just eat something sweet without following it up with something salty. Otherwise, you won't be satisfied. He's right. It works.

'I also drink a lot of water now. I used to drink a lot of fizzy drinks. I would always drink my eight glasses of water, but I'd have fizzy drinks at lunch and dinner. Not any more. Even at lunch, I drink water. I find fizzy drinks too sweet.

'I am amazed at how full I feel. I didn't make the desserts because most of the time, I was satisfied with dinner. I didn't need anything else.

'I feel so much better on this programme; I have much more energy, and I've been walking between 2 and 4 miles [3 and 6 km] every day. My clothes fit better, and people have been saying, "Oh, my God – look at you! You're so much thinner. You look so good." My colleagues have been particularly supportive. And a lot of people have asked me about the programme that I'm on; they can't wait to try it, too!' ■

The Universe of Foods

Try to choose foods from group B in the chart below. For overall health, the next best group is group A, foods dense in both nutrients and calories. Foods low in both nutrients and calories (group D) may not foster weight gain directly but can do so indirectly, as in the case of diet drinks (see 'Why Sugar Substitutes Don't Work' on page 34). These foods and beverages also offer few if any health benefits. Then there's group C: foods high in calories and low in nutrients. These badlands of the food universe are home to just about every junk food you can think of. If you spend too much time in group C, you'll fire up your brain's appetite meters, moving you away from the Flavour Point.

	HIGH NUTRIENT DENSITY	LOW NUTRIENT DENSITY
HIGH ENERGY DENSITY	A. High in both nutrients and calories: nuts, seeds, olives, avocados and some animal foods, such as fatty fish	C. Low in nutrients, high in calories: fast food, fried foods, crisps, processed meats, fizzy drinks, most sweets, doughnuts, biscuits, crackers, cream sauces, butter, mayonnaise, etc.
LOW ENERGY DENSITY	B. High in nutrients, low in calories: vegetables, fruits and whole grains	D. Low in both nutrients and calories: diet fizzy drinks and other diet beverages; celery; iceberg lettuce; fat-free, reduced-calorie spreads and dressings; etc.

but you'll swallow the cheese in a bite or two, whereas the apple will take you a while to eat. What do you think will happen if you opt for the cheese? Will you stop at just one slice? Probably not.

When foods pack lots of calories in a small space, as cheese does, it's easy to overeat. Because an apple takes longer to eat, your brain has time to register fullness. The apple's fibre and water also stimulate stretch receptors in the stomach more quickly.

Because fat has 9 calories per gram compared with carbohydrate or protein's 4 calories per gram, foods high in fat are energy dense. Processed foods with lots of sugar come in a close second. Processed foods loaded with both fat and sugar have dense concentrations of calories that are especially palatable and hard to resist. Because fibre takes up space in food but provides no calories, simply increasing your fibre consumption could help turn down your appetite – yet our highly processed food supply does just the opposite. Processed foods have been stripped of their fibre.

The overprocessing and increasing energy density of the Western diet is one of the leading causes of epidemic obesity. Energy-dense foods make it easy to squeeze too many calories into your stomach within a small amount of time and space. There is very little obesity seen in societies that rely on energy-dilute foods. Regrettably, there are fewer and fewer such societies as both highly processed, energy-dense foods and obesity relentlessly take over our planet.

The Flavour Point Diet relies on foods that are naturally low in fat, such as fruits, vegetables and whole grains. While reducing the amount of fat you consume can also reduce the energy density of your diet, it works only if you consume naturally low-fat foods. Too often, dieters turn to processed low-fat and fat-free foods. Because these foods contain lots of sugar, they are often nearly as energy dense as their high-fat cousins. Another consideration is that cutting out too much fat makes eating less enjoyable and renders a diet unsustainable. The Flavour Point Diet avoids this mistake.

(continued on page 32)

What Makes You Eat

Although the Flavour Point Meal Plan addresses all of the following influences on appetite to give you maximum control and mastery over your Flavour Point, you need to focus on only one thing: flavour. When you choose simply flavoured foods, all of the other influences fall into place.

INFLUENCE	HOW TO USE IT
Sensory-specific satiety	Avoid excess flavour variety in meals, snacks and processed into individual foods; group flavours into themes (see Chapter 3 for more details).
Energy density	Foods that pack lots of calories into small spaces are less filling and satisfying than foods that distribute calories in larger volumes. Avoid or limit highly processed foods that have lots of calories from fat and sugar and are devoid of water and fibre.
Volume	Foods high in volume, such as vegetables, fruits, soups and stews, fill you up with fewer calories. These wholesome foods are also generally rich in nutrients. Make them a regular part of a healthy diet.
Protein	Calorie for calorie, protein is the most filling of the nutrient categories, but too much can be harmful. The Flavour Point Meal Plan delivers protein at the upper end of the range recommended for lasting good health.

INFLUENCE	HOW TO USE IT
Glycaemic load	A better measure than the glycaemic index, the glycaemic load indicates how much foods tend to raise blood sugar. Swings in blood sugar overstimulate appetite and contribute to weight gain. The Flavour Point Meal Plan emphasizes foods with a low glycaemic load. By choosing less processed foods, you will lower the glycaemic load of your diet, speeding you to the Flavour Point.
Fibre content	Fibre reduces your risk of heart disease, diabetes and cancer, as well as helping to control appetite. Most people, however, eat less than half the recommended amount of about 30 milligrams a day. The Flavour Point Meal Plan consistently delivers an ideal dose of fibre each day. Found in cereal grains, fruit, vegetables, nuts, seeds, beans and lentils, fibre is plentiful in the Flavour Point Diet.
Fat content	Fat is less filling, calorie for calorie, than either protein or carbohydrate. It's also more energy dense, packing more calories into a smaller volume. Fat also serves as a vehicle for flavours. Sweet foods taste even sweeter, for example, when they are made with oil. The oil distributes the sweetness throughout the mouth. Even though added oils may not add a specific flavour to food, they enhance the potency of other added flavours. For these reasons, the Flavour Point Diet emphasizes foods naturally low in fat. The fats in this diet are almost all of the healthy, unsaturated variety.

THE MACRONUTRIENT CONNECTION

The appetite meters in our brains respond somewhat differently to the different nutrient classes we consume. For example, the more protein we eat, the more readily the meters register 'Full'. Although no one knows precisely why, I can guess. We need protein every day for good health, and our ancestors had to hunt – a dangerous activity – to procure it. So it makes sense that our brains and appetites not only motivate us to seek out protein but also let us know when we've had enough. Risking life and limb for protein we didn't need would be almost as ill advised as not risking life and limb for it at all.

Whatever the reasons, the science is clear that calorie for calorie, protein is the most satiating (filling) of the nutrient classes, followed by complex carbohydrates (those rich in fibre, such as whole grains, vegetables, and fruits), then simple carbohydrates (white flour and products containing added sugar), and finally, fat. This means it takes more calories from fat than from either carbohydrate or protein to make us feel comparably full. Because fat is the least satiating of the nutrient classes, high-fat foods can easily make you eat more than you intend to.

That said, when foods are mixed together, as they always are in any reasonable diet, even the satiating power of protein is reduced. Thus, relying on a low-carbohydrate, high-protein diet for weight control is not likely to work very well, and such diets are generally unbalanced. Finally, because restrictive diets get tedious, they tend to backfire. You lose weight for as long as you can stand the tedium, but when you can stand it no longer and go off the diet, you gain back the weight with interest.

The Flavour Point Diet avoids these pitfalls, providing the perfect balance of macronutrients for nutrition and health while controlling appetite with the powerful and permanent force of flavour. The breakdown, designed for lifelong health and weight control, looks like this.

- Roughly 55 per cent of calories from mostly complex carbohydrate
- Roughly 20 per cent of calories from lean sources of protein

---

Flavour Pointer

A RECKONING OF RENEGADE CALORIES

On the Flavour Point Diet, you needn't count calories, because you'll use food to fill up on fewer calories automatically. That said, you do need to stay vigilant. Don't let hidden, overlooked calories sneak into your day and on to your hips or waist. Pay attention to handfuls of nuts or potato crisps or sweets you may tend to grab on the go. Be attentive to spreads, dressings and sauces. And don't forget the calories you're drinking. Counting calories for weight control? Tiresome. You can fuhgeddaboudit, as long as you remember that all calories do count.

- Roughly 25 per cent of calories from fat, most from healthy sources such as vegetable oils, nuts, seeds and fish and very little from animal sources or processed foods

Here's my reasoning. First, this is the dietary pattern that many major health organizations and an abundance of research indicate is optimal for lifelong health. Second, foods high in complex carbohydrates, such as vegetables, fruits and whole grains, tend to be rich in fibre, water or both. Fibre may be particularly important because it increases food volume without added calories and can slow the absorption of nutrients into the bloodstream, thereby lowering blood sugar and stabilizing blood insulin levels. For lasting weight control, it makes far more sense to choose carbohydrate foods wisely than to simply abandon them altogether.

There's one caveat to all of this. High-carbohydrate foods are more filling and satiating than high-fat foods only if they contain water and fibre. Once processing removes the natural water and fibre content of a high-carbohydrate food and then adds sugar and refined starch, these foods trigger overeating just as fatty foods do. In other words, those reduced-fat biscuits aren't doing your waistline any good.

Why Sugar Substitutes Don't Work

Although sugar and fat substitutes allow you to enjoy sweet and creamy tastes and textures without consuming sweet and creamy calories, the use of these substitutes often backfires.

Studies show that we often compensate for these missing calories by eating more at other times. A fascinating study on this matter was recently carried out with mice. Researchers fed genetically identical mice either diet or regular fizzy drinks and then offered the rodents sweet gruel. The mice given the diet drink overate the gruel and became obese, whereas the mice given the regular fizzy drink were better able to judge the calories in the gruel, ate less of it, and stayed lean. The artificial sweetener in the diet drink disrupted the mice's ability to regulate their intake of calories.

All artificial sweeteners can produce this effect. The more you eat of any desired flavour over time, the higher it tends to drive your threshold for satisfaction. Although the science of sensory-specific satiety proves that eating the same flavour in one sitting turns down the appetite, eating a lot of the same flavour on a regular basis raises your appetite for that flavour. In the case of artificial sweeteners, this propagates a sweet tooth. The best way to tame a sweet tooth is not by feeding it but by weaning it. The Flavour Point Diet will help you remove sugar from places in your diet it simply doesn't need to be, such as in breads, sauces, spreads and dressings. As long as you don't replace this sweet taste with artificial sweeteners, you'll reduce your exposure not only to sugar but also to sweetness. That lowers your preference for sweet tastes so you're satisfied with less.

THE GLYCAEMIC CONNECTION

The glycaemic index is a measure of how much various foods raise blood sugar levels in comparison to a specific food used as a reference standard (usually a slice of white bread). In general, foods with high glycaemic indexes are considered bad for weight control because a rapid rise in blood sugar leads to a brisk rise in blood insulin, which in turn may increase appetite by causing blood sugar levels to dip back down. In contrast, foods with low glycaemic indexes are generally considered to help you lose weight because they produce smaller, slower variations in blood sugar and insulin levels. Although some studies show that foods with high glycaemic indexes tend to be less filling than foods with low glycaemic indexes, you really can't use the index to guide your food choices – for several reasons.

Perhaps the most straightforward reason is that the glycaemic index compares a fixed dose of sugar in one food with the same dose in another. This is unfair. Getting the test dose of sugar from ice cream requires eating very little ice cream, whereas getting it from carrots requires eating a whole lot of carrots. The result? Ice cream has a lower glycaemic index than white bread, and carrots have a higher one!

Unless you're prepared to believe that eating lots of ice cream and steering clear of carrots will enhance your health or control your weight, I trust you can see the limitations of the glycaemic index. Still, the effects of foods on blood sugar and blood insulin levels are important and can play a role in weight loss. As I mentioned in Chapter 1, to turn down appetite, you need slow, even increases in blood sugar and insulin.

A more useful measure for guiding dietary choices is something called the glycaemic load, which takes into account the dose of sugar found naturally in a food. The glycaemic index compares sugar in foods the same way a tape measure compares the heights of a boy and a man. Let's say a 35-year-old man is 1.57 m/5 ft 2 in tall, and a 5-year-old boy is 1.35 m/ 4 ft 6 in tall. The tape measure tells us the man is tall and the boy short. In fact, the opposite is true! For his age, the man is relatively short; for his age, the boy is quite tall. Adjusting height for age reveals the truth about

Satisfaction at the Flavour Point

THE FLAVOUR FACTS

Name: Chris Cornell

Age: 25

Family status: Married

Occupation: Field service technician

Starting weight: 99 kg/15 st 7 lb

Weight lost: 4.5 kg/10 lb in 12 weeks

Health stats: Blood pressure dropped 7 points; resting heart rate improved; $5^1/_2$ per cent decline in body fat

'I was looking for something new – something that would not just help me lose weight but make me feel better overall. I had tried losing weight on my own and had also tried another diet with modest success, but I didn't stick with it. When I heard about Dr Katz's plan, I decided to give it a try. I'm really glad I did, because it works.

'Overall, my favourite thing about the programme is the food. It's great, especially the fish dishes. And most of the recipes are fast and pretty easy to make. I often try to prepare some of the dishes ahead of time, so they're ready to go when I need them, which makes things even simpler.

'For breakfast and lunch, I use the Flavour-Friendly Alternatives, cereal and fruit in the morning and a salad for lunch. For dinners, the seafood dishes are my favourites, especially the almond-crusted fish and the grilled prawns. When I need a snack, I usually reach for raw veggies, fruit or yoghurt.

'I have also discovered new foods I never would have thought taste good and I found that I actually preferred Newman's Own light salad dressing!

'A number of people have commented on my weight loss and told me I look smaller, which has reinforced that the programme is working. My clothes also fit much better. Plus, I have more energy now, which is a bonus.

'In a perfect world, I'd like to be around 12 st 12 lb [82 kg], but I'm happy with the amount of weight I've lost in 12 weeks with Dr Katz's programme.' ■

height much more accurately. The glycaemic load does the same for the effects of food on blood sugar and insulin responses; it adjusts the effects of the food according to how its sugar content is concentrated. Whereas the glycaemic index of carrots is comparable to that of fizzy drinks, the glycaemic load of carrots is less than one-tenth as much. Now that makes much more sense.

To use glycaemic load to your advantage, you don't have to take a glycaemic load chart with you each time you head to the supermarket. To consume a diet low in foods with high glycaemic loads, you need only limit highly processed foods and maximize your consumption of vegetables, fruits, whole grains and lean protein. The Flavour Point Diet does exactly that.

THE POWER OF FLAVOUR, PLUS MORE

The Flavour Point Diet meal plan uses all of these important appetite regulators – volume, energy density, macronutrient content, glycaemic load and more – to help you fill up on the fewest calories. Of all the variables that influence appetite, however, flavour exerts the strongest influence, both in those of us who struggle with our weight and in those of us who do not. More important, foods with simple, satisfying flavours tend to include all of the appetite-subduing variables I just mentioned. In other words, when you follow the Flavour Point Meal Plan and subscribe to the Flavour Point principles, you will soon learn that you don't need to pay attention to calories, volume, macronutrients and other variables. Appetite management will happen naturally, behind the scenes, without effort on your part.

Quite simply, flavour is the most important aspect of food. By using flavour strategically, you can use your meals to turn off your appetite centre sooner. Turn to Chapter 3 to find out how.

Satisfaction at the Flavour Point

THE FLAVOUR FACTS

Name: Brenda Gibbs

Age: 57

Family status: Married with two children, ages 18 and 28

Occupation: Registered nurse

Starting weight: 152 kg/23 st 8 lb

Weight lost: 7.6 kg/17 lb in 12 weeks

Health stats: Blood pressure dropped 28 points; resting heart rate decreased; blood sugar levels improved; waist measurement shrank 11 cm/4½ in

'I was in a car accident about 6 years ago, and a resulting back injury made movement difficult. The less I moved, the more weight I put on, and the more weight I put on, the less I moved. It was a vicious cycle.

'Before I started the programme, I ate anything and everything I wanted – cheese burgers, fries, pasta salad, you name it. I would also keep a few cookies next to my bed, and if I woke up hungry, I would eat them and go back to sleep.

'As a result, I put on *a lot* of weight since the accident, and I finally said to myself, "Something is going to have to change, or you're going to die." I have a 7-year-old granddaughter and a son who's going to college. I wanted to be around for them. So when Dr Katz's programme came along, I decided to give it a try. I reasoned with myself, "If I can change what I put in my mouth, maybe I will feel physically better and want to move more." That's exactly what this programme has done for me.

'Now that I'm into it, this new eating plan has become a habit, and I love it. I really do. My husband does the cooking, so he had to stock the kitchen with these new ingredients over the first 2 weeks, but once he did that, he found the recipes to be pretty easy. He hasn't stuck to the programme religiously, but he eats some of the dishes and finds them flavoursome.

'The foods on the programme please all your senses – sight, smell and taste. And I don't feel like I'm on a strict regime. This weekend, I went to a barbecue, and instead of having a hamburger on a bun, I just had a small burger without the bun and a salad.

'And there is *so much* food that I can't eat it all. For breakfast, I usually eat cereal, but I occasionally make one of the more elaborate recipes, like the French toast made with the wholemeal bread. I don't miss the bagel with butter and jelly I used to have for breakfast. The lentil salads are great for lunch, as are the egg and tuna salads. Because I'm heading to bed around lunchtime (I work shifts), I usually eat a few rye crackers with hummus and bean sprouts and I'm fine.

'My favourite dinners are the Pasta Fagioli with Spinach Marinara Sauce and the Portobello Mushrooms with Walnut Stuffing. I could eat the portobello dish 24/7. It's wonderful. To me, it tastes like stuffed lobster.

'I've also discovered some great new foods, like bulgur wheat. There are a lot of foods on this programme that I never thought I'd eat, but I love them.

'One of the best things about Dr Katz's programme is how I look. I've gotten so many compliments. People say, "Brenda, you look wonderful. You look so healthy." My mother has been inspired to try it, too. She started 3 weeks ago and has lost 11 lb [5 kg] so far!

'Physically, I feel great. I sleep better, and my energy level is incredible. At work, I used to delegate a lot of duties to other people, but now, I just get up and do a lot of the things myself.

'Both my husband and I are amazed that I not only stuck to the programme for the first 12 weeks but also want to continue with it. My husband recently said, "Brenda, I'm really shocked and pleased to see that you've taken to this so easily and that you're enjoying it." I'm a wholehearted advocate of this programme!' ■

3

REACHING THE FLAVOUR POINT

Fill up on fewer calories in three easy steps

Now that you have a working knowledge of the neuroscience of appetite and of the food industry's exploitation of your metabolic vulnerabilities, you may understand why weight control has been so difficult and elusive. That's the bad news.

Here's the good news: you can take advantage of the science of sensory-specific satiety and turn down your appetite without losing out on the flavour of your meals. You don't have to give up your favourite foods. In fact, quite to the contrary, you're going to eat more of them. You don't need to spend more time in the kitchen or at the supermarket. You needn't refrain from eating out. You don't have to prepare one meal for yourself and another for your family. You can subdue your appetite centre with easy to prepare, tasty foods that even your children will love.

The Flavour Point Meal Plan is completely balanced, totally satisfying, absolutely healthy, permanently sustainable and wonderfully effective for weight loss and lasting weight control. The plan helps turn down appetite on two levels.

1. You learn to drape a flavour theme over your meals, cooking simply but deliciously flavoured foods that help trigger fullness with fewer calories.

Names Can Be Misleading

As Shakespeare once asked, 'What's in a name?' Potentially, a great deal of deception. Some foods, such as salad, sound weight-loss friendly, but not all are. The same goes for soup and sandwiches. Take a look at this chart to see which ingredients form the soup, salad and sandwich categories that help you lower your Flavour Point and which do not. It's not what you call your food but what's in it that counts. Choose wisely.

FOOD	FLAVOUR POINT FRIENDLY	STEER CLEAR
SOUP	Vegetable or defatted chicken stock, clear broth or tomatoes as a base; abundance of fresh vegetables and natural spices to taste	Cream, beef or high-fat chicken stock as a base; addition of corn syrup or sugar; high sodium content (more than 500 mg per serving)
SALAD	Plenty of mixed greens with any other desired vegetables, such as tomatoes, peppers (capsicums), onions and cucumbers, and vinaigrette dressing	Salad made with iceberg lettuce, with cheese, croutons or cold cuts; cream or cheese-based dressing; added salt; large amounts of any oily dressing
SANDWICH	Wholemeal bread with no added sugar or fat and limited added salt (less than 1 mg sodium per calorie); lettuce, tomato and other vegetables or lean, minimally processed meat, such as sliced turkey breast; mustard	White bread or any bread with added sugar and fat and/or high sodium content (more than 2 mg per calorie), with mayonnaise, butter or block margarine; sliced cheese; processed deli meats, such as salami and sausage

2. You learn to shop for and stock your kitchen with simply flavoured – but very tasty – foods and ingredients. By the end of the plan, you will use these foods and ingredients to create your own simply flavoured meals, which will allow you to go off the meal plan without going off the diet – ever.

The recipes, ingredients and foods used in the meal plan not only supply your taste buds with the right flavours to subdue your appetite centre and induce weight loss, they also have many additional appetite-suppressing and health-promoting properties. For example, the plan's grain products are high in fibre and minimally processed. You'll consume lean meat and dairy products. The sauces, spreads and dressings are free of trans fats and low in saturated fats.

Before getting started on this delicious new way of eating, however, you need a little background. You'll soon be changing the way you shop, stock your kitchen, cook and eat. To do that, you need the answers to some important questions. What do you look for on a food label to choose the best, Flavour Point Diet–approved products? What should be in your larder and refrigerator? How do you address making dietary changes with your teenager? I'll show you.

This knowledge will enable you to apply the benefits of the Flavour Point Diet with maximum flexibility, whatever the composition of your household, whatever ethnic food you prefer, and whatever your income or schedule. This way, you'll have a shortcut to the Flavour Point wherever you go.

THREE PHASES, ONE ULTIMATE GOAL

Depending on your genes, metabolism and dedication, you'll lose roughly 4 to 7.2 kg/9 to 16 lb or more during the next 6 weeks as you follow the meal plan. After that, as long as you stick with the Flavour Point way of eating, you'll continue to lose weight until you reach your goal.

Phase 1 imposes the greatest degree of dietary discipline, with the later phases a bit less restrictive. Because the Flavour Point Diet is based on the principle of flavour management rather than on cutting foods and food categories out of your diet, everything that helps you lose weight continues as you move from the more restrictive phases to the less restrictive ones. Rather than taking away foods, then adding them back (and doing the same with weight), as other diets do, the Flavour Point Diet teaches you to use flavour to organize how you eat in a permanent way. The discipline is more obvious at first, then slowly fades into the background as it becomes part of who you are and how you eat. It never goes away. Rather, it goes from obvious to subtle, from regimented to routine.

The programme moves from a *daily flavour theme* in Phase 1 to a *meal- and snack-specific flavour theme* in Phase 2. After Phase 2, you'll no longer need the meal plan. You'll remain on the Flavour Point Plan for life, however, sticking with Phase 3 until you reach your weight-loss goal – and forever. In Phase 3, the maintenance phase outlined in Chapter 6, you use individual foods to control appetite. From day to meal to food, you will take simple steps toward lifelong mastery of appetite – and permanent weight control.

Flavour Pointer

CEREAL AT THE FLAVOUR POINT

Cereal can be one of the best foods you can eat, combining the nutrients and fibre of whole grains with the benefits of the skimmed milk you pour over it and perhaps the fruit you add. However, it is vital that you choose a cereal that is high in fibre, with no added sugar and the minimum amount of salt (see page 48).

Some of the best cereals can be a bit pricey. If cost is a factor for you, here's another option. Use any combination of the cooking grains recommended in the meal plan. Make a bit extra when you prepare them for another meal, mix a few varieties together if you like, and – *voilà!* – you have multigrain cereal for pennies a bowl! Eat them plain with milk or sweeten them with a bit of juice or high-fruit preserves.

HOW TO USE THE MEAL PLAN

For best results on the Flavour Point Diet, follow these pointers.

- Respect each flavour theme, but feel free to make substitutions using the Flavour-Friendly Alternatives on pages 123–125. In counselling many people who tried many types of diets, I've discovered that few people stick to meal plans. Quite often, dieters look over a meal plan and then alter it to their preferences and lifestyle. In other words, they go on their own version of the plan. In some cases, they still manage to lose weight; in other cases, they don't. Because of this, I've devised a system that allows you to 'cheat' and still lose weight. For any breakfast, snack or lunch item on the menu, you can substitute a Flavour-Friendly Alternative. These items fit into any flavour theme. They're also quick and nearly effortless to prepare. *Note:* One of the flavour-friendly breakfast options is eggs, but you should limit your egg intake to six or fewer per week. Dietary cholesterol is not nearly as harmful as once feared, but too much of almost anything is a bad idea. Also, with the exception of Chow Now options (see page 64), there are no alternatives for dinners and desserts. For these, you must adhere to the plan.

- Refrain from eating fast food during the programme. Most fast foods combine the two most addictive flavours – sweet and salty – in one package. If you find you must break this rule (you're at a rest stop on the motorway, for example, and McDonald's is your only option), break it as gently as possible. Follow the tips for eating out (see page 54) and order a meal that's simple and minimally processed and has few if any flavour additions (such as special sauce). Also, make sure the foods you choose fit into your flavour theme.

- Don't frequent buffet-style restaurants during the programme. The human brain is too easily tempted by this type of food variety. Also, most of us tend to justify overeating at an all-you-can-eat buffet because we think it's a bargain. Change your thinking on this. Where's the bargain if, in eating more for free, you gain weight (at no extra charge) that you must later spend money to lose?

- Exercise moderately for 30 minutes most days of the week. Exercise certainly helps with weight loss, and even more with lasting weight control. Equally important, if not more so, it improves your health. Whether you walk, run, cycle, swim or dance in your bedroom, get some movement into your days. Increase your breathing and heart rate noticeably as you work out, but don't push yourself so hard that you can't talk comfortably in full sentences. You can complete the 30 or more minutes of activity all at once or accumulate that much over the course of the day. Your activity may be exercise, a sport, housework, walking your dog, dancing or just climbing stairs. The key is to move it if you want to lose it (weight), and gain it (health).

  Combine your aerobic activity with resistance training (weight lifting). Resistance exercise – such as lifting weights, pulling against elastic bands or doing circuit training – builds muscle. Each 455 g/1 lb of muscle you build through weight training burns roughly 30 to 50 calories a day, every day. That's right; when you build muscle by working out a few times a week, you burn more calories in your sleep. That's quite a return on investment.

  It's never too soon to begin being active, but it's never too late either. Studies of people well into their eighties show clear benefits of physical activity. Start slowly, giving yourself a chance to acclimatize. These bodies of ours were made to move, so there's a good chance you'll find physical activity habit forming once you give it a chance.

- Drink roughly six 240-ml/8-fl-oz glasses of water throughout the day and have water instead of other beverages, such as fizzy drinks.

- Whenever possible, finish lunch and dinner with a hot beverage, and sip it slowly. It will help give your brain time to register that you are full and satisfied and will provide a nice sense of closure.

- Always start dinner with a mixed green salad. Rich in nutrients and low in calories, salads turn down your appetite and keep you from overeating other, higher-calorie items.

- Save alcoholic beverages until near the end of a meal. Although a moderate amount of alcohol is healthy and pleasurable, it lowers your

Your Family at the Flavour Point
Finessing our Adolescents

Catherine and I have two adolescents in our home: Rebecca, 17, and Corinda, 16. I have to confess that we encouraged healthy eating before they became teenagers, but if you don't have this same advantage, don't despair.

Adolescents are somewhat autonomous because they're often out of your control and making their own decisions. They also need to push that autonomy to the limits because gaining independence is the very mission of adolescence. Can you respect that and still guide your teens towards the Flavour Point? Absolutely.

First, negotiate. You can find many nutritious substitutes for popular foods that almost all teens will readily accept. To get them to make some changes, allow them to reject others. Show some flexibility.

Set some limits, too, as well as an example. Adolescents are mature enough to deserve some independence but immature enough to need some rules. You do the shopping, after all, so you can agree to still have potato crisps in the house, but you decide which ones.

Don't be judgmental, and don't focus on a child's weight. Rather, make it clear that you care what they eat because you care about their health – because you love them! Talk the talk, and make it about love and family solidarity. Walk the walk, so they have an example to follow.

inhibitions, leading to overindulgence. If you wait until the end of the meal, however, you'll circumvent alcohol's appetite-stimulating effect.

- If you decide to have dessert, which is optional in the plan, wait a half hour after dinner. This gives your brain, stomach and intestines time to communicate your level of fullness. By delaying your gratification, you also enhance the pleasure you get from dessert.

- Choose brands of bread, crackers, cereal and other packaged foods that have the least amount of added salt and flavour enhancers – and no added sugars. Avoid products containing partially hydrogenated oils and more than 1.5 mg of sodium for every calorie. Breads, crackers and cereals should list whole grains as the first item on the ingredients list and should have at least 2, and preferably 3, grams of fibre per 100 calories.

STOCKING A FLAVOUR-FRIENDLY KITCHEN

Before embarking on the meal plan, you need to get your house in order – literally. By buying the following staples and stocking them in your refrigerator, freezer and cupboards, you'll have on hand almost everything you need for the meal plan. The following shopping list remains basically the same from week to week on the plan, so once you get used to buying these ingredients, you'll be able to shop by rote and get through the store faster and faster. Buying the Flavour Point foundation ingredients will become so second nature to you that you'll no longer need to carry a shopping list, and you'll head for all the right aisles without a moment's hesitation!

VEGETABLES

You'll need a lot of vegetables each week, as they always accompany the main course of dinner. Whenever you shop, throw fresh or frozen vegetables into your trolley. Unless the flavour theme is based on that veggie, feel free to sauté the same amount of whatever veggie you happen to have on hand in the freezer; that way, when you're shopping, you don't have to stop and think what veggies to get. Just get some!

Some of the recipes call for garlic cloves. Peel several at one go, to save on preparation time and store them in the refrigerator placed in a tightly sealed zip-top bag. You'll also occasionally need ginger. Get fresh ginger (rather than the dry powder, which isn't as fragrant) and, again, finely chop ahead of time. You can also store fresh ginger in a zip-top bag and grate it as needed. Despite popular belief, you don't have to peel it.

VEGETABLES

- Fresh or frozen precut broccoli florets
- Fresh or frozen cauliflower florets
- Fresh or frozen green beans
- Fresh or frozen precut peppers (capsicums)
- Frozen diced onions
- Frozen sweetcorn kernels
- Frozen oven chips (unprocessed – just potato and non-hydrogenated oil)
- Frozen peas
- Frozen precut or fresh baby carrots
- Frozen spinach
- Piece of fresh ginger
- Garlic bulb

SALAD INGREDIENTS

You'll eat a salad every evening of the week, so get used to having those ingredients in your fridge at all times. Because the following ingredients are prewashed and precut or grated in resealable packages, you can easily throw handfuls of this and that into a big salad bowl with only minimal rinsing and chopping.

SALAD INGREDIENTS

- Alfalfa sprouts
- Cherry tomatoes
- Grated cabbage/carrots
- Grated carrots
- Grated red cabbage
- Prewashed baby spinach
- Prewashed mixed greens

GRAINS, LENTILS AND BEANS

You'll use these staples throughout the meal plan. They have a long shelf life, so have some handy at all times. You may find canned fat-free chicken and vegetable stocks in the same aisle as the pulses, so toss some into the trolley to use in soups and stews. Alternatively, use good quality organic stock cubes that are free from artificial additives.

GRAINS, LENTILS, BEANS

- Brown rice
- Bulgur wheat
- Canned black beans
- Canned cannellini beans
- Canned chickpeas
- Canned chopped tomatoes
- Dry lentils
- Dry quinoa
- Light brown flour
- Oat bran flour
- Rolled oats (quick cooking or traditional) and oatcakes
- Wholemeal bread
- Wholegrain cereal
- Wholegrain crackers
- Wholewheat pasta

DAIRY PRODUCTS AND EGGS

You will use skimmed milk and natural yoghurt throughout the plan for breakfasts and snacks. You'll also need fat-free or low-fat buttermilk to thicken sauces and non-fat dried milk as a natural sweetener for baking and as creamer for coffee. Store dried milk in an airtight container or in its original jar. Keep eggs on hand for meals and baking. The fromage frais and cottage cheese are good alternatives as a snack.

DAIRY PRODUCTS AND EGGS

- Eggs (organic, with omega-3s)
- Fat-free fromage frais
- Fat-free natural yoghurt
- Less-than-2%-fat cottage cheese
- Fat-free or low-fat buttermilk
- Non-fat dried milk
- Skimmed milk

LEAN PROTEIN

Keep a pack of chicken breasts and a pack of cod fillets in your freezer to use on a Chow Now day (you'll learn more about these in Chapter 4). Freeze the ground turkey and use it as needed. Also keep frozen prawns on hand at all times; they're used in several of the recipes.

LEAN PROTEIN

- Cod fillets
- Extra-lean ground turkey
- Frozen raw prawns
- Skinless chicken breasts

MISCELLANEOUS

Keep the following items on hand for cooking or baking. You'll use them occasionally throughout the Flavour Point Meal Plan.

MISCELLANEOUS INGREDIENTS

- Almonds
- Apple sauce (unsweetened)
- Balsamic vinegar
- Basil pesto
- Canned peaches (in juice)
- Canned pineapple (in juice)
- Dijon mustard
- Dried fruit (raisins, cranberries, prunes, etc.)
- Dried spices
- Flax meal and/or flaxseed (refrigerate after opening)
- Fresh fruit
- High-fruit jam or preserves
- Honey
- Hummus (plain)
- Margarine (trans-fat-free)*
- Natural almond butter
- Natural peanut butter
- Newman's Own Light Italian Dressing
- Nuts/seeds
- Olive oil (extra virgin)
- 100% natural orange juice
- 100% natural pineapple juice
- Rapeseed (canola) oil
- Salsa, mild (with no added sugar, and low in salt and oil)

* Avoid hard margarines, which are full of harmful trans fats, and instead choose margarines such as Benecol, which are trans-fat free and designed to lower your cholesterol

READING FOOD LABELS FOR FLAVOUR

Now that you know what types of foods to buy, it's time to talk about choosing the best brands, especially of packaged foods. In every food category, from bread to salad dressing, you can choose from better brands and worse brands. To choose the best brands consistently, you must learn how to read the fine print on food labels.

To interpret a food label with minimal effort, follow this general rule: for every 100-calorie serving of a packaged food, the amount of sodium should be less than 1.5 milligrams per calorie, fat should be 3 or fewer grams, added sugars should be 3 or fewer grams, and fibre should be more than 2 grams. If, for example, a 110-calorie serving of a food provides 220 milligrams of sodium, it's too salty. This is okay if it's supposed to be a salty food, but certainly not if it's breakfast cereal!

In addition to that general rule, follow these pointers.

- Often, the Nutrition Facts pertain to just a portion of the contents. A 'serving' may have 100 calories, but if there are 2.5 servings per package, the entire package has 250 calories.

- Calories count! If you are judging a product on the number of calories per serving, pay attention to serving size. Calories come from protein (4 calories per gram), carbohydrate (4 calories per gram) and fat (9 calories per gram).

- Both the total amount and type of fat are important. Avoid foods with saturated and trans fats (partially hydrogenated oil).

- Fibre is your friend! It helps you reach the Flavour Point faster. Whole grains provide it in abundance; refined grains do not.

- If a product is packed full of added vitamins and minerals (which is often the case with processed cereals) it may look impressive, but it generally means that the equivalent of a multivitamin was mixed into the ingredients in an attempt to 'make up' for the vitamins that have been lost in the refining process!

- The ingredients list is separate from but usually printed near the Nutrition Facts label. It lists ingredients in order of abundance. In other words, packaged foods contain more of the ingredients near the beginning of the list and less of those near the end.

- Avoid buying packaged foods that have high-fructose corn syrup on the ingredient list. This is a long-winded way of saying 'added sugars'. Although this product is not as widespread elsewhere as it is in the US, its use is increasing.
- Choose foods with short ingredient lists. This is crucial. Generally, the longer the ingredient list, the more the food has been processed, and the more unnecessary flavours it contains. Wholesome, minimally processed foods with simple, uncluttered flavours tend to have short ingredient lists. One exception is foods made from multiple whole grains, but you'll soon learn to tell the difference.

STAYING ON POINT IN RESTAURANTS

Ideally, you'll cook most of your Flavour Point meals at home. That said, let's be realistic. Everyone goes out to eat from time to time. I know – we do it, too.

When you eat out, either order dishes that match the flavour theme of the day or choose dishes that resemble the Flavour-Friendly Alternatives (see page 123). I recommend that you avoid eating out during Phase 1 of the meal plan, when you're maintaining a day-long flavour theme. You'll more easily fit restaurant meals into the plan during Phases 2 and 3. Going out to eat is fine, but going off the plan is not, because if you do, you of course lose some of its benefits.

Try to choose restaurants that:

- Offer a variety of dishes made with wholegrain products (such as pasta), fish, seafood, vegetables and poultry.
- Are willing to modify dishes to suit your preferences.
- Indicate nutritious, low-calorie/low-fat or heart-healthy (i.e. olive oil rather than butter) choices on the menu.
- Offer a variety of vegetable salads.
- Tend to use low-fat sauces, such as vinaigrettes, wine sauces, citrus-juice sauces and tomato sauces.

• Provide adequate but not excessive portions. Refer to the portion sizes given throughout the meal plan for an idea of what reasonable portions look like.

Avoid restaurants that:

• Serve only or mostly fried food.
• Won't modify dishes to suit your preferences.
• Use mostly cream- or cheese-based sauces.
• Offer buffets or all-you-can-eat options.
• Provide especially large portions.
• Don't offer nutritious, heart-healthy or low-calorie/low-fat options on the menu.

Once you're inside the restaurant and seated at the table, you can take additional steps to stay on point. When the server comes to your table, ask the following questions.

1. Do you have any healthy dishes to recommend?
2. Does the menu give complete information about what's in a dish?
3. Is the chef/cook willing to modify dishes to make them healthier?

Then, before ordering any item from the menu, ask the server:

1. What's in the sauce of this dish? Does it contain butter, cream or cheese?
2. Is this dish rich or light in your opinion?
3. Are there any ingredients in this dish not listed on the menu, such as cream, cheese or meat?

STAYING ON POINT AT FAST-FOOD RESTAURANTS

I'd like to tell you to stop eating fast food altogether. Most fast-food restaurants offer selections that are very high in fat and calories, high in saturated fat and trans fat, high in sugar or salt, and very limited in nutri-

Your Restaurant Survival Guide

Use these pointers when eating at the following types of restaurants.

ITALIAN: Choose pasta, fish, seafood or poultry dishes with tomato-, olive oil- or wine-based sauces. Avoid excessive cheese, cream sauces or meat.

ASIAN: Choose vegetarian, tofu, seafood and poultry dishes. Ask for low-oil preparation.

MEXICAN: Avoid fried items, including tortilla chips, and dishes with excessive cheese. Choose soft tortillas instead of hard taco shells.

FRENCH: Avoid dishes with excessive cream, butter or cheese. Select restaurants offering southern French, or Provençal, cooking, which tends to be much lighter than northern French cuisine.

SNACK BARS: Choose wholemeal breads and lean cold meats such as sliced turkey breast. Avoid fatty, highly processed meats such as pastrami and corned beef. Use mustard instead of butter or mayonnaise.

FAST FOOD: Avoid fried foods and burgers. Take advantage of the wide selection to choose salads (avoid cheese and croutons), vegetable side dishes, fish, poultry, pasta or vegetarian dishes.

tional value. Most of their options combine too many flavours and calories in small packages. They are not flavour friendly.

That said, fast-food restaurants are convenient and inexpensive, and you may find them irresistible from time to time. Even as you work to reduce the role of fast food in your diet, use the following tips to improve the choices you make.

- Choose franchises such as Subway that offer and identify nutritious dishes instead of franchises that specialize in burgers or fried foods.

- Don't order deep-fried foods.
- At any fast-food restaurant or franchise you intend to visit repeatedly, ask to see a chart showing the calorie and nutritional content of the dishes you order. (You can often find the nutritional composition of foods on the websites of leading fast-food restaurants.) Identify and stick with minimally processed items with the fewest unnecessary additions of flavour enhancers. For example, a plain burger is better than a bacon cheeseburger smeared with mystery sauce.
- Don't order large or super sizes. These may give you more food for your money, but they also provide more calories, more fat, more salt and more sugar than any human being could possibly need in a meal.
- Choose water instead of fizzy drinks. They add many empty calories to a meal as well as increase the variety of flavours.
- Always make a salad with low-fat dressing part of your meal.
- Always add extra vegetables (such as lettuce, sliced tomato and onion) to your meal.
- Refrain from additions such as cheese or bacon.
- Choose dishes that are grilled, baked or poached. Also look for lean meat, fish, vegetarian and heart-healthy options.

STAYING ON POINT AT WORK

Don't let your company's cafeteria or vending machine options dictate how well you stick to the Flavour Point Meal Plan. Instead, get into the habit of using an insulated lunch bag to take nutritious lunch and snack items with you to work each day. This needn't take a lot of time. Consider the following quick and easy options.

Wholegrain cereal. Pick a good wholegrain cereal (see guidelines on page 48) and pack 20 g/ ¾ oz in a large zip-top bag to have as a morning snack. Either munch on it plain or mix it with fat-free yoghurt. Don't pack most major brands of cereal or breakfast bars. Although they claim to be wholegrain cereal, in fact, they're nothing more than confectionery filled with sugar, salt, hydrogenated oils and flavour enhancers.

Your Family at the Flavour Point
Betwixt with Tweens

If you have children between the ages of 10 and 13, you have tweens! Congratulations. We have them, too. Two, in fact: Valerie, age 11, and Natalia, age 10.

Tweens are still very dependent on you for their food choices; they can't just take off to McDonald's with their friends. That said, they are certainly old enough to have strong opinions. To take them to the Flavour Point, follow these tips.

- Give your kids an active voice in food selection. The more involved they are, the more cooperative they will be.
- If possible, let them help with food preparation. Tweens are much more willing to try a new food if they've had a hand in its preparation.
- Ask them to try the same new food repeatedly to give them a chance to acclimatize to it.

The Flavour Point Meal Plan will ease the way. Some of our pilot study participants told me that their kids had never really liked their cooking until they started following the Flavour Point Diet. Don't leave your children behind, betwixt and between. Take them by the hand and set them securely on the path to the Flavour Point right along with you.

Fresh fruit. Refreshing, sweet, relatively low in calories and generally rich in both nutrients and fibre, just about all types of fresh fruit make great snacks or accompaniments to lunch. Wash and cut or section fruit in advance so it's ready to eat. Match the fruit to the flavour theme of the day during Phases 1 and 2 and stick to one fruit at a time for Phase 3.

Dried fruit. Choose fruits that contain no added oils or sugar. Dates, figs, raisins, apricots, pears, prunes and dried bananas taste as sweet and chewy as confectionery but are great sources of nutrients, vitamins and fibre. Match the dried fruit with the theme of the day in Phases 1 and 2 and stick with one type at a time for Phase 3.

Canned fruit. Fruit packed in natural fruit juices is convenient to carry. Don't buy fruit packed in any kind of syrup, even light syrup. Stay away from so-called fruit snacks in the form of little gummy characters or chewy 'fruits'. They offer no nutrition and lots of added sugar, dyes and flavour enhancers. If you must indulge your sweet tooth, 100 per cent organic fruit leather made from concentrated fruit with no added sugar or oils fits into the plan.

Yoghurt. Fat-free natural yoghurt makes a great snack. Combine 120 ml/4 fl oz with dried fruit, fresh fruit and/or cereal, and you have a meal. Yoghurt provides plenty of calcium and is convenient to carry in single-serving containers. Check the serving size on tubs of yoghurt to make sure you're not exceeding the specified amount.

Wholemeal bread. Opt for a brand that has at least 2 grams of fibre per 100 calories and no trans fats (partially hydrogenated oil). Use two slices to create your own signature flavour-friendly sandwiches.

Wholegrain crackers. Pick a brand that has at least 2 grams of fibre per 100 calories. Spread with 2 tablespoons of plain hummus for an afternoon snack.

Veggies. Crunchy and satisfying to chew, raw vegetables are generally very low in calories and high in nutrients and fibre. Choose from convenient prewashed, packaged veggies in the produce section, such as baby carrots, broccoli, cauliflower and green beans. Eat them plain or with fat-free yoghurt dips from the meal plan, or try dipping them in store-bought hummus or fat-free salsa that you've packed in a small container. Consider purchasing a special container designed to hold a salad and a specific amount of dressing. Put packaged grated carrots, coleslaw or broccoli and baby spinach and other greens in the bottom section and fill the top with 2 capfuls of Newman's Own Light Italian Dressing.

Dips. For a great afternoon snack, take along some dip and wholemeal bread, crackers or veggies. Make your own dips from beans or veggies or buy prepared dips, hummus, salsa or less-than-2-per-cent fat cottage cheese, fat-free yoghurt or fromage frais.

Nuts and seeds. Packed with healthy essential natural oils, raw nuts make a convenient snack food. Because they're easy to overeat, however, pack only a small portion and take along only one variety per day. You can also buy packaged trail mixes, which are combinations of dried fruits, nuts, seeds and cereals, but avoid mixes that include any added sugar or oil, coconut or chocolate chips.

Lean protein. Use the following lean protein foods for your lunches.

90 g/3 oz canned light tuna in springwater

1 hard-boiled egg packed in a zip-top bag

65 g/2¼ oz rinsed and drained chickpeas or beans mixed with salad greens packed in a bag or container

3 slices plain, unprocessed roasted turkey breast packed in a zip-top bag

Drinks. Always take a bottle filled with iced water. Don't pack sports drinks, juice cocktails or fizzy drinks.

Your Family at the Flavour Point
Pacifying Your Pipsqueaks

I have been surprised at the number of times parents have told me their 3- or 4-year-olds simply refuse to eat the right foods. What would you do if your child simply refused not to play in traffic?

To encourage your young children to eat healthier foods, be assertive. How your kids eat is every bit as important to their health as being vaccinated or getting enough exercise. Second, keep trying. Familiarity breeds preference! We all like what we're used to, and your children will dislike new foods just because they are new. Stick with them for a while. Once your chil-dren adjust, they'll be much more accepting.

Third, no one, including a child, likes to be duped. Your kids will doubtless want the products they see peddled on TV. As soon as they're old enough to under-stand (our 6-year-old son cer-tainly is), tell them that food ads may be deceiving them into eat-ing things that really aren't good for them.

Discuss, explain, set limits, occasionally compromise and, above all, set a good example. Your child will follow you towards a lifetime of health. There is no greater gift a parent can give!

PART 2

THE PLAN

4

THE FLAVOUR POINT
MEAL PLAN

6 weeks of delicious, convenient and flavour-friendly
meals that turn down the Flavour Point

Are you a busy parent who sometimes doesn't have time to microwave a frozen dinner, much less pull out the pots and pans and become reacquainted with your oven? Have you always wanted to lose weight but just couldn't find the internal motivation, energy and time to pull it off?

Even if you answered yes to both questions, you can still succeed on the Flavour Point Diet. A busy mother of five developed and tested all of the recipes in this meal plan. With a 6-year-old taking Tae Kwon Do and football, a 10- and 11-year-old needing help with homework and rides to dance classes, two teens with active social lives, three dogs, two rabbits and me to look after, my wife and writing partner, Catherine doesn't exactly have spare time on her hands. Over the years, she's developed many time-saving tricks that help her create delicious, mouthwatering, healthy and *convenient* meals night after night after night. She buys prechopped vegetables, has developed many quick-preparation cooking techniques, and has learned to always have all the right ingredients at hand.

She shares those time-saving tricks with you throughout this meal plan and in the recipes in Chapter 5. In less time than it would take to get to and from the take-away, you can prepare a Flavour Point Diet meal.

Whenever possible, we suggest breakfasts, lunches and snacks that require minimal preparation. Although dinners require slightly more prep work, these too will become a convenient way of life once you properly stock your kitchen and begin to make certain meals and side dishes by rote. In our test group, we found that most participants were able to significantly decrease their prep time by week 2.

Unlike many meal plans you may find in other diet books, this one also offers you plenty of choices. You can follow the standard plan, sticking to each suggested breakfast, lunch, dinner and snack exactly. Or you can go off the beaten path slightly, depending on your goals. Let's say you'd like to lose weight more quickly. Perhaps you have a school reunion coming up, and you want to look your best. In the meal plan, you'll find suggestions to make that happen. Or maybe you've had a busy week and haven't had time to shop for food. Not to worry. The plan includes emergency rations that you can turn to when you're pushed for time.

The more you make the plan fit your needs, the more successful you'll become. If you find a meal you particularly like or one you don't like, go ahead and replace that meal with another from the same week. It's that flexible. Every dieter I've ever counselled has changed the diet plan they were on to suit their particular needs. Since I know you're just as likely to modify this meal plan, I've built in tips for doing so right from the start. Let's take a look at how the plan allows you to customize it to your needs.

CN)   CHOW NOW MEALS

Most Flavour Point Diet dinners are simple and relatively quick to prepare, but some of them do require time to cook or bake – from 15 minutes to 1 hour (in the case of roast chicken). On days when you know you're going to walk in the door at 7 in the evening, and the whole family is going to want 'chow now', we designed 1 or 2 days per week where dinner requires 15 minutes or less, including cooking time, from start to finish. That's probably less time than it takes to get to a fast-food restaurant, which is why I like to call these Chow Now meals. Plan to have these dinners on days when you know you'll be busy; just look for the symbol next to a recipe.

You don't need to follow the exact sequence of the meal plan; you simply must stick with the choices for that week. Thus, if you have a busy day on a Wednesday, but you see a meal with a Chow Now symbol on a Tuesday, go ahead and cook Tuesday's suggested meal on Wednesday. If you plan ahead, you can save even more time. For example, when you prepare any dinner, make twice as much and use the leftovers later in the week. Do that twice in a week, and you'll cut out 2 days of food preparation. You may find that preparing dinners on the weekend and having them handy in the refrigerator or freezer to repeat on a busy day during the week also works well.

SPECIAL INDULGENCE DAYS

At the end of the meal plan, you will find two special days, one based on chocolate and the other on coconut. Yummy, right? Even these indulgences are Flavour Point approved – and nutritious, too. Any time during or after week 3 of the plan, you can select up to one indulgence day per week.

Our group of 20 men and women who tested the meal plan loved these meals and turned to them regularly. The chocolate lovers in particular told me that the indulgence days were a great aspect of this diet because eating their favourite flavour repeatedly on just one day during the week subdued their cravings for that flavour the rest of the week. So don't feel guilty. Just indulge!

FLAVOUR-FRIENDLY ALTERNATIVES

Many nutritious foods, such as wholegrain breakfast cereals, are relatively flavour neutral and fit into any flavour theme. In addition to cereal, fresh fruits and vegetables work for any phase of any week of the meal plan.

I've included a list of flavour-friendly options, which you can mix and match with any flavour theme, on pages 123–125. This provides you with more control over your daily menu, more choices and more convenience. All of the Flavour-Friendly Alternatives require little or no preparation and no special shopping, and they even adapt to restaurant eating. For example, when you're eating out for breakfast, pick the cereal option with skimmed milk, the wholemeal toast, the porridge or two eggs. When eating lunch at a restaurant, you can choose the salad with oil and vinegar on the side and grilled fish or chicken breast. Just stick with the amount specified in the menu plan. You can use these options at any time for any meal during any week or phase of the plan.

⫴WLE   WEIGHT-LOSS EXPRESS

The Flavour Point Diet will help you lose weight at a brisk but reasonable pace and then help you keep it off forever. When I tested the diet on 20 participants, however, I learned that for some people, the meal plan provides more food than they need to feel full and satisfied. If you fall into that category, don't try to stuff yourself silly in order to lose weight. If you don't mind cutting a few more calories and losing weight even faster, use the Weight-Loss Express options. You can make these lower-calorie substitutions for various meals throughout the plan; just look for the symbol.

THE FAMILY PLAN

Any weight-loss programme is designed especially for the person who is trying to lose weight – you! If you have a family, you know how difficult it is to go on a diet while serving different food to everyone else. The Flavour Point Meal Plan will help you avoid this problem. Catherine tested all of her recipes on our family of seven people, including children ranging from age 6 to 17. Also, during our pilot test of the diet, participants took their whole families along with them and reported that, for the most part, their spouses and kids loved the food. We have incredible reports of spouses and children losing weight (sometimes as much as or more than the actual dieter!) and improving their health. If, however, your children object to certain meals on the plan, look to the Flavour-Friendly Alternatives for help. Make these quick and easy meals for your children and something more adult and delicious for yourself.

To make the plan as family friendly as possible, most dinners serve four unless otherwise noted. If you have fewer people to feed, either prepare single servings or freeze the leftovers for a meal later during the week or for other phases of the plan. Every recipe in the plan will be just as delicious after spending a few weeks in your freezer.

As with dinner, desserts also always serve four (and sometimes six). Dessert is, of course, optional, but it's available on every day of the plan, and the nutritional analysis you'll find at the bottom of each daily menu always includes dessert. Feel free to indulge if you need something sweet to end your meal or as an evening snack. You can, of course, omit dessert to accelerate your weight loss.

(continued on page 70)

Can You Drink Coffee?

Although some diets recommend that you cut back on caffeine in order to lose weight, I don't see any need for this. First, going without caffeine may make you tired, and if you're tired, you'll have more difficulty sticking with your new habits. Second, research shows that caffeine probably facilitates weight loss. So there's no need to give up that morning cup. Just be careful what you put in it, since the calories in sugar and cream can quickly add up. That's why I recommend using undiluted non-fat dried milk (unlike skimmed milk, it won't turn your coffee grey).

Satisfaction at the Flavour Point

THE FLAVOUR FACTS

Name: Patty Finn

Age: 45

Family status: Single

Occupation: Assistant director of
economic development

Starting weight: 106 kg/16 st 10 lb

Weight lost: 11 kg/24 lb in 12 weeks

Health stats: Blood pressure
dropped 21 points; cholesterol
dropped 0.62 points; lost 18
cm/7 in from waist; over 7 per
cent decline in body fat

'My slip fell down at work again
today. I reached up for something,
and it fell right down to the floor.
That's a good thing. It fell down
because I lost 24 lb [11 kg]! Until
I have a chance to go out and get
some new ones, I guess I'll just have
to safety-pin my slips to my skirts.

'I've struggled with fad diets in
the past. I tried low-carb diets, and
I'm not a meat eater, so I just found
them to be gross. Then I tried
xenadrine supplements to boost my
metabolism. They turned me into a
total monster. I lost weight fast with
both plans, but when I stopped them,
the weight came back twofold.

'I knew of Dr Katz and was very
impressed with what I had heard
about him, so I knew his plan was
probably not only effective but also
realistic and healthy. I went for it.

'I think the most important
thing Dr Katz taught, which I'll take
with me for life, is to examine what
I'm eating, to take a packet and
read every ingredient that I'm
putting in my body. Before this
plan, I was constantly on the run, so
I often ate things that were
quick . . . and not so good for me.
I'm still just as busy, but Dr Katz
has shown me how to make better
choices. For instance, he taught me
that even though the packaging
leads unsuspecting customers (like
me) to believe they're healthy, cereal
bars are loaded with sugar. He
taught me a quick and easy way to
choose better foods: look at the list
of ingredients. The fewer ingredients
listed, the more nutritious and less

appetite-stimulating the food.

'I also think the plan worked well for me because it incorporated foods I like. There is nothing in it that I got sick of. Whenever a sweet tooth strikes, I now have healthy foods I can eat to satisfy it. Plus, I now enjoy sitting down for a good meal instead of constantly eating on the go.

'For breakfast and lunch, I usually chose one of the flavour-friendly options, like cereal or a salad with chicken breast or soup. For dinner, I loved the chicken dishes. I'm a chicken person. My favourite dish was the Roast Chicken with Currant Wine Glaze and Caramelized Onions.

'As far as the snacks are concerned, I've never been a big snacker. Most of the time, I don't even eat the snacks – or the desserts – because I'm too full. There is almost too much food on the programme; I can't finish it all.

'Overall, I can honestly say my food preferences have changed. Now I look at a plate of fries, and I don't want them any more.

'When I'm eating out, I now truly see that restaurant portions are at least three times too big. When I go out to a restaurant, I ask for foods to be grilled instead of fried, and I never finish my whole meal.

'One of the best outcomes of the programme is that I no longer take my prescription medication for heartburn. I haven't had heartburn at all since I started the programme 12 weeks ago! I've also noticed that my energy level has gone through the roof, and I've been walking every morning as a result.

'People have really noticed my weight loss and have been encouraging me. My boyfriend works out a lot and watches what he eats. He was happy that I tried Dr Katz's programme instead of yet another fad diet – he wants me to lose weight sensibly and healthily, and that's exactly what this programme has helped me to do.

'I will most definitely stay on Dr Katz's programme. I will never ever go back to the weight I was at before I started. This programme makes complete sense, and I'm sticking with it for life!' ■

LEARNING BY ROTE

Each dinner in the plan includes a source of protein along with the following quick and easy staples. If, some evening, you find yourself with absolutely no time to make dinner, you can throw a nutritious meal together for the whole family by grabbing a ready-made roast chicken at your local supermarket and serving it (without the skin) with the salad, whole grain and veggies below in less than 5 minutes.

Salad. Every day with dinner, you'll have a salad, something you throw together without even a thought. To make this truly effortless, keep packaged, prewashed baby greens and precut veggies in your fridge, ready to go every day. Just mix with olive oil and vinegar or Newman's Own Light Italian Dressing.

Bulgur wheat. With almost every dinner, you'll make a wholegrain side dish. Bulgur wheat, or cracked wheat, is a great choice. This delicious wholegrain side dish takes 5 minutes to prepare, and it will become a hit with your kids. It's relatively low in calories and high in fibre and protein. It also never clumps. Double the recipe and keep leftovers handy to use cold for a lunch salad. You can also reheat it for 2 minutes in the microwave for a subsequent dinner side dish. Bulgur keeps well for 1 week in an airtight container in the fridge.

Vegetables. You'll also have veggies every evening, either as part of the sauce for the main course or separately, sautéed in olive oil. Feel free to use packaged, precut vegetables, either frozen or fresh. The recipe for sautéing is always the same: heat 1 to 2 teaspoons of olive oil in a frying pan on a high heat, add the veggies, a pinch of salt, and cook for 5 minutes. That's it. Unless the flavour theme is based on a particular vegetable, feel free to sauté the same amount of whatever veggies you happen to have on hand. That way, you don't have to stop and think about which veggies to get when shopping.

PHASE 1

WEEK 1

DAY 1 **RAISIN/CURRANT DAY**

DAY 2 **PINEAPPLE DAY**

DAY 3 **CRANBERRY DAY**

DAY 4 **LEMON DAY**

DAY 5 **PEACH DAY**

DAY 6 **ORANGE DAY** CN

DAY 7 **APPLE DAY**

DAY 1 **RAISIN/CURRANT DAY**

BREAKFAST

45 g/1½ oz wholegrain cereal with 2 tbsp raisins and 120 ml/4 fl oz skimmed milk

OR

⫷≡**WLE** Grape-Banana Smoothie (page 141)

MIDMORNING SNACK

240 ml/8 fl oz fat-free natural yoghurt with 1 tbsp raisins or currants

LUNCH

Spinach and Lentil Salad with Feta, Walnuts and Currants (page 158)

MIDAFTERNOON SNACK

Grape-Banana Smoothie (page 141)

OR

⫷≡**WLE** about 25 red or green grapes

DINNER FOR 4

Roast Chicken with Currant Wine Glaze and Caramelized Onions (page 178)

455 g/1 lb sautéed fresh or frozen green beans

Tossed Garden Salad (page 201; add 1 tbsp currants)

DESSERT FOR 4 (OPTIONAL)

Raisin-Muesli Parfait (page 230)

OR

⫷≡**WLE** about 25 red or green grapes

Daily Nutrition Facts

REGULAR

1,499 calories/6,266 kJ: 19% from fat (3% from sat fat), 25% from protein, 54% from carbohydrate; 30 g fibre, 1,850 mg sodium

WEIGHT-LOSS EXPRESS

1,301 calories/5,438 kJ: 21% from fat (4% from sat fat), 23% from protein, 53% from carbohydrate; 23 g fibre, 1,423 mg sodium

DAY 2 **PINEAPPLE DAY**

BREAKFAST

45 g/1½ oz wholegrain cereal with 120 ml/4 fl oz skimmed milk

180 ml/6 fl oz 100% pineapple juice

OR

 Pineapple Smoothie (page 141)

MIDMORNING SNACK

180 ml/6 fl oz low-fat pineapple yoghurt

LUNCH

Pineapple-Walnut Chicken Salad (page 167)

10 g/½ oz multi- or whole-grain crackers (see page 48)

MIDAFTERNOON SNACK

90 g/3 oz fresh or canned unsweetened pineapple chunks

OR

 300 ml/10 fl oz pineapple fizz (180 ml/6 fl oz fizzy mineral water and 120 ml/4 fl oz 100% pineapple juice)

DINNER FOR 4

Pineapple Prawns (page 200)

285 g/10 oz bulgur wheat, cooked (page 218)

455 g/1 lb sautéed fresh or frozen sugar snap peas

Tossed Garden Salad (page 201)

DESSERT FOR 4 (OPTIONAL)

Caramelized Pineapple Rings (page 224)

OR

 2 fresh or canned unsweetened pineapple rings per person

Daily Nutrition Facts
REGULAR

1,459 calories/6,099 kJ: 19% from fat (5% from sat fat), 20% from protein, 62% from carbohydrate; 33 g fibre, 1,392 mg sodium

WEIGHT-LOSS EXPRESS

1,281 calories/5,354 kJ: 18% from fat (3% from sat fat), 20% from protein, 62% from carbohydrate; 25 g fibre, 1,142 mg sodium

DAY 3 **CRANBERRY DAY**

BREAKFAST

2 Cranberry-Banana Soft Wheat Muffins (page 134)

240 ml/8 fl oz skimmed milk

OR

⊱≡WLE Cranberry-Banana Smoothie (page 141)

MIDMORNING SNACK

120 ml/4 fl oz fat-free natural yoghurt with 2 tsp dried cranberries and 1 tbsp low-fat, fruit-free muesli

LUNCH

Mixed Greens and Lentil Salad with Feta, Pecans and Cranberries (page 159)

MIDAFTERNOON SNACK

Cranberry-Banana Smoothie (page 141)

DINNER FOR 4

Cranberry and Sweet Onion Turkey Breast Steaks (page 187)

Baked sweet potatoes (wrap 2 whole sweet potatoes in aluminium foil and bake at 190°C/375°F/gas 5 until tender; unwrap and cut each in half for 1 serving)

Tossed Garden Salad (page 201; add 2 tsp dried cranberries)

DESSERT FOR 4 (OPTIONAL)

Cranberry-Vanilla Soft Ice Cream (page 232)

OR

⊱≡WLE No dessert

Daily Nutrition Facts

REGULAR

1,453 calories/6,088 kJ: 20% from fat (3% from sat fat), 23% from protein, 57% from carbohydrate; 24 g fibre, 1,272 mg sodium

WEIGHT-LOSS EXPRESS

1,272 calories/5,317 kJ: 17% from fat (3% from sat fat), 23% from protein, 60% from carbohydrate; 24 g fibre, 1,062 mg sodium

DAY 4 **LEMON DAY**

BREAKFAST

2 Lemon-Poppy Soft Wheat Muffins (page 136)

OR

⟨≡**WLE** Lemon-Orange Smoothie (page 142)

MIDMORNING SNACK

180 ml/6 fl oz fat-free lemon yoghurt with 15 g/½ oz wholegrain cereal

LUNCH

Lemon Tabbouleh Salad (page 157)

MIDAFTERNOON SNACK

Lemon-Orange Smoothie (page 142)

OR

⟨≡**WLE** 90 g/3 oz less-than-2%-fat cottage cheese

350 ml/12 fl oz lemon fizz (300 ml/10 fl oz fizzy mineral water and juice of ½ lemon)

DINNER FOR 4

Pan-Seared Cod with Lemon Chives and Capers (page 193)

455 g/1 lb sautéed fresh or frozen asparagus with grated lemon zest

425 g/15 oz unprocessed oven chips (baked according to packet directions)

Tossed Garden Salad (page 201; add juice of ½ lemon)

DESSERT FOR 4 (OPTIONAL)

500 g/1 lb 2 oz fresh blueberries with lemon zest

Daily Nutrition Facts

REGULAR

1,415 calories/5,915 kJ: 23% from fat (3% from sat fat), 19% from protein, 57% from carbohydrate; 30 g fibre, 1,281 mg sodium

WEIGHT-LOSS EXPRESS

1,257 calories/5,254 kJ: 20% from fat (3% from sat fat), 23% from protein, 57% from carbohydrate; 27 g fibre, 1,551 mg sodium

DAY 5 **PEACH DAY**

BREAKFAST

45 g/1½ oz wholegrain cereal with 120 ml/4 fl oz skimmed milk

1 fresh peach or 90 g/3 oz canned unsweetened peaches

MIDMORNING SNACK

120 ml/4 fl oz fat-free peach yoghurt with 1 tbsp chopped pecans

LUNCH

Peanut butter and peach jam sandwich (2 slices wholemeal bread, 1 tbsp natural peanut butter and 1 tbsp high-fruit peach jam)

240 ml/8 fl oz skimmed milk

OR

≡WLE Peach-Banana Smoothie (page 141)

MIDAFTERNOON SNACK

90 g/3 oz canned unsweetened peaches

DINNER FOR 4

Peach-Coriander Turkey with Oven-Roasted Potatoes and Turnips (page 188)

Tossed Garden Salad (page 201)

DESSERT FOR 6 (OPTIONAL)

Peach Flat Cake (page 225)

OR

≡WLE 1 ripe peach per person

Daily Nutrition Facts

REGULAR

1,493 calories/6,241 kJ: 23% from fat (4% from sat fat), 19% from protein, 57% from carbohydrate; 37 g fibre, 1,825 mg sodium

WEIGHT-LOSS EXPRESS

1,204 calories/5,032 kJ: 17% from fat (3% from sat fat), 18% from protein, 64% from carbohydrate; 31 g fibre, 1,438 mg sodium

DAY 6 **ORANGE DAY**

BREAKFAST

45 g/1½ oz wholegrain cereal with 120 ml/4 fl oz skimmed milk

180 ml/6 fl oz 100% orange juice

OR

WLE Orange-Banana Smoothie (page 141)

MIDMORNING SNACK

120 ml/4 fl oz fat-free natural yoghurt with 1 sliced orange and 2 tsp raisins

OR

WLE Omit the yoghurt and raisins

LUNCH

Spinach and Orange-Lentil Salad with Feta and Pecans (page 159)

MIDAFTERNOON SNACK

Orange-Banana Smoothie (page 141)

OR

WLE 300 ml/10 fl oz orange fizz (180 ml/6 fl oz fizzy mineral water and 120 ml/4 fl oz 100% orange juice)

DINNER FOR 4

CN *Orange Grilled Tuna (page 195)*

285 g/10 oz bulgur wheat, cooked (page 218)

455 g/1 lb sautéed fresh or frozen green beans with grated orange zest

Tossed Garden Salad (page 201; add juice of ½ orange)

DESSERT FOR 4 (OPTIONAL)

Fat-free orange sorbet; 120 ml/4 fl oz per person

OR

WLE 1 sliced orange per person

Daily Nutrition Facts

REGULAR

1,499 calories/6,266 kJ: 18% from fat (3% from sat fat), 20% from protein, 62% from carbohydrate; 38 g fibre, 1,248 mg sodium

WEIGHT-LOSS EXPRESS

1,214 calories/5,075 kJ: 22% from fat (3% from sat fat), 21% from protein, 58% from carbohydrate; 34 g fibre, 928 mg sodium

DAY 7 **APPLE DAY**

BREAKFAST

Apple-Raisin Porridge (page 133)

OR

 Apple-Banana Smoothie (page 140)

MIDMORNING SNACK

120 ml/4 fl oz unsweetened apple sauce

120 ml/4 fl oz fat-free natural yoghurt

LUNCH

Apple-Walnut Chicken Salad (page 166)

10 g/½ oz multi- or whole-grain crackers (see page 48)

MIDAFTERNOON SNACK

½ sliced apple spread with 1 tbsp natural peanut butter

OR

 300 ml/10 fl oz apple fizz (180 ml/6 fl oz fizzy mineral water and 120 ml/4 fl oz 100% apple juice)

DINNER FOR 4

Apple-Butternut Squash Soup (page 207)

2 slices wholemeal bread per person

Tossed Garden Salad (page 201)

DESSERT FOR 4 (OPTIONAL)

Warm Apple Crisp (page 231)

Daily Nutrition Facts

REGULAR

1,424 calories/5,952 kJ: 22% from fat (3% from sat fat), 18% from protein, 60% from carbohydrate; 40 g fibre, 1,361 mg sodium

WEIGHT-LOSS EXPRESS

1,236 calories/5,166 kJ: 18% from fat (3% from sat fat), 17% from protein, 65% from carbohydrate; 33 g fibre, 1,313 mg sodium

WEEK 2

DAY 8 **TOMATO DAY**

DAY 9 **CARROT DAY**

DAY 10 **MUSHROOM DAY**

DAY 11 **ONION DAY**

DAY 12 **PUMPKIN DAY** CN

DAY 13 **SPINACH DAY**

DAY 14 **PEPPER (CAPSICUM) DAY**

DAY 8 **TOMATO DAY**

BREAKFAST

Tomato and egg sandwich (2 slices wholemeal bread, 1 soft-boiled egg, 2 slices tomato and 1 tbsp grated light mozzarella, melted)

OR

WLE Use 1 slice bread and omit the cheese and 1 slice tomato

MIDMORNING SNACK

12 cherry tomatoes with 2 tbsp hummus

OR

WLE Omit the hummus

LUNCH

Tomato and Black Bean Mediterranean Salad (page 163) in ½ whole-wheat pitta

OR

WLE Omit the pitta

MIDAFTERNOON SNACK

12 baked corn chips with 60 g/2 oz tomato salsa

OR

WLE Replace the chips with 12 baby carrots

DINNER FOR 4

Baked Monkfish with Tomatoes, Olives and Capers (page 192)

285 g/10 oz bulgur wheat, cooked (page 218)

340 g/12 oz sautéed fresh or frozen cauliflower florets

Tossed Garden Salad (page 201; add 300 g/10½ oz rinsed and drained chickpeas)

DESSERT FOR 4 (OPTIONAL)

Peach-blueberry salad (340 g/12 oz fresh or canned peach slices and 250 g/9 oz blueberries)

Daily Nutrition Facts

REGULAR

1,535 calories/6,416 kJ: 24% from fat (5% from sat fat), 20% from protein, 56% from carbohydrate; 53 g fibre, 2,186 mg sodium

WEIGHT-LOSS EXPRESS

1,289 calories/5,388 kJ: 27% from fat (5% from sat fat), 22% from protein, 52% from carbohydrate; 44 g fibre, 1,884 mg sodium

DAY 9 **CARROT DAY**

BREAKFAST

45 g/1½ oz wholegrain cereal with 120 ml/4 fl oz skimmed milk

180 ml/6 fl oz 100% carrot-orange juice

OR

 Carrot-Pineapple Smoothie (page 141)

MIDMORNING SNACK

Up to 18 baby carrots with 90 g/3 oz less-than-2%-fat cottage cheese

LUNCH

Carrot, hummus, tomato and avocado sandwich (2 slices wholemeal bread, 2 tbsp hummus, 60 g/2 oz grated carrots, ¼ sliced avocado, ½ sliced tomato and alfalfa sprouts to taste)

OR

 Omit the avocado

MIDAFTERNOON SNACK

Up to 18 baby carrots with 80 ml/3 fl oz fat-free bean dip

OR

Omit the bean dip

DINNER FOR 4

Carrot Cider-Glazed Chicken (page 170)

500 g/1 lb 2 oz cooked brown rice (page 218)

455 g/1 lb sautéed fresh or frozen broccoli

Tossed Garden Salad (page 201)

DESSERT FOR 4 (OPTIONAL)

Oranges with honey yoghurt drizzle (peel and slice 4 oranges; whisk together 120 ml/4 fl oz fat-free natural yoghurt and 1 tbsp honey)

Daily Nutrition Facts

REGULAR

1,515 calories/6,333 kJ: 19% from fat (3% from sat fat), 21% from protein, 60% from carbohydrate; 41 g fibre, 2,115 mg sodium

WEIGHT-LOSS EXPRESS

1,244 calories/5,200 kJ: 17% from fat (3% from sat fat), 21% from protein, 62% from carbohydrate; 29 g fibre, 1,591 mg sodium

DAY 10 **MUSHROOM DAY**

BREAKFAST

Mushroom, Thyme and Cheese Omelette (page 139)

1 slice wholemeal toast, plain or with 1 tsp trans-fat-free margarine

MIDMORNING SNACK

10 baby carrots with Mushroom Dip (page 146)

OR

WLE 2 sliced celery sticks with Mushroom Dip

LUNCH

Portobello Mushroom, Gorgonzola and Sun-Dried Tomato Sandwich (page 165)

OR

WLE Omit the Gorgonzola

MIDAFTERNOON SNACK

20 g/¾ oz multi- or whole-grain crackers (see page 48) with Mushroom Dip (page 146)

OR

WLE 10 pepper strips with Mushroom Dip

DINNER FOR 4

Chicken in Creamy Dijon Mushroom Sauce (page 174)

500 g/1 lb 2 oz cooked brown rice (page 218)

455 g/1 lb sautéed fresh or frozen broccoli florets

Tossed Garden Salad (page 201; add fresh mushrooms)

DESSERT FOR 4 (OPTIONAL)

Fruit salad (1 sliced banana; 2 medium apples, cored and cut into small chunks; and 24 grapes)

Daily Nutrition Facts

REGULAR

1,469 calories/6,140 kJ: 22% from fat (5% from sat fat), 25% from protein, 52% from carbohydrate; 38 g fibre, 2,013 mg sodium

WEIGHT-LOSS EXPRESS

1,347 calories/5,630 kJ: 21% from fat (5% from sat fat), 26% from protein, 51% from carbohydrate; 37 g fibre, 1,851 mg sodium

DAY 11 **ONION DAY**

BREAKFAST

Spring Onion and Cheese Omelette (page 139)

1 slice wholemeal toast, plain or with 1 tsp trans-fat-free margarine

MIDMORNING SNACK

10 baby carrots and celery sticks with Spring Onion Yoghurt Dip (page 147)

LUNCH

Red Onion, White Bean, Lentil and Tomato Salad (page 161)

4 light wholemeal pitta chips

OR

WLE Omit the beans and pitta chips and add 1 tomato

MIDAFTERNOON SNACK

20 g/¾ oz multi- or whole-grain crackers (see page 48) with Spring Onion Yoghurt Dip (page 147)

OR

WLE Replace the crackers with 1 cucumber cut into sticks

DINNER FOR 4

Grilled Chicken with Caramelized Onion on Pitta (page 179)

Cucumber, Tomato, Olive and Red Onion Salad (page 202)

DESSERT FOR 4 (OPTIONAL)

Fruit salad (1 sliced banana; 2 medium apples, cored and cut into small chunks; and 24 grapes)

Daily Nutrition Facts

REGULAR

1,436 calories/6,002 kJ: 31% from fat (6% from sat fat), 21% from protein, 48% from carbohydrate; 35 g fibre, 2,127 mg sodium

WEIGHT-LOSS EXPRESS

1,298 calories/5,426 kJ: 32% from fat (6% from sat fat), 22% from protein, 46% from carbohydrate; 33 g fibre, 1,749 mg sodium

Satisfaction at the Flavour Point

THE FLAVOUR FACTS

Name: Carol Borger

Age: 46

Family status: Married with two children, aged 15 and 17

Occupation: Phlebotomist

Starting weight: 83 kg/13 st 1 lb

Weight lost: 7.6 kg/17 lb in 12 weeks

Health stats: Blood pressure dropped 15 points; cholesterol dropped 1.39 points; irritable bowel flare-ups have disappeared; 5½ per cent decline in body fat

'Until recently, I only knew how to cook meat and potatoes. That's what my mother cooked, so that's what I cooked. When I found out that my cholesterol was very high, and my husband's and two kids' levels were high too, I said, "That's it – we have to do something." When I heard about Dr Katz's programme, I knew I had found that something.

'For the most part, my family has been on board because they know I'm doing this for the right reasons. They liked the food I used to cook, but they're learning to accept the fact that it was horrible for us and that we all needed to make a change. I can't say they've been as strict as I have, but they've been doing most of the programme with me. My husband has lost 21 lb [9.4 kg] so far.

'I've been choosing flavour-friendly options for breakfast and lunch, but when it comes time for dinner, I'm amazed at how easy it is to cook healthily. I made peanut butter prawns the other night, and other than peeling the prawns, it was simple, and it tasted absolutely amazing. The coconut chicken has also been a big hit, along with the stuffed peppers with bulgur wheat and ground turkey and the cod with lemon sauce. I've also started improvising with some of the recipes. I created breading with flour and crackers and made great breaded haddock and chicken Parmesan with it.

'All the flavours on the programme help make it more interesting and satisfying, and the themes have introduced me to new foods and spices. I've also learned some great tricks for saving calories, like using natural yoghurt instead of mayo in chicken salad and ground turkey instead of ground beef. I slipped some ground turkey into a recipe and told my husband it was beef – he had no idea! I've also stocked my kitchen with healthy snacks. Now, when my kids come home from school, they munch on high-fibre cereal instead of crisps. We've also been making a lot of the smoothies with fresh fruit and vanilla yoghurt. The blender gets a lot of use in our house.

'I'm totally satisfied on the plan. There is more food on our table than ever before, but fewer calories. If I do start to feel a little hungry, I reach for a piece of fruit. It's amazing. I don't miss the red meat at all. I haven't craved red meat since I started. I also don't crave sweets like I used to. My son just headed out the door to get some ice cream, and I wasn't the least bit tempted to ask him to pick something up for me.

'Health-wise, the programme has done wonders for me. Not only have I lost 17 lb [7.6 kg], but my cholesterol and triglycerides dropped, and I've lost more than 4 in [10 cm] off my waist. Before I started, I had regular symptoms of irritable bowel syndrome, and they've completely disappeared. The other night, I had a piece of pizza and felt uncomfortable and bloated for 2 days. It reminded me of how bad my old eating habits used to make me feel.

'I also love the way I look. The other day, I was shopping for new clothes with my daughter, and I caught a glimpse of myself in a mirror. I backed up to take a second look and said, "Wow!" I'm 46 years old, I just lost 17 lb [7.6 kg], and I'm fitting into a size 12. I'm pretty happy with that. And everybody notices the change, especially in my face. I've lost a few chins, and my bum looks cute now.

'This programme has truly changed my life. It's so rewarding to see my cholesterol and triglycerides go down without medication. I know I can stick with this. I've made the change, and this is the way I and my whole family are going to eat from now on.' ■

DAY 12 **PUMPKIN DAY**

BREAKFAST

2 Pumpkin-Banana Soft Wheat Muffins (page 135)

OR

╒≡WLE 1 slice wholemeal toast spread with 2 tsp natural peanut butter mixed with 1 tbsp canned pumpkin

MIDMORNING SNACK

Pumpkin-Allspice Smoothie (page 142)

LUNCH

Pumpkin and Chocolate Grilled Panini (page 168)

180 ml/6 fl oz skimmed milk

MIDAFTERNOON SNACK

Pumpkin-Allspice Smoothie (page 142)

DINNER FOR 4

CN *Pumpkin Soup (page 213)*

2 slices wholemeal bread per person

OR

╒≡WLE Omit 1 slice bread per person

Tossed Garden Salad (page 201; add 300 g/10½ oz rinsed and drained chickpeas and 60 g/2 oz feta)

DESSERT FOR 4 (OPTIONAL)

Pumpkin Soft Ice Cream (page 233)

Daily Nutrition Facts

REGULAR

1,461 calories/6,107 kJ: 22% from fat (4% from sat fat), 18% from protein, 61% from carbohydrate; 50 g fibre, 1,855 mg sodium

WEIGHT-LOSS EXPRESS

1,290 calories/5,392 kJ: 19% from fat (4% from sat fat), 18% from protein, 63% from carbohydrate; 47 g fibre, 1,762 mg sodium

DAY 13 **SPINACH DAY**

BREAKFAST

Spinach and Feta Omelette (page 139)

1 slice wholemeal toast, plain or with 1 tsp trans-fat-free margarine

OR

⟨≡WLE 30 g/1 oz wholegrain cereal with 120 ml/4 fl oz skimmed milk

MIDMORNING SNACK

20 g/¾ oz multi- or whole-grain crackers (see page 48) with Spinach Yoghurt Dip (page 148)

LUNCH

Spinach and Turkey Salad (page 162)

MIDAFTERNOON SNACK

Up to 18 baby carrots with Spinach Yoghurt Dip (page 148)

DINNER FOR 4

Pasta Fagioli with Spinach Marinara Sauce (page 205)

Tossed Garden Salad (page 201; make with spinach)

DESSERT FOR 4 (OPTIONAL)

Mixed-berry salad (125 g/4½ oz each fresh blueberries, raspberries and blackberries)

OR

⟨≡WLE No dessert

Daily Nutrition Facts

REGULAR

1,449 calories/6,057 kJ: 27% from fat (5% from sat fat), 20% from protein, 54% from carbohydrate; 47 g fibre, 2,715 mg sodium

WEIGHT-LOSS EXPRESS

1,284 calories/5,367 kJ: 21% from fat (3% from sat fat), 19% from protein, 59% from carbohydrate; 43 g fibre, 2,284 mg sodium

DAY 14 **PEPPER (CAPSICUM) DAY**

BREAKFAST

Pepper and Cheese Omelette (page 138)

1 slice wholemeal toast, plain or with 1 tsp trans-fat-free margarine

OR

WLE 30 g/1 oz wholegrain cereal with 120 ml/4 fl oz skimmed milk

MIDMORNING SNACK

Up to 18 baby carrots with Sweet Pepper Yoghurt Dip (page 145)

LUNCH

Roasted pepper, avocado and hummus sandwich (2 slices whole-meal bread, 60 g/2 oz roasted peppers/capsicums, 3 tbsp hummus, ¼ ripe avocado and alfalfa sprouts to taste)

MIDAFTERNOON SNACK

2 dark rye crispbreads with Sweet Pepper Yoghurt Dip (page 145)

DINNER FOR 4

Mexican Stuffed Peppers (page 183)

455 g/1 lb sautéed frozen whole-kernel sweetcorn

Tossed Garden Salad (page 201; add ½ red pepper/capsicum, chopped)

DESSERT FOR 4 (OPTIONAL)

Fruit salad (340 g/12 oz each cantaloupe melon, cubed and honey-dew melon, cubed, and 230 g/8 oz fresh or frozen raspberries)

Daily Nutrition Facts

REGULAR

1,427 calories/5,965 kJ: 25% from fat (6% from sat fat), 17% from protein, 58% from carbohydrate; 50 g fibre, 2,340 mg sodium

WEIGHT-LOSS EXPRESS

1,246 calories/5,208 kJ: 22% from fat (4% from sat fat), 17% from protein, 62% from carbohydrate; 47 g fibre, 1,870 mg sodium

WEEK 3

DAY 15 **APPLE DAY**

DAY 16 **TOMATO DAY**   CN⋑

DAY 17 **ALMOND DAY**

DAY 18 **THYME DAY**

DAY 19 **WALNUT DAY**

DAY 20 **SESAME DAY**   CN⋑

DAY 21 **BASIL DAY**

DAY 15 **APPLE DAY**

BREAKFAST

Apple-Raisin Porridge (page 133)

OR

≶≡**WLE** Apple-Banana Smoothie (page 140)

MIDMORNING SNACK

120 ml/4 fl oz unsweetened apple sauce mixed with 120 ml/4 fl oz fat-free natural yoghurt

OR

≶≡**WLE** Omit the yoghurt

LUNCH

Apple, Fennel, Walnut and Barley Salad (page 153)

MIDAFTERNOON SNACK

1 small apple

OR

≶≡**WLE** 300 ml/10 fl oz apple fizz (180 ml/6 fl oz fizzy mineral water and 120 ml/4 fl oz 100% apple juice)

DINNER FOR 4

Apple-Prune Chicken (page 186)

285 g/10 oz bulgur wheat, cooked (page 218)

340 g/12 oz sautéed spinach

Tossed Garden Salad (page 201)

DESSERT FOR 4 (OPTIONAL)

Baked Cinnamon Apples (page 221)

Daily Nutrition Facts

REGULAR

1,459 calories/6,099 kJ: 19% from fat (3% from sat fat), 17% from protein, 64% from carbohydrate; 48 g fibre, 1,697 mg sodium

WEIGHT-LOSS EXPRESS

1,285 calories/5,371 kJ: 18% from fat (3% from sat fat), 15% from protein, 67% from carbohydrate; 41 g fibre, 1,329 mg sodium

DAY 16 **TOMATO DAY**

BREAKFAST

Tomato, Basil and Feta Omelette (page 139)

1 slice wholemeal toast, plain or with 1 tsp trans-fat-free margarine

OR

 1 slice wholemeal bread, 1 thick slice tomato, and ½ tbsp grated light mozzarella, melted

MIDMORNING SNACK

12 cherry tomatoes with 2 tbsp hummus

OR

 Omit the hummus

LUNCH

Tomato and Black Bean Mediterranean Salad (page 163) in ½ whole-wheat pitta

MIDAFTERNOON SNACK

12 baked corn chips with 60 g/2 oz tomato salsa

OR

 Replace the chips with 12 baby carrots

DINNER FOR 4

 Pasta with Marinara Sauce (page 206)

Tossed Garden Salad (page 201; add 400 g/14 oz rinsed and drained chickpeas)

Wholemeal Garlic Bread (page 217)

DESSERT FOR 4 (OPTIONAL)

Peach-blueberry salad (340 g/12 oz fresh or canned peach slices and 250 g/9 oz blueberries)

OR

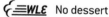 No dessert

---

Daily Nutrition Facts

REGULAR

1,508 calories/6,303 kJ: 25% from fat (5% from sat fat), 15% from protein, 60% from carbohydrate; 53 g fibre, 1,889 mg sodium

WEIGHT-LOSS EXPRESS

1,307 calories/5,463 kJ: 23% from fat (5% from sat fat), 15% from protein, 63% from carbohydrate; 51 g fibre, 1,430 mg sodium

DAY 17 **ALMOND DAY**

BREAKFAST

2 slices Almond French Toast with Sliced Strawberries (page 132)

MIDMORNING SNACK

Almond-Banana Smoothie (page 141)

OR

≡WLE 120 ml/4 fl oz fat-free natural yoghurt with 6 whole almonds

LUNCH

Almond, Green Bean and Quinoa Salad (page 152)

MIDAFTERNOON SNACK

10–12 whole almonds and 1 fresh pear or 90 g/3 oz canned unsweetened pears

OR

≡WLE 6 whole almonds and 1 tbsp raisins

DINNER FOR 4

Almond-Crusted Haddock (page 191)

455 g/1 lb sautéed fresh or frozen broccoli florets with 1 tbsp sliced almonds

Tossed Garden Salad (page 201)

DESSERT FOR 4 (OPTIONAL)

Amaretto strawberry salad (340 g/12 oz strawberries, sliced, 4 tsp amaretto liqueur and 4 tsp chopped almonds)

Daily Nutrition Facts

REGULAR

1,479 calories/6,182 kJ: 36% from fat (5% from sat fat), 21% from protein, 42% from carbohydrate; 43 g fibre, 1,272 mg sodium

WEIGHT-LOSS EXPRESS

1,309 calories/5,472 kJ: 39% from fat (6% from sat fat), 22% from protein, 39% from carbohydrate; 38 g fibre, 1,226 mg sodium

DAY 18 **THYME DAY**

BREAKFAST

Mushroom, Thyme and Cheese Omelette (page 139)

1 slice wholemeal toast, plain or with 1 tsp trans-fat-free margarine

OR

 Scrambled Eggs with Thyme (page 137)

1 slice wholemeal toast, plain or with 1 tsp trans-fat-free margarine

MIDMORNING SNACK

Up to 18 baby carrots with Thyme Yoghurt Dip (page 149)

LUNCH

Stuffed Tomato with Thyme Tuna Salad (page 164)

10 g/½ oz multi- or whole-grain crackers (see page 48)

OR

 Omit the crackers

MIDAFTERNOON SNACK

6 mini oat bran sticks or 2 oatcakes

45 g/1½ oz less-than-2%-fat cottage cheese with ¼ tsp dried or 1 tsp fresh thyme

DINNER FOR 4

Grilled Chicken with White Beans Provençal (page 180)

285 g/10 oz bulgur wheat, cooked (page 218)

Tossed Garden Salad (page 201)

DESSERT FOR 4 (OPTIONAL)

Fruit salad (1 sliced banana; 2 medium apples, cored and cut into small chunks; and 24 grapes)

Daily Nutrition Facts

REGULAR

1,422 calories/5,944 kJ: 22% from fat (5% from sat fat), 26% from protein, 50% from carbohydrate; 41 g fibre, 2,472 mg sodium

WEIGHT-LOSS EXPRESS

1,255 calories/5,246 kJ: 20% from fat (4% from sat fat), 28% from protein, 49% from carbohydrate; 34 g fibre, 2,287 mg sodium

DAY 19 **WALNUT DAY**

BREAKFAST

Apple-Raisin Porridge sprinkled with 2 tsp chopped walnuts

OR

≡WLE 180 ml/6 fl oz fat-free natural yoghurt with 4 tbsp low-fat muesli and 1 tsp chopped walnuts

MIDMORNING SNACK

120 ml/4 fl oz fat-free natural yoghurt with 1 tbsp chopped walnuts and 1 tbsp raisins

OR

≡WLE 1 tbsp chopped walnuts and 1 dried apricot

LUNCH

Walnut Chicken Salad (page 166)

5 light wholemeal pitta chips

OR

≡WLE Omit the pitta chips

MIDAFTERNOON SNACK

6 walnut halves and 16 grapes

OR

≡WLE Omit the grapes

DINNER FOR 4

Portobello Mushrooms with Walnut Stuffing (page 210)

340 g/12 oz baby spinach sautéed in 1 tsp olive oil with 1 tbsp chopped walnuts

Lentil and Bean Salad with Coriander (page 203) over mixed greens

DESSERT FOR 4 (OPTIONAL)

Baked Cinnamon-Walnut Apples (page 221)

Daily Nutrition Facts

REGULAR

1,526 calories/6,379 kJ: 35% from fat (5% from sat fat), 20% from protein, 46% from carbohydrate; 32 g fibre, 1,459 mg sodium

WEIGHT-LOSS EXPRESS

1,289 calories/5,388 kJ: 36% from fat (5% from sat fat), 21% from protein, 43% from carbohydrate; 28 g fibre, 1,139 mg sodium

DAY 20 **SESAME DAY**

BREAKFAST

2 slices Sesame French Toast with Sliced Strawberries (page 133)

MIDMORNING SNACK

115 g/4 oz chopped fresh vegetables (baby carrots and celery sticks) with Tahini Dip (page 147)

LUNCH

Carrot, hummus, lettuce and tomato sandwich (2 slices wholemeal bread, 2 tbsp hummus, 60 g/2 oz carrots, grated, ½ sliced tomato and lettuce)

MIDAFTERNOON SNACK

2 100% wholewheat crackers with Tahini Dip (page 147)

OR

⨕≡WLE Replace the crackers with 10 celery sticks

DINNER FOR 4

CN⊃ *Sesame-Soy Chicken (page 169)*

455 g/1 lb sautéed bean sprouts

Tossed Garden Salad (page 201)

DESSERT FOR 4 (OPTIONAL)

4 sliced fresh pears or 250 g/9 oz canned pear slices sprinkled with 30 g/1 oz sesame seeds

OR

⨕≡WLE No dessert

Daily Nutrition Facts

REGULAR

1,471 calories/6,149 kJ: 30% from fat (5% from sat fat), 19% from protein, 50% from carbohydrate; 46 g fibre, 1,802 mg sodium

WEIGHT-LOSS EXPRESS

1,291 calories/5,396 kJ: 31% from fat (6% from sat fat), 21% from protein, 47% from carbohydrate; 42 g fibre, 1,901 mg sodium

DAY 21 **BASIL DAY**

BREAKFAST

Tomato, Basil and Feta Omelette (page 139)

1 slice wholemeal toast, plain or with 1 tsp trans-fat-free margarine

OR

 1 slice wholemeal bread with ½ chopped tomato, 5 chopped fresh basil leaves and 1 tbsp grated light mozzarella, melted

MIDMORNING SNACK

10 green beans, 6 baby carrots and 6 cauliflower florets with Basil-Ricotta Dip (page 144)

LUNCH

Turkey sandwich with basil, lettuce and tomato (2 slices wholemeal bread, 2 slices unprocessed roast turkey, 2 tsp basil pesto, lettuce and ½ sliced tomato)

MIDAFTERNOON SNACK

6 mini oat bran sticks or 2 oatcakes with 2 tbsp hummus mixed with 5 chopped fresh basil leaves

OR

 Replace the oat bran sticks or oatcakes with 10 celery sticks

DINNER FOR 4

Prawn Pasta Primavera with Basil Pesto (page 199)

Tossed Garden Salad (page 201; add fresh basil to taste)

DESSERT FOR 4 (OPTIONAL)

Strawberry-kiwi salad (340 g/12 oz strawberries, sliced, and 3 sliced kiwi fruit)

Daily Nutrition Facts

REGULAR

1,490 calories/6,228 kJ: 34% from fat (6% from sat fat), 21% from protein, 45% from carbohydrate; 46 g fibre, 2,232 mg sodium

WEIGHT-LOSS EXPRESS

1,297 calories/5,421 kJ: 31% from fat (5% from sat fat), 20% from protein, 50% from carbohydrate; 47 g fibre, 1,734 mg sodium

WEEK 4

DAY 22 **SPINACH DAY**

DAY 23 **ORANGE DAY**   CN

DAY 24 **MINT DAY**

DAY 25 **LEMON DAY**

DAY 26 **PECAN DAY**

DAY 27 **DILL DAY**

DAY 28 **CRANBERRY DAY**

DAY 22 **SPINACH DAY**

BREAKFAST

Spinach and Feta Omelette (page 139)

1 slice wholemeal toast, plain or with 1 tsp trans-fat-free margarine

OR

WLE 30 g/1 oz wholegrain cereal with 120 ml/4 fl oz skimmed milk

MIDMORNING SNACK

20 g/¾ oz multi- or whole-grain crackers (see page 48) with Spinach Yoghurt Dip (page 148)

LUNCH

Spinach and Turkey Salad (page 162)

MIDAFTERNOON SNACK

12 baby carrots with Spinach Yoghurt Dip (page 148)

DINNER FOR 4

Pasta Fagioli with Spinach Marinara Sauce (page 205)

Tossed Garden Salad (page 201; make with spinach)

DESSERT FOR 4 (OPTIONAL)

Mixed-berry salad (125 g/4½ oz each fresh blueberries, raspberries and blackberries)

OR

WLE No dessert

Daily Nutrition Facts

REGULAR

1,449 calories/6,057 kJ: 27% from fat (5% from sat fat), 20% from protein, 54% from carbohydrate; 47 g fibre, 2,715 mg sodium

WEIGHT-LOSS EXPRESS

1,284 calories/5,367 kJ: 21% from fat (3% from sat fat), 19% from protein, 59% from carbohydrate; 43 g fibre, 2,284 mg sodium

DAY 23 **ORANGE DAY**

BREAKFAST

45 g/1½ oz wholegrain cereal with 120 ml/4 fl oz skimmed milk

180 ml/6 fl oz 100% orange juice

OR

WLE Orange-Banana Smoothie (page 141)

MIDMORNING SNACK

120 ml/4 fl oz fat-free natural yoghurt with 1 sliced orange

LUNCH

Spinach and Orange-Lentil Salad with Feta and Pecans (page 159)

MIDAFTERNOON SNACK

Orange-Banana Smoothie (page 141)

OR

WLE 300 ml/10 fl oz orange fizz (180 ml/6 fl oz fizzy mineral water and 120 ml/4 fl oz 100% orange juice)

DINNER FOR 4

CN *Orange Cod (page 194)*

455 g/1 lb sautéed fresh or frozen green beans with grated orange peel

285 g/10 oz bulgur wheat, cooked (page 218)

Tossed Garden Salad (page 201; add juice of ½ orange)

DESSERT FOR 4 (OPTIONAL)

Fat-free orange sorbet; 120 ml/4 fl oz per person

OR

WLE 1 orange

Daily Nutrition Facts

REGULAR

1,431 calories/5,982 kJ: 20% from fat (3% from sat fat), 16% from protein, 64% from carbohydrate; 39 g fibre, 1,509 mg sodium

WEIGHT-LOSS EXPRESS

1,196 calories/4,999 kJ: 23% from fat (3% from sat fat), 17% from protein, 61% from carbohydrate; 34 g fibre, 1,256 mg sodium

DAY 24 **MINT DAY**

BREAKFAST

60 g/2 oz wholegrain cereal with 180 ml/6 fl oz skimmed milk

1 cup peppermint tea with 1 tsp honey

MIDMORNING SNACK

170 g/6 oz fresh strawberries, sliced, sprinkled with chopped fresh mint

1 cup peppermint tea with 1 tsp honey

LUNCH

Fresh Mint Salade Niçoise (page 156)

MIDAFTERNOON SNACK

1 banana

1 cup peppermint tea with 1 tsp honey

DINNER FOR 4

Mint, Sweet Pea and Spinach Soup (page 212)

1 slice wholemeal bread per person

Minty Tabbouleh Salad (page 204)

OR

≡WLE Omit the bread

DESSERT FOR 4 (OPTIONAL)

Mint Chocolate Chip Shake (page 232)

OR

≡WLE No dessert

Daily Nutrition Facts

REGULAR

1,498 calories/6,262 kJ: 19% from fat (3% from sat fat), 20% from protein, 61% from carbohydrate; 52 g fibre, 2,423 mg sodium

WEIGHT-LOSS EXPRESS

1,319 calories/5,513 kJ: 21% from fat (4% from sat fat), 21% from protein, 59% from carbohydrate; 46 g fibre, 2,258 mg sodium

DAY 25 **LEMON DAY**

BREAKFAST

2 Lemon-Poppy Soft Wheat Muffins (page 136)

OR

≡WLE Lemon-Orange Smoothie (page 142)

MIDMORNING SNACK

180 ml/6 fl oz fat-free lemon yoghurt with 15 g/½ oz wholegrain cereal

LUNCH

Lemon Tabbouleh Salad (page 157)

MIDAFTERNOON SNACK

Lemon-Orange Smoothie (page 142)

OR

≡WLE 90 g/3 oz less-than-2%-fat cottage cheese and 350 ml/12 oz lemon fizz (300 ml/10 fl oz fizzy mineral water and juice of ½ lemon)

DINNER FOR 4

Lemon Salmon with Garlic Spinach (page 196)

Sautéed Spaghetti Squash (page 215)

1 slice wholemeal bread per person

Tossed Garden Salad (page 201; add juice of ½ lemon)

OR

≡WLE Omit the bread

DESSERT FOR 4 (OPTIONAL)

500 g/1 lb 2 oz fresh blueberries with lemon zest

Daily Nutrition Facts

REGULAR

1,456 calories/6,086 kJ: 24% from fat (3% from sat fat), 20% from protein, 56% from carbohydrate; 36 g fibre, 1,532 mg sodium

WEIGHT-LOSS EXPRESS

1,238 calories/5,175 kJ: 21% from fat (3% from sat fat), 25% from protein, 54% from carbohydrate; 29 g fibre, 1,722 mg sodium

Satisfaction at the Flavour Point

THE FLAVOUR FACTS

Name: Cindy Garafolo

Age: 46

Family status: Married with two children, aged 19 and 20

Occupation: Medical assistant

Starting weight: 78 kg/12 st 3 lb

Weight lost: 6 kg/13½ lb in 12 weeks

Health stats: Cholesterol dropped 0.46 points; blood pressure dropped 8 points; waist measurement shrank 6 cm/2½ in; 5 per cent decline in body fat

'My husband and I both wanted to lose weight, so Dr Katz's programme just came up at the right time. I had no idea what I was getting into, but it has really worked. My husband and I both lost about 14 lb [6.4 kg] in the first 12 weeks.

'Before I started the programme, I would eat more out of boredom than hunger. I didn't even think about it. Dr Katz has taught me to be more conscious of whether or not I'm really hungry. If I think I'm genuinely hungry, I now grab a piece of fruit or one of the snacks, like a fruit and yoghurt parfait or a smoothie rather than chocolate.

'For breakfast, I usually choose one of the flavour-friendly options, like porridge. For lunch, my whole family's favourite is the chicken salad with yoghurt and mustard. My daughter asks me to make it for her all the time. For dinner, I love the chicken recipes, especially Roast Chicken with Currant Wine Glaze and Caramelized Onions. The currants cook down and make the sauce thick, like gravy. This recipe would be great for a party.

'Overall, my food preferences have absolutely changed on Dr Katz's programme. This meal plan has turned my entire family on to foods we wouldn't have tried otherwise. I never set foot in the health food section of the supermarket before, and now I'm in there all the time. It has totally changed the way we cook and eat. There's no white bread in my house any more! We've just learned to live without it, and I've replaced vegetable oil with olive oil.

'I also picked up some new tricks, like using fat-free chicken stock as a base. When I make a salad, instead of using plain old iceberg lettuce, I use a mix of dark green, leafy vegetables.

'Others have noticed that I'm getting thinner and told me my trousers are fitting better. My daughter has also lost some weight and had some comments on it.

'The best thing about the whole experience is that it works. And it's not that big a deal – I don't feel like I'm on a diet, because it's so easy.' ■

DAY 26 **PECAN DAY**

BREAKFAST

Apple-Pecan Porridge (page 133)

OR

 180 ml/6 fl oz fat-free natural yoghurt with 4 tbsp low-fat muesli and 1 tsp chopped pecans

MIDMORNING SNACK

4 pecan halves and 2 dried figs

LUNCH

Mixed Greens and Lentil Salad with Tomato and Pecans (page 159)

MIDAFTERNOON SNACK

6 pecan halves and 1 fresh peach or 90 g/3 oz canned unsweetened peaches

OR

 Omit the peaches

DINNER FOR 4

Pecan-Crusted Chicken (page 182)

285 g/10 oz bulgur wheat, cooked (page 218)

Roasted Asparagus with Pecans and Sun-Dried Tomatoes (page 216)

Tossed Garden Salad (page 201)

DESSERT FOR 4 (OPTIONAL)

Baked Bananas with Rum-Pecan Topping (page 220)

OR

 No dessert

Daily Nutrition Facts

REGULAR

1,479 calories/6,182 kJ: 36% from fat (4% from sat fat), 16% from protein, 47% from carbohydrate; 42 g fibre, 1,035 mg sodium

WEIGHT-LOSS EXPRESS

1,226 calories/5,125 kJ: 38% from fat (5% from sat fat), 19% from protein, 43% from carbohydrate; 34 g fibre, 1,123 mg sodium

DAY 27 **DILL DAY**

BREAKFAST

Asparagus and Dill Cheese Omelette (page 138)

1 slice wholemeal toast, plain or with 1 tsp trans-fat-free margarine

OR

⌇≣WLE 1 slice wholemeal bread with ½ chopped tomato, ½ tsp dried dill and
1 tbsp grated light mozzarella, melted

MIDMORNING SNACK

Up to 18 baby carrots with Dill Yoghurt Dip (page 144)

LUNCH

Dill Chicken Salad Sandwich (page 167) on wholemeal bread

OR

⌇≣WLE Replace the bread with 2 pieces wholemeal Melba toast

MIDAFTERNOON SNACK

*6 mini oat bran sticks or 2 oatcakes with 2 tbsp hummus mixed
with a pinch of dried dill*

DINNER FOR 4

Poached Salmon with Cucumber-Dill Sauce (page 197)

Dill Potatoes (page 214)

Tossed Garden Salad (page 201)

DESSERT FOR 4 (OPTIONAL)

*Fruit salad (1 sliced banana; 2 medium apples, cored and cut into
small chunks; and 24 grapes)*

Daily Nutrition Facts

REGULAR

1,492 calories/6,237 kJ: 25% from fat (6%
from sat fat), 26% from protein, 46% from
carbohydrate; 37 g fibre, 2,570 mg sodium

WEIGHT-LOSS EXPRESS

1,236 calories/5,166 kJ: 21% from fat (4%
from sat fat), 26% from protein, 49% from
carbohydrate; 28 g fibre, 2,067 mg sodium

DAY 28 **CRANBERRY DAY**

BREAKFAST

2 Cranberry-Banana Soft Wheat Muffins (page 134)
240 ml/8 fl oz skimmed milk

OR

◁≡WLℰ Cranberry-Banana Smoothie (page 141)

MIDMORNING SNACK

120 ml/4 fl oz fat-free natural yoghurt with 2 tsp dried cranberries
and 1 tbsp low-fat, fruit-free muesli

LUNCH

Mixed Greens and Lentil Salad with Feta, Pecans and Cranberries
(page 159)

MIDAFTERNOON SNACK

Cranberry-Banana Smoothie (page 141)

DINNER FOR 4

Cranberry and Sweet Onion Turkey Breast Steaks (page 187)

Baked sweet potatoes (wrap 2 whole sweet potatoes in aluminium
foil and bake at 190°C/375°F/gas 5 until tender; unwrap and cut
each in half for 1 serving)

Tossed Garden Salad (page 201; add 2 tsp dried cranberries)

DESSERT FOR 4 (OPTIONAL)

Cranberry-Vanilla Soft Ice Cream (page 232)

OR

◁≡WLℰ No dessert

Daily Nutrition Facts

REGULAR

1,453 calories/6,074 kJ: 20% from fat (3%
from sat fat), 23% from protein, 57% from
carbohydrate; 24 g fibre, 1,272 mg sodium

REGULAR

1,272 calories/5,317 kJ: 17% from fat (3%
from sat fat), 23% from protein, 60% from
carbohydrate; 24 g fibre, 1,062 mg sodium

PHASE 2: **WEEKS 5 AND 6**

DAY 29

BREAKFAST

45 g/1½ oz wholegrain cereal with 120 ml/4 fl oz skimmed milk

180 ml/6 fl oz 100% orange juice

OR

 Orange-Banana Smoothie (page 141)

MIDMORNING SNACK

4 large strawberries with Sweet Cinnamon Yoghurt Dip (page 148)

LUNCH

Red Onion, White Bean, Lentil and Tomato Salad (page 161)

4 light wholemeal pitta chips

OR

 Omit the beans and pitta chips and add 1 tomato

MIDAFTERNOON SNACK

Up to 18 baby carrots with 90 g/3 oz less-than-2%-fat cottage cheese

DINNER FOR 4

CN) *Pistachio-Crusted Chicken (page 177)*

285 g/10 oz bulgur wheat, cooked (page 218)

Sautéed Spaghetti Squash (page 215)

Tossed Garden Salad (page 201; add 3 tbsp shelled pistachios)

DESSERT FOR 4 (OPTIONAL)

Peanut Katz Flax Crisps (page 228); 1 square per person

Daily Nutrition Facts

REGULAR

1,446 calories/6,044 kJ: 26% from fat (4% from sat fat), 21% from protein, 53% from carbohydrate; 37 g fibre, 1,745 mg sodium

WEIGHT-LOSS EXPRESS

1,239 calories/5,179 kJ: 29% from fat (4% from sat fat), 21% from protein, 51% from carbohydrate; 27 g fibre, 1,266 mg sodium

DAY 30

BREAKFAST

Mushroom, Thyme and Cheese Omelette (page 139)

1 slice wholemeal toast, plain or with 1 tsp trans-fat-free margarine

MIDMORNING SNACK

120 ml/4 fl oz fat-free natural yoghurt with 1 sliced small apple

OR

≡WLE Omit the yoghurt

LUNCH

Dill Chicken Salad Sandwich (page 167) on wholemeal bread

OR

≡WLE Replace the bread with 2 pieces wholemeal Melba toast

MIDAFTERNOON SNACK

1 cucumber cut into strips

90 g/3 oz less-than-2%-fat cottage cheese

OR

≡WLE Omit the cottage cheese

DINNER FOR 4

Portobello Mushrooms with Walnut Stuffing (page 210)

340 g/12 oz sautéed baby spinach with 1 tbsp chopped walnuts

Lentil and Bean Salad with Coriander (page 203) over mixed greens

DESSERT FOR 4 (OPTIONAL)

Baked Cinnamon Apples (page 221)

Daily Nutrition Facts

REGULAR

1,478 calories/6,178 kJ: 24% from fat (6% from sat fat), 24% from protein, 52% from carbohydrate; 48 g fibre, 2,429 mg sodium

WEIGHT-LOSS EXPRESS

1,265 calories/5,288 kJ: 28% from fat (7% from sat fat), 22% from protein, 50% from carbohydrate; 38 g fibre, 1,845 mg sodium

DAY 31

BREAKFAST

2 slices Almond French Toast with Sliced Strawberries (page 132)

OR

✟≡WLE 1 slice wholemeal toast with 1 tbsp almond butter

MIDMORNING SNACK

120 ml/4 fl oz fat-free natural yoghurt with 1 tbsp chopped walnuts and 1 tbsp raisins

OR

✟≡WLE Omit the yoghurt and replace the raisins with 1 dried apricot

LUNCH

Turkey sandwich with basil, lettuce and tomato (2 slices wholemeal bread, 2 slices unprocessed roast turkey, 2 tsp basil pesto, lettuce and ½ sliced tomato)

MIDAFTERNOON SNACK

18 baked corn tortilla chips with 60 g/2 oz salsa

OR

✟≡WLE 45 g/1½ oz air-popped popcorn

DINNER FOR 4

Baked Monkfish with Tomatoes, Olives and Capers (page 192)

285 g/10 oz bulgur wheat, cooked (page 218)

285 g/10 oz sautéed fresh or frozen cauliflower florets

Tossed Garden Salad (page 201)

DESSERT FOR 4 (OPTIONAL)

Amaretto strawberry salad (500 g/1 lb 2 oz strawberries, sliced, 4 tsp amaretto liqueur, and 4 tsp chopped almonds)

Daily Nutrition Facts
REGULAR

1,474 calories/6,161 kJ: 26% from fat (5% from sat fat), 22% from protein, 52% from carbohydrate; 48 g fibre, 2,533 mg sodium

WEIGHT-LOSS EXPRESS

1,243 calories/5,196 kJ: 28% from fat (4% from sat fat), 22% from protein, 49% from carbohydrate; 43 g fibre, 2,041 mg sodium

DAY 32

BREAKFAST

Spinach and Feta Omelette (page 139)

1 slice wholemeal toast, plain or with 1 tsp trans-fat-free margarine

OR

WLE 1 slice wholemeal bread with 1 soft-boiled egg, 1 slice tomato, ½ tsp olive oil and ½ tbsp grated light mozzarella, melted

MIDMORNING SNACK

170 g/6 oz fresh or canned unsweetened pineapple chunks

OR

WLE 300 ml/10 fl oz pineapple fizz (180 ml/6 fl oz fizzy mineral water and 120 ml/4 fl oz 100% pineapple juice)

LUNCH

Stuffed Tomato with Thyme Tuna Salad (page 164)

10 g/½ oz multi- or whole-grain crackers (see page 48)

OR

WLE Omit the crackers

MIDAFTERNOON SNACK

120 ml/4 fl oz fat-free natural yoghurt with 12 whole almonds

DINNER FOR 4

CN *Pumpkin Soup (page 213)*

2 slices wholemeal bread per person

Tossed Garden Salad (page 201; add 400 g/14 oz rinsed chickpeas)

OR

WLE Omit 1 slice of bread

DESSERT FOR 4 (OPTIONAL)

Raisin-Muesli Parfait (page 230)

Daily Nutrition Facts

REGULAR

1,492 calories/6,237 kJ: 21% from fat (5% from sat fat), 22% from protein, 57% from carbohydrate; 45 g fibre, 2,567 mg sodium

WEIGHT-LOSS EXPRESS

1,225 calories/5,120 kJ: 21% from fat (4% from sat fat), 23% from protein, 56% from carbohydrate; 37 g fibre, 1,941 mg sodium

DAY 33

BREAKFAST

45 g/1½ oz wholegrain cereal with 120 ml/4 fl oz skimmed milk

1 fresh peach or 90 g/3 oz canned unsweetened peaches

OR

WLE Peach-Banana Smoothie (page 141)

MIDMORNING SNACK

120 ml/4 fl oz fat-free natural yoghurt with 1 sliced orange

OR

WLE Omit the yoghurt

LUNCH

Lemon Tabbouleh Salad (page 157)

MIDAFTERNOON SNACK

1 pepper (capsicum) cut into strips with 2 tbsp hummus

DINNER FOR 4 (OPTIONAL)

Carrot Cider-Glazed Chicken (page 170)

285 g/10 oz bulgur wheat, cooked (page 218)

455 g/1 lb sautéed fresh or frozen broccoli florets

Tossed Garden Salad (page 201; make with 60 g/2 oz carrots, grated)

DESSERT FOR 6 (OPTIONAL)

Peach Flat Cake (page 225)

OR

WLE 1 seasonal fresh fruit per person

Daily Nutrition Facts

REGULAR

1,443 calories/6,032 kJ: 22% from fat (4% from sat fat), 19% from protein, 58% from carbohydrate; 46 g fibre, 1,624 mg sodium

WEIGHT-LOSS EXPRESS

1,283 calories/5,363 kJ: 19% from fat (4% from sat fat), 19% from protein, 62% from carbohydrate; 41 g fibre, 1,282 mg sodium

DAY 34

BREAKFAST

45 g/1½ oz wholegrain cereal with 120 ml/4 fl oz skimmed milk

180 ml/6 fl oz 100% orange juice

OR

⫘**WLE** Orange-Banana Smoothie (page 141)

MIDMORNING SNACK

1 apple

LUNCH

Spinach and Lentil Salad with Feta, Walnuts and Currants
(page 158)

MIDAFTERNOON SNACK

Up to 18 baby carrots

DINNER FOR 4

Poppy Seed-Crusted Salmon (page 198)

375 g/13 oz quinoa, cooked (page 219)

455 g/1 lb sautéed courgettes (zucchini) topped with 1 tsp poppy seeds

Tossed Garden Salad (page 201)

DESSERT FOR 4 (OPTIONAL)

Mixed-berry salad (125 g/4½ oz each fresh blueberries, raspberries and blackberries)

OR

⫘**WLE** No dessert

Daily Nutrition Facts

REGULAR

1,498 calories/6,262 kJ: 29% from fat (4% from sat fat), 20% from protein, 51% from carbohydrate; 38 g fibre, 1,122 mg sodium

WEIGHT-LOSS EXPRESS

1,334 calories/5,576 kJ: 32% from fat (5% from sat fat), 20% from protein, 48% from carbohydrate; 27 g fibre, 886 mg sodium

DAY 35

BREAKFAST

45 g/1½ oz wholegrain cereal with 120 ml/4 fl oz skimmed milk

180 ml/6 fl oz 100% pineapple juice

OR

WLE Pineapple Smoothie (page 141)

MIDMORNING SNACK

120 ml/4 fl oz fat-free natural yoghurt

120 ml/4 fl oz unsweetened apple sauce

OR

WLE 1 small apple

LUNCH

Peanut-Cucumber Salad (page 160)

MIDAFTERNOON SNACK

6 mini oat bran sticks or 2 oatcakes with 2 tbsp hummus

DINNER FOR 4

Apple-Prune Chicken (page 186)

285 g/10 oz bulgur wheat, cooked (page 218)

340 g/12 oz sautéed spinach

Tossed Garden Salad (page 201)

DESSERT FOR 4 (OPTIONAL)

Fruit salad (340 g/12 oz each cantaloupe melon, cubed, honeydew melon, cubed, and 230 g/8 oz fresh or frozen raspberries)

Daily Nutrition Facts

REGULAR

1,432 calories/5,986 kJ: 17% from fat (3% from sat fat), 19% from protein, 64% from carbohydrate; 46 g fibre, 1,688 mg sodium

WEIGHT-LOSS EXPRESS

1,272 calories/5,316 kJ: 19% from fat (3% from sat fat), 18% from protein, 64% from carbohydrate; 42 g fibre, 1,377 mg sodium

DAY 36

BREAKFAST

Apple-Raisin Porridge (page 133)

OR

⟨≡**WLE** Apple-Banana Smoothie [page 140]

MIDMORNING SNACK

120 ml/4 fl oz fat-free fruit yoghurt with 1 tbsp chopped pecans

LUNCH

Tomato and Black Bean Mediterranean Salad (page 163) in ½ wholewheat pitta

OR

⟨≡**WLE** Omit the pitta

MIDAFTERNOON SNACK

20 g/¾ oz multi- or whole-grain crackers (see page 48) with Spinach Yoghurt Dip (page 148)

DINNER FOR 4

CN⟩   *Orange Cod (page 194)*

455 g/1 lb sautéed fresh or frozen green beans with grated orange zest

285 g/10 oz bulgur wheat, cooked (page 218)

Tossed Garden Salad (page 201; add juice of ½ orange)

DESSERT FOR 4 (OPTIONAL)

Peanut Katz Flax Crisps (page 228); 1 square per person

Daily Nutrition Facts

REGULAR

1,445 calories/6,040 kJ: 27% from fat [4% from sat fat], 19% from protein, 55% from carbohydrate; 38 g fibre, 1,572 mg sodium

WEIGHT-LOSS EXPRESS

1,294 calories/5,409 kJ: 26% from fat [4% from sat fat], 17% from protein, 57% from carbohydrate; 34 g fibre, 1,099 mg sodium

DAY 37

BREAKFAST

Apple-Pecan Porridge (page 133)

OR

WLE 180 ml/6 fl oz fat-free natural yoghurt with 4 tbsp low-fat muesli and 1 tsp chopped pecans

MIDMORNING SNACK

1 orange

LUNCH

Roasted pepper (capsicum), avocado and hummus sandwich (2 slices wholemeal bread, 60 g/2 oz roasted peppers, 3 tbsp hummus, ¼ ripe avocado and alfalfa sprouts to taste)

OR

WLE Omit the avocado

MIDAFTERNOON SNACK

12 cherry tomatoes

DINNER FOR 4

Turkey, Bean and Thyme Pot au Feu (page 190)

285 g/10 oz bulgur wheat, cooked (page 218)

Tossed Garden Salad (page 201)

DESSERT FOR 4 (OPTIONAL)

Fruit salad (1 sliced banana; 2 medium apples, cored and cut into small chunks; and 24 grapes)

OR

WLE No dessert

Daily Nutrition Facts

REGULAR

1,501 calories/6,274 kJ: 17% from fat (2% from sat fat), 22% from protein, 59% from carbohydrate; 53 g fibre, 1,462 mg sodium

WEIGHT-LOSS EXPRESS

1,274 calories/5,325 kJ: 13% from fat (2% from sat fat), 25% from protein, 59% from carbohydrate; 45 g fibre, 1,547 mg sodium

DAY 38

BREAKFAST

1 slice wholemeal cinnamon toast with 2 tsp almond or natural peanut butter and 3 slices banana (about ¼ banana)

180 ml/6 fl oz skimmed milk

MIDMORNING SNACK

120 ml/4 fl oz fat-free natural yoghurt with 1 tbsp chopped walnuts and 1 tbsp raisins

OR

⟜≡WLE Omit the yoghurt and replace the raisins with 1 dried apricot

LUNCH

Stuffed Tomato with Thyme Tuna Salad (page 164)

10 g/½ oz multi- or whole-grain crackers (see page 48)

OR

⟜≡WLE Omit the crackers

MIDAFTERNOON SNACK

12 baby carrots with 60 g/2 oz salsa

DINNER FOR 4

Prawn Pasta Primavera with Basil Pesto (page 199)

Tossed Garden Salad (page 201; add fresh basil to taste)

DESSERT FOR 4 (OPTIONAL)

1 seasonal fresh fruit per person

OR

⟜≡WLE No dessert

Daily Nutrition Facts

REGULAR

1,444 calories/6,036 kJ: 31% from fat (4% from sat fat), 21% from protein, 48% from carbohydrate; 30 g fibre, 1,791 mg sodium

WEIGHT-LOSS EXPRESS

1,273 calories/5,321 kJ: 35% from fat (5% from sat fat), 22% from protein, 44% from carbohydrate; 27 g fibre, 1,655 mg sodium

DAY 39

BREAKFAST

45 g/1½ oz wholegrain cereal with 120 ml/4 fl oz skimmed milk

1 fresh peach or 90 g/3 oz canned unsweetened peaches

MIDMORNING SNACK

180 ml/6 fl oz fat-free fruit yoghurt (flavour of choice)

OR

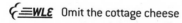 120 ml/4 fl oz fat-free natural yoghurt with 1 sliced orange

LUNCH

*Spinach and Lentil Salad with Feta, Walnuts and Currants
(page 158)*

MIDAFTERNOON SNACK

*Up to 18 baby carrots with 90 g/3 oz less-than-2%-fat cottage
cheese*

OR

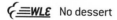 Omit the cottage cheese

DINNER FOR 4

Honey Curry-Glazed Chicken (page 181)

*455 g/1 lb sautéed fresh or frozen broccoli florets with a pinch of
mild curry powder*

340 g/12 oz cooked brown rice (page 218)

Tossed Garden Salad (page 201)

DESSERT FOR 4 (OPTIONAL)

Baked Cinnamon-Walnut Apples (page 221)

OR

WLE No dessert

Daily Nutrition Facts

REGULAR

1,515 calories/6,333 kJ: 22% from fat (4%
from sat fat), 23% from protein, 55% from
carbohydrate; 33 g fibre, 1,835 mg sodium

WEIGHT-LOSS EXPRESS

1,281 calories/5,355 kJ: 22% from fat (4%
from sat fat), 23% from protein, 56% from
carbohydrate; 34 g fibre, 1,367 mg sodium

DAY 40

BREAKFAST

180 ml/6 fl oz fat-free natural yoghurt with 4 tbsp fruit-free muesli, about 25 grapes and 1 tsp chopped pecans

OR

≡WLE Omit the grapes

MIDMORNING SNACK

90 g/3 oz canned unsweetened peaches

LUNCH

Dill Chicken Salad Sandwich (page 167) on wholemeal bread

OR

≡WLE Replace the bread with 2 pieces wholemeal Melba toast

MIDAFTERNOON SNACK

120 ml/4 fl oz fat-free natural yoghurt with 6 whole almonds

DINNER FOR 4

Pasta Fagioli with Spinach Marinara Sauce (page 205)

Tossed Garden Salad (page 201; make with spinach)

DESSERT FOR 4 (OPTIONAL)

Amaretto strawberry salad (500 g/1 lb 2 oz strawberries, sliced, 4 tsp amaretto liqueur and 4 tsp chopped almonds)

Daily Nutrition Facts

REGULAR

1,469 calories/6,140 kJ: 18% from fat (3% from sat fat), 18% from protein, 64% from carbohydrate; 48 g fibre, 1,997 mg sodium

WEIGHT-LOSS EXPRESS

1,298 calories/5,426 kJ: 20% from fat (3% from sat fat), 19% from protein, 60% from carbohydrate; 37 g fibre, 1,918 mg sodium

DAY 41

BREAKFAST

2 Banana-Chocolate Chip Soft Wheat Muffins (page 134)

MIDMORNING SNACK

120 ml/4 fl oz fat-free natural yoghurt with 3 dried apricots

OR

WLE Omit the yoghurt

LUNCH

Black Bean, Sweetcorn and Tomato Salad (page 156) in ½ whole-wheat pitta

OR

WLE Omit the pitta

MIDAFTERNOON SNACK

18 baked corn tortilla chips with 60 g/2 oz salsa

OR

WLE 45 g/1½ oz air-popped popcorn

DINNER FOR 4

Pan-Seared Cod with Lemon, Chives and Capers (page 193)

455 g/1 lb sautéed fresh or frozen asparagus with grated lemon zest

425 g/15 oz unprocessed oven chips (cooked according to package directions)

Tossed Garden Salad (page 201; add juice of 1 lemon)

DESSERT FOR 4 (OPTIONAL)

500 g/1 lb 2 oz fresh blueberries with lemon zest

Daily Nutrition Facts

REGULAR

1,449 calories/6,057 kJ: 28% from fat (4% from sat fat), 18% from protein, 54% from carbohydrate; 35 g fibre, 1,822 mg sodium

WEIGHT-LOSS EXPRESS

1,294 calories/5,409 kJ: 30% from fat (5% from sat fat), 18% from protein, 52% from carbohydrate; 35 g fibre, 1,424 mg sodium

DAY 42

BREAKFAST

Spring Onion and Cheese Omelette (page 139)

1 slice wholemeal toast, plain or with 1 tsp trans-fat-free margarine

MIDMORNING SNACK

Pineapple Smoothie (page 141)

LUNCH

Tuna salad sandwich (2 slices wholemeal bread with tuna salad on page 164)

OR

≡WLE Stuffed Tomato with Thyme Tuna Salad (page 174)

10 g/ ½ oz oz multi- or whole-grain crackers (see page 48)

MIDAFTERNOON SNACK

Up to 18 baby carrots with 90 g/3 oz less-than-2%-fat cottage cheese

DINNER FOR 4

Mexican Stuffed Peppers (page 183)

455 g/1 lb sautéed frozen whole-kernel sweetcorn

Tossed Garden Salad (page 201)

DESSERT FOR 4 (OPTIONAL)

Baked Bananas with Rum-Pecan Topping (page 220)

OR

1 seasonal fresh fruit per person

Daily Nutrition Facts

REGULAR

1,506 calories/6,295 kJ: 23% from fat (5% from sat fat), 23% from protein, 54% from carbohydrate; 42 g fibre, 2,584 mg sodium

WEIGHT-LOSS EXPRESS

1,343 calories/5,614 kJ: 22% from fat (6% from sat fat), 25% from protein, 53% from carbohydrate; 33 g fibre, 2,489 mg sodium

SPECIAL INDULGENCE DAY **CHOCOLATE DAY**

BREAKFAST

1 Banana-Chocolate Chip Soft Wheat Muffin (page 134)

180 ml/6 fl oz hot cocoa (180 ml/6 fl oz skimmed milk with 2 tbsp organic, ground pure cocoa and 60%-cocoa chocolate)

MIDMORNING SNACK

Chocolate chip trail mix (1 tbsp raisins, 1 tbsp good-quality chocolate chips and 3 whole almonds)

LUNCH

Chocolate and Banana Grilled Panini (page 168)

240 ml/8 fl oz skimmed milk

MIDAFTERNOON SNACK

Strawberries Dipped in Dark Chocolate (page 225)

DINNER FOR 4

Chicken with Chocolate Port Wine Sauce (page 172)

455 g/1 lb sautéed fresh baby spinach

DESSERT FOR 4 (OPTIONAL)

Chocolate Brownies (page 222); 1 brownie per person

Daily Nutrition Facts

1,500 calories/6,270 kJ: 28% from fat (11% from sat fat), 20% from protein, 49% from carbohydrate; 29 g fibre, 1,537 mg sodium

SPECIAL INDULGENCE DAY **COCONUT DAY**

BREAKFAST

Coconut-Pineapple Smoothie (page 141)

MIDMORNING SNACK

Coconut trail mix (2 tbsp raisins, 1 tbsp unsweetened flaked coconut and 3 whole almonds)

LUNCH

Coconut Prawn and Avocado Salad (page 154)

MIDAFTERNOON SNACK

240 ml/8 fl oz fat-free natural yoghurt with 5 large strawberries, sliced, and 1 tbsp unsweetened desiccated coconut

DINNER FOR 4

Coconut Thai Chicken (page 176)

500 g/1 lb 2 oz cooked brown rice (page 218)

455 g/1 lb sautéed sugar snap peas

Tossed Garden Salad (page 201)

DESSERT FOR 4 (OPTIONAL)

Piña Colada Frozen Dessert (page 228)

Daily Nutrition Facts

1,517 calories/6,341 kJ: 31% from fat (9% from sat fat), 18% from protein, 50% from carbohydrate; 26 g fibre, 1,592 mg sodium

FLAVOUR-FRIENDLY ALTERNATIVES

Any day of the week, in any phase of the plan, feel free to replace the breakfast, snacks or lunch on the menu with one of the flavour-friendly options on the following pages. Make sure, though, your breakfast cereal, bread and crackers have at least 2 grams of fibre per 100 calories, no trans fats (that means no partially hydrogenated oil) and no added sugar. Jam should have no added sugar.

BREAKFAST OPTIONS

BREAKFAST 1

65 g/2¼ oz wholegrain cereal with 180 ml/6 fl oz skimmed milk

Nutritional analysis (on average) per serving: 269 calories/1,124 kJ; 2 g fat (0 g sat fat), 15 g protein, 56 g carbohydrate, 11 g fibre; 245 mg sodium

BREAKFAST 2

2 slices wholemeal bread, plain or with 2 tsp trans-fat-free margarine or 2 tsp high-fruit jam (matching the flavour theme of the day)

240 ml/8 fl oz skimmed milk

Nutritional analysis (on average) per serving: 236 calories/986 kJ, 3 g fat (1 g sat fat), 15 g protein, 42 g carbohydrate, 7 g fibre, 385 mg sodium

BREAKFAST 3

1 bowl of porridge (page 133), plain or with 60 ml/2 fl oz fat-free fruit yoghurt or 90 g/3 oz fresh fruit (matching the flavour theme of the day)

Nutritional analysis (on average) per serving: 291 calories/1,216 kJ, 56 g fat (1 g sat fat), 13 g protein, 53 g carbohydrate, 6 g fibre, 74 mg sodium

BREAKFAST 4

2 eggs (organic, with omega-3s), soft-boiled, scrambled, or fried (cook in a non-stick frying pan coated with olive oil spray)

2 slices wholemeal toast, plain or with 1 tsp trans-fat-free margarine

Nutritional analysis (on average) per serving: 281 calories/1,175 kJ, 12 g fat (3 g sat fat), 19 g protein, 26 g carbohydrate, 7 g fibre, 388 mg sodium

MIDMORNING SNACK OPTIONS

SNACK

120 ml/4 fl oz fat-free natural yoghurt with 15 g/½ oz whole-grain unprocessed cereal (remember that it should have at least 2 grams of fibre per 100 calories and no added sugar)

Nutritional analysis (on average) per serving: 86 calories/359 kJ, 0 g fat (0 g sat fat), 6 g protein, 18 g carbohydrate, 2 g fibre, 96 mg sodium

LUNCH OPTIONS

SALAD

60–115 g/2–4 oz of favourite mixed greens or lettuce (preferably not iceberg lettuce)

As many raw vegetables as you can pile on – tomatoes, cucumbers, onions, pepper (capsicum) strips, alfalfa sprouts, and so on. (For ease and convenience, use packaged, prewashed grated carrots, grated cabbage, etc.)

A drizzle of olive oil (1½ tsp) and vinegar (1 tbsp) and a pinch of salt and pepper or no more than 2 tbsp (2 capfuls) Newman's Own Light Italian Dressing

Choose from the following toppings.

3 slices plain, unprocessed roasted turkey breast (no saturated fat or added sugar)

90 g/3 oz chicken breast or fillet (cooked in a cast-iron frying pan with olive oil spray)

115 g/4 oz cod fillet (cooked in a non-stick frying pan with olive oil spray)

90 g/3 oz drained water-packed tuna

1 hard-boiled egg and 1 sliced egg white

65 g/2¼ oz rinsed and drained chickpeas or beans

Nutritional analysis (on average) per serving: 278 calories/1,162 kJ, 10 g fat (2 g sat fat), 21 g protein, 29 g carbohydrate, 9 g fibre, 411 mg sodium

MIDAFTERNOON SNACK OPTIONS

SNACKS

2 tbsp plain hummus with your choice of either high-fibre, low-fat crackers (serving not to exceed 85 calories/355 kJ) or 75–150 g/ 2½–5½ oz of the following raw veggies in any combination.

VEGETABLES

Cauliflower florets

Sliced celery

Sliced cucumber

Edamame (fresh soya beans), a small handful after shelling

Green beans

Romaine (Cos) lettuce

Sugar snap peas

Nutritional analysis (on average) per serving: 98 calories/410 kJ, 3 g fat (0 g sat fat), 3 g protein, 15 g carbohydrate, 3 g fibre, 170 mg sodium

DINNER OPTIONS

Whole roasted chicken (skin removed) from the supermarket

OR

4 chicken breasts (115 g/4 oz each) or 4 cod fillets (145 g/5 oz each)

Heat 2 to 3 tsp olive oil in a cast-iron grill pan for chicken or a non-stick frying pan for fish (lightly dust fish with wholemeal flour). Grill or cook for 3 to 4 minutes on each side and season with a pinch of salt and pepper.

285 g/10 oz bulgur wheat, cooked (page 218)

Tossed Garden Salad (page 201)

Nutritional analysis (on average) per serving, with chicken: 463 calories/1,935 kJ, 8 g fat (<2 g sat fat), 45 g protein, 53 g carbohydrate, 15 g fibre, 212 mg sodium (not counting any added to chicken)

With fish: 421 calories/1,760 kJ, 7 g fat (<2 g sat fat), 40 g protein, 53 g carbohydrate, 15 g fibre, 194 mg sodium (not counting any added to fish)

Satisfaction at the Flavour Point

THE FLAVOUR FACTS

Name: Janet Mazur

Age: 50

Family status: Married with two
   children, aged 16 and 20

Occupation: Medical clerk

Starting weight: 90 kg/14 st 2 lb

Weight lost: 7.2 kg/16 lb in 12 weeks

Health stats: Blood pressure
   dropped 10 points; cholesterol
   dropped 1.24 points; waist measurement shrank 5 cm/2 in;
   4 per cent decline in body fat

'This programme came at the perfect time in my life. My brother was recently diagnosed with diabetes, and due to my age and weight of 14 st 2 lb [90 kg], I was also at high risk. I knew it was time to do something.

'As it turned out, the programme is perfect for me because I was looking for something that would help me lose weight and improve my overall health at the same time. I had tried Weight Watchers in the past, and it didn't work at all. It became more of a social hour, and some of the participants were fanatical. For instance, if I wore jeans to the meeting, they'd scold me because "jeans add weight". One woman wore the exact same outfit to every meeting to get weighed in – it was crazy. Plus, I only lost 6 lb [2.75 kg].

'But Dr Katz's programme is a completely different story. I feel so much better on it. The first few weeks were a little challenging, but then everything just fell into place; now I look at food in a totally different way.

'The best thing is that I have so much more energy. I used to come home from work and immediately sit down and read the paper. Now I'm bouncing around and doing things. Plus, I've been using my exercise bike for a half hour each day.

'As far as preparation is concerned, if you're organized, the recipes are really quick and easy. You buy the fish, throw half in the freezer, and you're set for the rest of the week.

'I enjoy almost all the dishes, as does my family. And it's simple to work around the programme – if my family doesn't want the bulgur wheat or sweet potatoes, I make them brown rice or regular mashed potatoes as a side dish and stick to the programme myself.

'My personal favourite recipe is the Mexican Stuffed Peppers, and it's great that I can use the stuffing as a dip for vegetables as well. I also love the stewed turkey – it's so tender and wonderful on top of the bulgur wheat. And the cod and turkey recipes are also high on my list of favourites.

'It was also an easy programme to customize to my life. I went out for dinner a few times and just ordered fish with steamed vegetables or a salad with chicken. Luckily, most restaurants have a number of healthy choices on their menus now, which helps.

'The snack foods on the programme not only help keep me from feeling hungry, they're enjoyable as well. When I want something to munch on at 2 in the afternoon, I have plenty of options (and they're the *right* options). So now, instead of reaching for empty calories (like a chocolate bar) during the day, I drink a glass of water or go for one of the snacks on the programme. I love the chips and salsa, unsweetened apple sauce and yoghurt. And the fizzy pineapple drink is delicious!

'I used to be a big dessert eater, but now I have to scrape icing off a piece of cake because it tastes too sweet to me. If a strong urge for something sweet strikes, I eat a piece of dark chocolate, half a cookie, or 2 tablespoons of ice cream, and that's enough to quell it.

'The best part is, I'm seeing results. A lot of people have noticed my weight loss, telling me I look skinnier and that I have more colour in my face. I had to buy two new pairs of trousers, and I think I'm going to have to buy yet another size smaller soon. I pulled an old pair of trousers out of my wardrobe that I couldn't wear for years and was happily able to button them.

'Even though my 12 weeks are over, I'm definitely going to stick with Dr Katz's programme.' ▪

5

THE FLAVOUR POINT DIET RECIPES

More than 100 options that are so delicious,
you won't believe they're this good for you

Many times over the years, I have heard people lament, 'If it tastes good, it's bad for you.' I've already discussed the hidden significance of how we register taste. Now, let's attack this regret head-on by noting, quite bluntly: it doesn't have to be that way.

Diets have long given weight control a deservedly bad reputation, since most of them are based on what you have to give up. Until the low-carb diets came along, diet food was often dismissively equated with rabbit (or some alternative rodent) food. True, the low-carb diets fixed this (I've never seen a rabbit eat bacon!). They did so, however, with diets that are, in my view, at odds with good health and unrealistically restrictive over the long term.

Well, folks, welcome to a new place. When I tell you that the Flavour Point Diet is based on the power of taste, I truly mean *tasty* taste! This food is, in a word, delicious.

The Flavour Point Diet recipes will show you that the joy of eating and the joy of weight loss can indeed come together at the same dinner table. I know, because it's *my* dinner table, too.

When Catherine and I married, the process of marrying my devotion to nutrition and her skill in the kitchen also began. In these recipes, you'll find the culinary offspring of this union. Like any relationship, this one took work. It took years of figuring out how to combine the very best of taste with the very best of nutrition. We did the trial and put up with some inevitable error, so now you don't have to. I really like good food and can personally vouch for every recipe in the Flavour Point Diet. I expect these flavoursome yet simple recipes to become a hit with everyone in your family, just as they have in ours.

I love Catherine's Banana Soft Wheat Muffins, and so do our kids, who often bake them by themselves.

I would happily eat Black Bean, Sweetcorn and Tomato Salad every day, except for the days when I might rather have Curried Spinach and Lentil Salad with Gorgonzola and Walnuts. All I can say about Almond-Crusted Haddock is 'Yum!' and in our household of seven, it's pretty much a scrum to see who can get to the Honey Curry-Glazed Chicken first. I could go on, but I trust you get the idea. This food is good.

The recipes are also convenient. For us to use them in our crazy schedules, they really have to be. Many take 15 minutes or less to prepare. Most use convenient ingredients, such as pre-chopped vegetables, to get you and your family to the dinner table with minimal time and effort. They all use the best, most healthy ingredients the food supply has to offer. From the types of fish to the types of vegetables used in each recipe, you will be consuming the most nutritious foods you can get. Not only will their simple, flavoursome preparation help lower your Flavour Point, it will also help improve your overall health and wellbeing.

The Flavour Point recipes are designed to transform your whole diet, forever. Just because we've focused on the big picture doesn't mean we didn't address every detail. Each recommendation in these recipes has a rationale. We recommend wild salmon over farm-raised salmon, for example, assuming you can find and afford it. (We always say, 'Don't make perfect the enemy of good'.) Wild salmon is more flavoursome, relatively free of contaminating chemicals and richer in healthy omega-3 fatty acids. We recommend natural over processed peanut butter to help you cut out unnecessary sugar, salt and harmful trans fat. We encourage organic foods if you can afford them, both for your benefit and for that of the planet. We encourage selecting eggs that are enriched with omega-3s. In every instance, our recommendations are directed towards optimizing your shopping trolley, larder and refrigerator on the way to optimizing your health and weight.

Which recipes will *you* like best? I don't know. That's a matter of . . . taste! I'm quite confident that you will find many future favourites here. As you master the Flavour Point principles, I'll bet you will cook up some real winners of your own. Eating well for enjoyment, health and lasting weight control is suited to everyone's tastes. You'll find the recipe for *that* in the recipes that follow – so *bon appétit!*

BREAKFASTS

Almond French Toast with Sliced Strawberries

Whenever you find the time to make French toast,
you'll love this recipe.

SERVES 1

1 egg
1 tbsp skimmed milk
1 drop almond extract
2 slices wholemeal bread
2 tsp Benecol margarine
$\frac{1}{2}$ tsp icing sugar
1 tsp finely ground almonds
3 large strawberries, sliced

1. In a shallow bowl, whisk the egg with the milk and almond extract.

2. Dip the bread in the egg mixture, coating both sides lightly. Set aside.

3. Heat the spread in a non-stick frying pan large enough to hold both pieces of bread. Add the bread and cook on medium heat for 1 to 2 minutes, then sprinkle with the ground almonds, turn and cook for 1 minute.

4. To serve, dust with the icing sugar and top with the strawberries.

Per serving: 281 calories/1,175 kJ, 13 g fat (3 g sat fat), 11 g protein, 34 g carbohydrate, 11 g fibre, 294 mg sodium

VARIATION

Sesame French Toast with Sliced Strawberries: Sprinkle with 1 teaspoon sesame seeds instead of almonds in step 3.

Per serving: 287 calories/1,120 kJ, 13g fat (3 g sat fat), 11 g protein, 35 g carbohydrate, 12 g fibre, 294 mg sodium

Apple-Raisin Porridge

A complete and heartwarming breakfast in a bowl.

SERVES 1

150 ml/5 fl oz water

60 ml/2 fl oz skimmed milk

1 tbsp non-fat dried milk

50 g/1³/₄ oz quick-cook oats

80 ml/3 fl oz unsweetened apple sauce

1 tbsp raisins

1–2 tsp brown sugar (optional)

1. In a small saucepan, bring the water and milk to the boil.

2. Add the dried milk and oats and cook for 1 to 2 minutes. Remove from the heat, cover, and let stand for 2 minutes.

3. Add the apple sauce and raisins. Spoon into a bowl and sprinkle with the brown sugar (if using).

Per serving: 261 calories/1,010 kJ, 3 g fat (<1 g sat fat), 11 g protein, 49 g carbohydrate, 5 g fibre, 68 mg sodium

VARIATION

Apple-Pecan Porridge: Add 2 teaspoons chopped pecans in step 3.

Per serving: 280 calories/1,170 kJ, 6 g fat (<1 g sat fat), 11 g protein, 46 g carbohydrate, 5 g fibre, 67 mg sodium

Banana Soft Wheat Muffins

These muffins are filled with fibre and fruit and are very low in fat and sugar — they also freeze well.

MAKES 12 MUFFINS

2 medium ripe bananas

1 egg

3 tbsp dark brown sugar

3 tbsp non-fat dried milk

3 tbsp rapeseed (canola) oil

170 g/6 oz light brown flour*

1 tsp baking powder

80 ml/2½ fl oz skimmed milk

1. Preheat the oven to 180°C/350°F/gas 4.

2. Place the bananas, egg, brown sugar, dried milk and oil in the bowl of an electric mixer and beat until well blended.

3. Add the flour and baking powder and beat on low, adding the milk slowly until well blended.

4. Place 12 foil baking cups on a baking sheet or line a 12-cup muffin tin with paper liners. Spoon in the batter, filling each cup ²/₃ full.

5. Bake for 15 to 20 minutes, or until golden.

Per muffin: 115 calories/481 kJ, 4 g fat (0 g sat fat), 3 g protein, 18 g carbohydrate, 2 g fibre, 50 mg sodium

* This type of flour is paler and lighter than wholemeal flour but contains more nutrients than white flour.

VARIATIONS

Banana-Chocolate Chip Soft Wheat Muffins: Add 15 g/½ oz good-quality chocolate chips in step 4.

Per muffin: 141 calories/589 kJ, 6 g fat (1 g sat fat), 3 g protein, 21 g carbohydrate, 2 g fibre, 50 mg sodium

Cranberry-Banana Soft Wheat Muffins: Add 65 g/2¼ oz fresh or frozen cranberries in step 4.

Per muffin: 118 calories/493 kJ, 4 g fat (0 g sat fat), 3 g protein, 18 g carbohydrate, 2 g fibre, 57 mg sodium

Pumpkin-Banana Soft Wheat Muffins

The sweet flavours of banana and pumpkin were made for each other.

MAKES 12 MUFFINS

1 small ripe banana

8 tbsp canned pumpkin (no added salt or sugar)

2 eggs

30 g/1 oz dark brown sugar

4 tbsp non-fat dried milk

3 tbsp rapeseed (canola) oil

170 g/6 oz light brown flour*

1 tsp baking powder

120 ml/4 fl oz skimmed milk

40 g/1¼ oz pecans, chopped

1. Preheat the oven to 180°C/350°F/gas 4.

2. Place the banana, pumpkin, eggs, brown sugar, dried milk and oil in the bowl of an electric mixer and beat until well blended.

3. Add the flour and baking powder and beat on low, adding the milk slowly until well blended.

4. Place 12 foil baking cups on a baking sheet or line a 12-cup muffin tin with paper liners. Spoon in the batter, filling each cup ⅔ full.

5. Bake for 15 to 20 minutes, or until golden.

Per muffin: 141 calories/589 kJ, 7 g fat (<1 g sat fat), 4 g protein, 17 g carbohydrate, 2 g fibre, 58 mg sodium

*This type of flour is paler and lighter than wholemeal flour but contains more nutrients than white flour.

Lemon-Poppy Soft Wheat Muffins

Simply delicious and nutritious. These muffins freeze well, so make a batch and keep the extras for another lemon- or poppy seed-theme day.

MAKES 12 MUFFINS

180 ml/6 fl oz fat-free lemon yoghurt

Grated zest of 1 lemon

2 eggs

60 g/2 oz granulated sugar

4 tbsp non-fat dried milk

1 tbsp poppy seeds

3 tbsp rapeseed (canola) oil

170 g/6 oz light brown flour*

1 tsp baking powder

80 ml/2½ fl oz skimmed milk

1. Preheat the oven to 180°C/350°F/gas 4.

2. Place the yoghurt, lemon zest, eggs, sugar, dried milk, poppy seeds and oil in the bowl of an electric mixer and beat until creamy.

3. Add the flour and baking powder and beat on low speed, adding the milk slowly until well blended.

4. Place 12 foil baking cups on a baking sheet or line a 12-cup muffin tin with paper liners. Spoon in the batter, filling each cup ⅔ full.

5. Bake for 15 to 20 minutes, or until golden.

Per muffin: 120 calories/502 kJ, 5 g fat (<1 g sat fat), 4 g protein, 16 g carbohydrate, 1 g fibre, 70 mg sodium

*This type of flour is paler and lighter than wholemeal flour but contains more nutrients than white flour.

Scrambled Eggs with Thyme

Herbs such as thyme hint at saltiness to our taste buds
but don't add sodium to our diets.

SERVES 1

2 eggs
1 tbsp skimmed milk
Pinch of salt
Pinch of dried thyme

1. Coat a non-stick frying pan with olive oil spray.

2. In a cup, stir together the eggs and milk. Add the eggs to the frying pan
   with the salt and thyme and scramble over a medium heat.

Per serving: 146 calories/610 kJ, 9 g fat (3 g sat fat), 13 g protein, 1 g carbohydrate, 0 g fibre,
429 mg sodium

Pepper and Cheese Omelette

Because cheese tends to provide calories and saturated fat that no one needs, we use it only in moderation in the Flavour Point Meal Plan. That said, cheese is delicious, and when used thoughtfully, it's a flavoursome, high-calcium addition to the diet. As for eggs, they're an ideal protein source, and more and more research suggests that in the context of a healthy diet, cholesterol content isn't a real worry. So enjoy.

SERVES 1

2 large eggs
1 tbsp skimmed milk
Pinch of salt
Pinch of garlic granules
1 tbsp grated light mozzarella cheese
60 g/2 oz roasted peppers (capsicums)

1. Coat a non-stick frying pan with olive oil spray and place over a medium heat.

2. In a small bowl, whisk the eggs, milk, salt and garlic granules.

3. Pour the eggs into the frying pan. As they start to set around the edges, use a spatula to lift the edges and tilt the pan so the uncooked egg in the middle flows around the edges. Continue until the eggs no longer flow freely.

4. Spoon the cheese and peppers on to one half of the omelette, then fold in half and cook on both sides until golden.

Per serving: 184 calories/769 kJ, 10 g fat (4 g sat fat), 14 g protein, 7 g carbohydrate, <1 g fibre, 573 mg sodium

VARIATIONS

Asparagus and Dill Cheese Omelette: Wash and slice 3 asparagus spears. Sauté for 2 to 3 minutes in the heated frying pan, then remove and set aside. Cook the omelette as directed, then add the asparagus and a pinch of dried dill (or 1 teaspoon fresh) instead of the peppers (capsicums) in step 4.

Per serving: 181 calories/757 kJ, 11 g fat (4 g sat fat), 15 g protein, 3 g carbohydrate, <1 g fibre, 437 mg sodium

Spring Onion and Cheese Omelette: Add 1 chopped spring onion instead of the peppers (capsicums) in step 4.

Per serving: 170 calories/711 kJ, 10 g fat (4 g sat fat), 15 g protein, 2 g carbohydrate, 1 g fibre, 319 mg sodium

Mushroom, Thyme and Cheese Omelette: Wash and slice 4 fresh medium mushrooms. Sauté for 2 to 3 minutes in the heated frying pan, then remove and set aside. Cook the omelette as directed, then add the mushrooms and a pinch of dried thyme instead of the peppers (capsicums) in step 4.

Per serving: 183 calories/765 kJ, 11 g fat (4 g sat fat), 16 g protein, 4 g carbohydrate, <1 g fibre, 437 mg sodium

Spinach and Feta Omelette: Add 2 teaspoons feta cheese instead of the mozzarella and 30 g/1 oz raw baby spinach instead of the peppers (capsicums) in step 4.

Per serving: 167 calories/698 kJ, 10 g fat (4 g sat fat), 14 g protein, 2 g carbohydrate, <1 g fibre, 518 mg sodium

Tomato, Basil and Feta Omelette: Add 2 teaspoons feta cheese instead of the mozzarella and 1/2 chopped tomato and 5 rinsed and dried fresh basil leaves instead of the peppers (capsicums) in step 4.

Per serving: 173 calories/723 kJ, 10 fat (4 g sat fat), 14 g protein, 4 g carbohydrate, 1 g fibre, 480 mg sodium

Apple-Banana Smoothie

Use the variations of this recipe to adapt it to the flavour theme of the day.

SERVES 1

180 ml/6 fl oz 100% apple juice

½ ripe banana

1 tbsp fat-free natural or vanilla yoghurt

8 tbsp crushed ice

Place the juice, banana, yoghurt and ice in a blender and process until smooth.

Per serving: 156 calories/652 kJ, 0.5 g fat (0 g sat fat), 2 g protein, 38 g carbohydrate, 2 g fibre, 17 mg sodium

VARIATIONS

Carrot-Pineapple Smoothie: Replace the apple juice with 120 ml/4 fl oz each carrot juice and pineapple juice. Omit the banana.
Per serving: 130 calories/543 kJ, 0 g fat (0 g sat fat), 2 g protein, 32 g carbohydrate, 1 g fibre, 49 mg sodium

Coconut-Pineapple Smoothie: Use 100% pineapple juice instead of the apple juice. Replace the banana with 90 g/3 oz drained crushed pineapple. Replace the yoghurt with 60 ml/2 fl oz light unsweetened coconut milk.
Per serving: 208 calories/869 kJ, 3 g fat (3 g sat fat), 2 g protein, 45 g carbohydrate, 1 g fibre, 27 mg sodium

Cranberry-Banana Smoothie: Use 100% cranberry juice instead of the apple juice and add 2 tablespoons natural yoghurt.
Per serving: 145 calories/606 kJ, 0 g fat (0 g sat fat), 4 g protein, 35 g carbohydrate, 3 g fibre, 34 mg sodium

Grape-Banana Smoothie: Use 100% grape juice instead of the apple juice.
Per serving: 177 calories/740 kJ, 0 g fat (0 g sat fat), 2 g protein, 44 g carbohydrate, 2 g fibre, 14 mg sodium

Orange-Banana Smoothie: Use 100% orange juice instead of the apple juice.

Per serving: 154 calories/644 kJ, 0 g fat (0 g sat fat), 1 g protein, 37 g carbohydrate, 1 g fibre, 31 mg sodium

Peach-Banana Smoothie: Replace the apple juice with 170 g/6 oz canned unsweetened peaches with juice.

Per serving: 170 calories/710 kJ, 0 g fat (0 g sat fat), 3 g protein, 43 g carbohydrate, 4 g fibre, 21 mg sodium

Pineapple Smoothie

Along with its wonderful flavour and an aroma that evokes swaying palm trees and pristine beaches, pineapple provides an abundance of potassium and vitamin C and moderate amounts of fibre, folic acid and calcium.

SERVES 1

170 g/6 oz fresh pineapple chunks or juice-packed canned pineapple
1 tbsp fat-free natural yoghurt
8 tbsp crushed ice

Place the pineapple, yoghurt and ice in a blender and process until smooth.

Per serving: 156 calories/652 kJ, 0 g fat (0 g sat fat), 2 g protein, 40 g carbohydrate, 2 g fibre, 11 mg sodium

Lemon-Orange Smoothie

A little tart and surprisingly delicious.

SERVES 1

180 ml/6 fl oz fat-free lemon yoghurt
120 ml/4 fl oz 100% orange juice
4 tbsp fresh lemon juice
8 tbsp crushed ice

Place the yoghurt, orange juice, lemon juice and ice in a blender and process until smooth.

Per serving: 170 calories/711 kJ, 0 g fat (0 g sat fat), 6 g protein, 37 g carbohydrate, 0 g fibre, 100 mg sodium

Pumpkin-Allspice Smoothie

This creamy smoothie has a delicious blend of flavours.

SERVES 2

4 tbsp canned pumpkin (no added salt or sugar)
60 ml/2 fl oz fat-free vanilla yoghurt
4 tbsp non-fat dried milk
180 ml/6 fl oz skimmed milk
8 tbsp crushed ice
Pinch of ground allspice

Place the pumpkin, yoghurt, dried milk, skimmed milk, ice and allspice in a blender and process until smooth.

Per serving: 105 calories/439 kJ, 0 g fat (0 g sat fat), 9 g protein, 37 g carbohydrate, 1g fibre, 122 mg sodium

Almond-Banana Smoothie

This unusual smoothie will quickly become a rich and satisfying favourite. Almonds are a great source of calcium, magnesium, potassium and fibre as well as healthy unsaturated oils. Bananas provide plenty of potassium and fibre, as well as moderate amounts of vitamin A, folic acid and magnesium.

SERVES 1

1 tsp natural almond butter

$^1/_3$ ripe banana

2 tbsp fat-free vanilla yoghurt

2 tbsp non-fat dried milk

80 ml/2$^1/_2$ fl oz skimmed milk

Drop of almond extract

8 tbsp crushed ice

1. Spread the almond butter on the tip of the banana.

2. Place the banana, yoghurt, dried milk, skimmed milk, almond extract and ice in a blender and process until smooth.

Per serving: 160 calories/669 kJ, 3 g fat (<1 g sat fat), 9 g protein, 25 g carbohydrate, 1 g fibre, 116 mg sodium

DIPS

Basil-Ricotta Dip

We eat them only in small quantities, but herbs and spices tend to be nutritional powerhouses. For example, calorie for calorie, basil is higher in fibre than most grains, richer in calcium than spinach, and higher in potassium than a banana. It just happens to taste great, too.

SERVES 1

45 g/1$\frac{1}{2}$ oz light ricotta cheese
10 fresh basil leaves, chopped

In a small bowl, stir together the ricotta and basil until blended. Refrigerate until ready to serve.

Per serving: 51 calories/213 kJ, 0 g fat (0 g sat fat), 5 g protein, 5 g carbohydrate, 0 g fibre, 65 mg sodium

Dill Yoghurt Dip

Dill is rich in vitamin A, calcium and potassium.

SERVES 1

60 ml/2 fl oz fat-free natural yoghurt
1 tsp fresh dill or $\frac{1}{8}$ tsp dried
Pinch of garlic granules
Pinch of salt

In a small bowl, stir together the yoghurt, dill, garlic granules and salt until blended. Refrigerate until ready to serve.

Per serving: 26 calories/109 kJ, 0 g fat (0 g sat fat), 3 g protein, 5 g carbohydrate, 0 g fibre, 189 mg sodium

Sweet Pepper Yoghurt Dip

Fat-free yoghurt is a great alternative to traditional mayonnaise as a base for dips. Whereas mayonnaise provides a large load of fat and calories, yoghurt provides neither of these and is a great source of calcium and those famous active cultures.

SERVES 1

$\frac{1}{2}$ red pepper (capsicum), cored and de-seeded
120 ml/4 fl oz fat-free natural yoghurt
Pinch of garlic granules
Pinch of salt

Finely chop the pepper in a small food processor. In a small bowl, stir together the pepper, yoghurt, garlic granules and salt until blended. Refrigerate until ready to serve.

Per serving: 67 calories/280 kJ, 0 g fat (0 g sat fat), 6 g protein, 14 g carbohydrate, 1 g fibre, 146 mg sodium

Mushroom Dip

Low-fat cottage cheese is a great calcium source, while mushrooms provide plenty of fibre, potassium, selenium and vitamin D. Are we taking good care of you, or what?

SERVES 1

45 g/1½ oz mushrooms, sliced
45 g/1½ oz less-than-2%-fat cottage cheese
Pinch of garlic granules
Pinch of dried dill

1. Grind the mushrooms in a small food processor.

2. In a small bowl, stir together the cottage cheese, mushrooms, garlic granules and dill until blended. Refrigerate until ready to serve.

Per serving: 89 calories/372 kJ, 0 g fat (0 g sat fat), 14 g protein, 8 g carbohydrate, 1 g fibre, 442 mg sodium

Spring Onion Yoghurt Dip

Spring onions are as nutritious as they are flavoursome. They're a concentrated source of vitamin K, antioxidant carotenoids, vitamin A, folic acid, potassium and calcium.

SERVES 1

½ spring onion
60 ml/2 fl oz fat-free natural yoghurt
⅛ tsp onion powder
Pinch of salt

1. Finely chop the spring onion in a small food processor.

2. In a small bowl, stir together the spring onion, yoghurt, onion powder and salt until blended. Refrigerate until ready to serve.

Per serving: 28 calories/117 kJ, 0 g fat (0 g sat fat), 3 g protein, 6 g carbohydrate, 0 g fibre, 180 mg sodium

Tahini Dip

Tahini, a Mediterranean staple, is a paste made from sesame seeds. It's a great source of calcium and healthy monounsaturated oils.

SERVES 1

2 tsp tahini
1 tbsp lemon juice
1 tbsp water
Pinch of garlic granules
Pinch of salt

In a small bowl, stir together the tahini, lemon juice, water, garlic granules and salt until blended. Refrigerate until ready to serve.

Per serving: 64 calories/268 kJ, 5 g fat (<1 g sat fat), 2 g protein, 4 g carbohydrate, <1 g fibre, 150 mg sodium

Spinach Yoghurt Dip

Spinach is on every nutritionist's short list of superstar foods. It's an exceptional source of fibre, vitamin A, vitamin K, potassium, magnesium, vitamin C and calcium.

SERVES 1

15 g/½ oz baby spinach
60 ml/2 fl oz fat-free natural yoghurt
Pinch of garlic granules
1 tsp finely grated Parmesan

1. Grind the spinach in a small food processor.

2. In a small bowl, stir together the spinach, yoghurt, garlic granules and cheese until blended. Refrigerate until ready to serve.

Per serving: 38 calories/159 kJ, <1 g fat (0 g sat fat), 3 g protein, 6 g carbohydrate, <1 g fibre, 84 mg sodium

Sweet Cinnamon Yoghurt Dip

Cinnamon provides a concentrated dose of antioxidants, along with calcium, potassium, fibre and iron. But hey — we're only interested in its great taste!

SERVES 1

120 ml/4 fl oz fat-free natural yoghurt
1 tsp natural honey
Pinch of ground cinnamon

In a small bowl, stir together the yoghurt, honey and cinnamon until blended. Refrigerate until ready to serve.

Per serving: 72 calories/301 kJ, 0 g fat (0 g sat fat), 5 g protein, 15 g carbohydrate, 0 g fibre, 68 mg sodium

Thyme Yoghurt Dip

Thyme is a rich source of calcium, iron, magnesium and potassium, and a good source of antioxidants and vitamin K. Its slightly 'salty' spiciness can be helpful in reducing sodium intake.

SERVES 1

60 ml/2 fl oz fat-free natural yoghurt
1 tsp fresh thyme or $\frac{1}{4}$ tsp dried
Pinch of garlic granules
Pinch of salt

In a small bowl, stir together the yoghurt, thyme, garlic granules and salt until blended. Refrigerate until ready to serve.

Per serving: 27 calories/113 kJ, 0 g fat (0 g sat fat), 3 g protein, 5 g carbohydrate, 0 g fibre, 189 mg sodium

Satisfaction at the Flavour Point

THE FLAVOUR FACTS

Name: Ron Steeves

Age: 55

Family status: Married with three adult children, aged 29, 30 and 31

Occupation: Locksmith

Starting weight: 109 kg/17 st

Weight lost: 9.6 kg/21 lb in 12 weeks

Health stats: Blood pressure dropped 16 points; waist measurement shrank 6 cm/2½ in

'I went on the programme simply because I needed to lose weight – I was about 40 lb [18 kg] overweight when I started. My old habits weren't good. I didn't eat breakfast. I would have coffee at 6.30 am and then go until noon without eating. Then I'd eat a meal, like a pie, for lunch and not eat again until dinner – and I'd eat a big dinner.

Before starting the Flavour Point Diet, I never was able to stick with a diet and lose weight. I thought the theory about the flavour themes and how they work in the brain to control hunger sounded interesting. I thought, "This just might work."

'It did, which is especially impressive because I went on holiday twice during my 12 weeks. I've been on diets before, but I've never been re-educated like this. I lost 21 lb [9.6 kg], and I'm thrilled. My wife has been doing it with me, and she's lost about 10 lb [4.5 kg].

'Overall, my tastes have definitely changed. I like more nutritious foods, and I have adopted better habits. I've cut way back on processed bread. I've also moved away from all the juices and fizzy drinks; I drink a lot of water or iced tea instead. I've also stopped eating highly processed potatoes, chips, pasta and doughnuts.

'For breakfast, I usually choose one of the plan's flavour-friendly options and eat cereal. I was never a big breakfast person, and I can just eat the cereal quickly and go. For lunch, I usually have a salad. The cafeteria where I work serves some awesome salads with chicken, tuna or egg, so I grab one of those. Later in the afternoon, I'll have some fruit, and that carries me through until it's time for dinner.

'Snack-wise, I love the carrots. If I'm looking for a snack when I get home from work, I'll throw a bunch of baby carrots on a dish and take them outside with me – I just love them. If I want something sweet, I now walk through the kitchen and grab a banana or an orange instead of a brownie.

'Speaking of brownies and desserts, although they looked really good, my wife and I have chosen not to make the desserts on the programme. I knew if I kept the sweets around, my craving for sweets wouldn't go away. I grew up in a household where we had pie or cake after dinner every night, so I knew if I did away with sweets altogether, I'd lose weight faster.

'I've also been doing a lot of walking. Even while on holiday, I walked about 2 to 3 miles [3 to 5 km] a day, which has helped to speed up my weight loss.

'I found the programme very flexible. When I was on a cruise a few weeks ago, I had fresh fruit in the morning and then a salad for lunch. At dinner, I ate what they served, but I had one serving, and that was it.

'The flavour themes were a unique aspect of Dr Katz's programme, and they worked. My favourites were the tomato day and most of the nut days. I also loved the recipes that included strawberries.

'People have noticed my weight loss and told me I look great. I've really noticed the loss in my stomach – my waistline is shrinking, which is a really good thing. I'm going to stick with it. I plan to lose the other 20 lb [9 kg] within the next few months – and, with the help of this programme, keep the weight off for life.' ■

LUNCHES

Almond, Green Bean and Quinoa Salad

To save time when preparing this delicious recipe, cook the quinoa ahead of time and refrigerate it to use on a regular basis. You can substitute bulgur wheat for the quinoa if you like.

SERVES 1

170 g/6 oz frozen green beans

1 tsp Dijon mustard

2 tsp balsamic vinegar

2 tsp extra-virgin olive oil

Pinch of salt

Freshly ground black pepper to taste

90 g/3 oz cooked quinoa

1 tsp crumbled feta cheese

½ red onion, thinly sliced

2 tbsp chopped almonds

1. Bring 480 ml/16 fl oz of water to the boil in a medium saucepan. Add the green beans and cook for 2 minutes. Drain and set aside.

2. In a large bowl, whisk the mustard, vinegar, oil, salt and pepper. Add the green beans and toss to coat.

3. Add the quinoa, cheese, onion and almonds and toss to combine.

Per serving: 363 calories/1,517 kJ, 18 g fat (2 g sat fat), 12 g protein, 43 g carbohydrate, 12 g fibre, 398 mg sodium

Apple, Fennel, Walnut and Barley Salad

The combination of tart apple and cooked barley creates a perfect blend. Cook the barley ahead of time and refrigerate it so you can have this lunch ready in the time it takes to chop the apple and fennel. If you like, you can substitute wheat berries for the barley.

SERVES 1

65 g/2¼ oz hulled barley

1 apple, rinsed, cored and chopped

1 bulb fennel, rinsed, trimmed and thinly sliced

1 tbsp chopped walnuts

2 tbsp Newman's Own Light Italian Dressing

Fresh rocket leaves, rinsed and patted dry

1. Bring 350 ml/12 fl oz water to the boil in a medium saucepan. Add the barley and cook for 15 minutes. Drain in a colander and rinse with cold water.

2. In a medium bowl, combine the barley, apple, fennel, walnuts and dressing. Mix well and serve over the rocket.

Per serving: 358 calories/1,496 kJ, 13 g fat (2 sat fat), 7 g protein, 60 g carbohydrate, 16 g fibre, 388 mg sodium

Coconut Prawn and Avocado Salad

Our family loves this nutritious tropical delight.

SERVES 1

6 frozen large prawns

1 tsp extra-virgin olive oil

$\frac{1}{2}$ avocado, peeled and sliced

Juice of 2 limes (about 3 tbsp)

2 tbsp light unsweetened coconut milk

1 spring onion, diced

Pinch of salt

Chopped fresh coriander to taste

1. Quickly thaw the prawns by rinsing in cold water. Peel and pat dry.

2. Heat the oil in a cast-iron grill pan over a high heat. When the oil is very hot, add the prawns and cook for 2 to 3 minutes on each side (do not overcook).

3. Place the prawns and avocado in a salad bowl or on a salad plate.

4. In a small bowl, combine the lime juice, coconut milk, spring onion, salt, and coriander.

5. Pour over the prawns and avocado and stir gently to blend.

Per serving: 285 calories/1,191 kJ, 22 g fat (5 g sat fat), 10 g protein, 17 g carbohydrate, 6 g fibre, 231 mg sodium

Black Bean, Sweetcorn and Tomato Salad

*If you have time to open a can, you have time to throw this complete lunch
together in a flash. If canned black beans are not available,
substitute kidney beans.*

SERVES 1

150 g/5½ oz canned black beans, rinsed and drained

100 g/3½ oz canned or frozen sweetcorn, rinsed and drained

1 medium tomato, sliced

60 g/2 oz baby spinach

2 tsp extra-virgin olive oil

2 tsp balsamic vinegar

⅛ tsp ground cumin

Pinch of salt*

Freshly ground black pepper to taste

In a medium bowl, combine the beans, sweetcorn, tomato, spinach, oil, vinegar and cumin. Toss well and season with the salt and pepper.

Per serving: 257 calories/1,074 kJ, 10 g fat (1 g sat fat), 10 g protein, 34 g carbohydrate, 12 g fibre, 588 mg sodium

*You don't need to use much, if any, salt in this dish because the residual sodium in the canned beans and sweetcorn adds flavour.

Fresh Mint Salade Niçoise

The fresh mint adds a refreshing touch to this classic salad.

SERVES 1

½ tsp Dijon mustard

2 tsp extra-virgin olive oil

2 tsp vinegar

Pinch of salt

Freshly ground black pepper to taste

½ head round (butterhead) lettuce, rinsed and drained

60 g/2 oz tuna, packed in spring water, drained

1 hard-boiled egg, sliced

½ tomato, sliced

2 tbsp chopped fresh mint

1. In a small bowl, whisk the mustard, olive oil, vinegar, salt and pepper.

2. Place the lettuce in a salad bowl or on a salad plate and top with the tuna, egg, tomato and mint. Pour on the dressing.

Per serving: 242 calories/1,012 kJ, 14 g fat (3 g sat fat), 21 g protein, 5 g carbohydrate, 1 g fibre, 453 mg sodium

Lemon Tabbouleh Salad

A delicious classic salad bursting with lemon flavour, tabbouleh is made with bulgur wheat, a form of steam-cooked, dried, cracked wheat that's an excellent source of fibre.

SERVES 1

60 g/2 oz bulgur wheat, cooked (page 218)
1 medium tomato, chopped
2 spring onions, chopped
Juice of 1 lemon
1 tsp extra-virgin olive oil
Pinch of onion powder
Pinch of garlic granules
Pinch of salt
1 tbsp chopped fresh mint or 1 tsp dried
75 g/2½ oz mixed greens

In a medium bowl, combine the bulgur, tomato, spring onions, lemon juice, oil, onion powder, garlic granules, salt and mint. Refrigerate until ready to serve over the greens.

Per serving: 222 calories/928 kJ, 6 g fat (<1 g sat fat), 7 g protein, 41 g carbohydrate, 10 g fibre, 333 mg sodium

Spinach and Lentil Salad with Feta, Walnuts and Currants

Cook the lentils ahead of time and refrigerate them so you can assemble this salad at the last minute. The amounts of cheese and dressing in this recipe are just enough to provide rich taste without endangering your waistline, so don't cheat. Use the variations to adapt it to the flavour theme of the day.

SERVES 1

60 g/2 oz baby spinach (prewashed)

75 g/2½ oz lentils, cooked (page 219), well drained

1 tsp Dijon mustard

2 tsp vinegar

2 tsp extra-virgin olive oil

1 tbsp water

Pinch of salt

Freshly ground black pepper to taste

1 tbsp chopped walnuts

2 tbsp dried currants or raisins

2 tsp feta cheese, crumbled

1. In a medium bowl, combine the spinach and lentils.

2. In a small bowl, stir together the mustard, vinegar, oil, water, salt and pepper.

3. Add the dressing to the spinach mixture and toss to combine. Sprinkle with the nuts, currants and cheese.

Per serving: 293 calories/1,225 kJ, 16 g fat (3 g sat fat), 10 g protein, 32 g carbohydrate, 9 g fibre, 343 mg sodium

VARIATIONS

Mixed Greens and Lentil Salad with Feta, Pecans and Cranberries: Replace the spinach with mixed greens. Replace the walnuts with pecans and add 1 tablespoon dried cranberries instead of the currants in step 3.

Per serving: 301 calories/1,258 kJ, 17 g fat (3 g sat fat), 10 g protein, 31 g carbohydrate, 9 g fibre, 381 mg sodium

Curried Spinach and Lentil Salad with Gorgonzola and Walnuts: Add $1/8$ teaspoon mild curry powder to the dressing in step 2. Omit the currants and replace the feta with Gorgonzola in step 3.

Per serving: 254 calories/1,062 kJ, 16 g fat (3 g sat fat), 10 g protein, 20 g carbohydrate, 8 g fibre, 424 mg sodium

Spinach and Orange-Lentil Salad with Feta and Pecans: Use the juice of $1/2$ orange (about 4 tablespoons) instead of the water. Replace the walnuts with pecans and omit the currants.

Per serving: 278 calories/1,162 kJ, 16 g fat (2 g sat fat), 9 g protein, 28 g carbohydrate, 8 g fibre, 452 mg sodium

Mixed Greens and Lentil Salad with Tomato and Pecans: Replace the spinach with mixed greens. Replace the walnuts with pecans and add $1/2$ sliced tomato instead of the cheese in step 3.

Per serving: 263 calories/1,099 kJ, 16 g fat (2 g sat fat), 10 g protein, 25 g carbohydrate, 10 g fibre, 399 mg sodium

Peanut-Cucumber Salad

Peanuts provide a good amount of healthy polyunsaturated and monounsaturated oils, as well as magnesium and vitamin E. Cucumbers are exceptionally low in calories and a good source of beta-carotene and potassium.

SERVES 1

½ cucumber, seeded and thinly sliced into half-moons

½ small red onion, thinly sliced

2 tbsp rice wine vinegar or red wine vinegar

2 tbsp chopped dry-roasted unsalted peanuts

¼ tsp red pepper flakes

Pinch of salt

1 wholewheat pitta

In a medium bowl, stir together the cucumber, onion, vinegar, peanuts, pepper flakes and salt. Refrigerate until ready to serve with the pitta.

Per serving: 332 calories/1,388 kJ, 10 g fat (1 g sat fat), 15 g protein, 50 g carbohydrate, 12 g fibre, 389 mg sodium

Red Onion, White Bean, Lentil and Tomato Salad

This salad is perfect for a summer picnic – even one in your kitchen – and provides a wonderful combination of nutrients. Onion and tomato are rich sources of anti-oxidants, while beans and lentils provide protein and soluble fibre.

SERVES 1

60 g/2 oz canned white cannellini beans, rinsed and drained

75 g/2½ oz lentils, cooked (page 219)

1 medium tomato, chopped

½ red onion, thinly sliced

2 tsp extra-virgin olive oil

2 tsp red wine vinegar

Pinch of salt

Freshly ground black pepper to taste

In a medium bowl, combine the beans, lentils, tomato, onion, oil, vinegar, salt and pepper. Refrigerate until ready to serve.

Per serving: 349 calories/1,459 kJ, 13 g fat (1 g sat fat), 12 g protein, 46 g carbohydrate, 12 g fibre, 403 mg sodium

Spinach and Turkey Salad

This healthy salad delivers great taste along with great nutrition.

SERVES 1

2 tsp extra-virgin olive oil

1 tsp Dijon mustard

1 tbsp balsamic vinegar

Pinch of salt

Freshly ground black pepper to taste

60 g/2 oz baby spinach

1 tomato, sliced

3 slices roast turkey, cut into strips*

1. In a small bowl, combine the oil, mustard, vinegar, salt and pepper.

2. Place the spinach in a salad bowl or on a salad plate and top with the tomato and turkey. Pour on the dressing.

Per serving: 240 calories/1,003 kJ, 11 g fat (1 g sat fat), 19 g protein, 16 g carbohydrate, 4 g fibre, 573 mg sodium

*Choose turkey with no added fat, sugar or water.

Tomato and Black Bean Mediterranean Salad

Easy, quick and very filling!

SERVES 1

150 g/5¹/₂ oz canned black beans*, rinsed and drained

1 medium fresh tomato, chopped

2 tsp extra-virgin olive oil

1 tsp balsamic vinegar

2 tsp feta cheese

Freshly ground black pepper to taste

¹/₂ wholewheat pitta

In a medium bowl, stir together the beans, tomato, oil, vinegar, feta and pepper. Stuff the filling into the pitta.

Per serving: 334 calories/1,396 kJ, 12 g fat (3 g sat fat), 13 g protein, 46 g carbohydrate, 12 g fibre, 256 mg sodium

* If black beans are unavailable, use chickpeas

Stuffed Tomato with Thyme Tuna Salad

The ground crackers in this tuna salad create the perfect consistency
and provide plenty of fibre and flavour.

SERVES 1

10 g/¹/₂ oz multi- or whole-grain crackers (i.e. Kashi 7-grain or Dr
   Karg's wholegrain 3-seed)
1 large tomato
90 g/3 oz tuna packed in spring water, drained
1 tsp Dijon mustard
1¹/₂ tbsp fat-free natural yoghurt
Chopped celery to taste
1 tsp fresh thyme or ¹/₄ tsp dried
Pinch of salt

1. Grind the crackers in a coffee grinder or small food processor or crush with
   your fingers. Cut the tomato in half and core it.

2. In a medium bowl, combine the tuna, mustard, yoghurt, cracker crumbs,
   celery, thyme and salt to blend. Stuff both halves of the tomato with the
   tuna salad.

Per serving: 189 calories/790 kJ, 2 g fat (0 g sat fat), 25 g protein, 17 g carbohydrate,
3 g fibre, 615 mg sodium

Portobello Mushroom, Gorgonzola and Sun-Dried Tomato Sandwich

The Gorgonzola cheese does make this sandwich a bit indulgent, but like everything else at the Flavour Point, the overall nutrition is top-notch. If it also happens to taste sinfully delicious, don't worry — you don't need to feel guilty.

SERVES 1

2 portobello mushrooms, sliced*

2 slices wholemeal bread

1 tbsp oil-packed sun-dried tomatoes, drained and cut into strips

1 tbsp Gorgonzola cheese

Alfalfa sprouts to taste

1. Coat a cast-iron grill pan with olive oil spray. Add the mushrooms and cook over a high heat for a few minutes on each side until tender.

2. Place the mushrooms on 1 slice of bread, top with the tomatoes, cheese and sprouts, and add the second slice of bread.

Per serving: 236 calories/986 kJ, 5 g fat (2 g sat fat), 11 g protein, 41 g carbohydrate, 14 g fibre, 327 mg sodium

*Look for packaged presliced mushrooms.

Walnut Chicken Salad

Cook the chicken ahead and refrigerate it to save time when you assemble this delicious salad, or use 90 g/3 oz of ready-cooked, skinless chicken breast. Use the variations of this recipe to adapt it to the flavour theme of the day.

SERVES 1

1/2 tsp salt + pinch of salt

90 g/3 oz chicken breast

1 tbsp chopped walnuts

2 tsp fat-free natural yoghurt

1 tsp Dijon mustard

1 tsp extra-virgin olive oil

1/2 tsp cider vinegar

Pinch of garlic granules

Freshly ground black pepper to taste

1. Bring 350 ml/12 fl oz water to a simmer in a medium saucepan and add the 1/2 teaspoon of salt. Add the chicken and cook for 10 minutes, or until cooked through. Alternatively, cook it in a cast-iron grill pan coated with olive oil spray. Let cool and finely chop.

2. In a small bowl, combine the chicken, walnuts, yoghurt, mustard, oil, vinegar, garlic granules, salt and pepper. Refrigerate until ready to serve.

Per serving: 243 calories/1,141 kJ, 13 g fat (2 g sat fat), 28 g protein, 4 g carbohydrate, 1 g fibre, 314 mg sodium

VARIATIONS

Apple-Walnut Chicken Salad: Add 1/2 tart green apple, finely chopped.

Per serving: 273 calories/1,016 kJ, 13 g fat (2 g sat fat), 28 g protein, 12 g carbohydrate, 2 g fibre, 169 mg sodium

Pineapple-Walnut Chicken Salad: Add 1 tablespoon drained canned unsweetened crushed pineapple.

Per serving: 253 calories/1,058 kJ, 13 g fat (2 g sat fat), 28 g protein, 6 g carbohydrate, 1 g fibre, 325 mg sodium

Dill Chicken Salad Sandwich

Our version of chicken salad steers clear of mayonnaise and adds wholegrain goodness and fibre using crackers, but still delivers great taste. Judge for yourself.

SERVES 1

10 g/$\frac{1}{2}$ oz multi- or whole-grain crackers (i.e. Kashi 7-grain or Dr Karg's wholegrain 3-seed)

90 g/3 oz skinless cooked chicken, chopped

1 tsp Dijon mustard

1$\frac{1}{2}$ tbsp natural fat-free yoghurt

Chopped celery to taste

1 tsp fresh dill or $\frac{1}{8}$ tsp dried

$\frac{1}{2}$ tomato, sliced

Lettuce

2 slices wholemeal bread or 2 pieces wholemeal melba toast

1. Grind the crackers in a coffee grinder or small food processor or crush them with your fingers.

2. In a medium bowl, combine the chicken, mustard, yoghurt, cracker crumbs, celery and dill.

3. Spread between the slices of bread, or serve with melba toast.

Per serving: 298 calories/1,246 kJ, 5 g fat (2 g sat fat), 23 g protein, 43 g carbohydrate, 13 g fibre, 669 mg sodium

Pumpkin and Chocolate Grilled Panini

This probably isn't a recipe you would have come up with on your own. It's unusual, we admit, but give it a try. We're pretty sure you'll love it (our test subjects did). Both pumpkin and chocolate are rich in antioxidant nutrients and fibre.

SERVES 1

1 tsp Benecol margarine

2 slices wholemeal bread

2 tbsp canned pumpkin (no added salt or sugar)

16 good-quality chocolate chips

1 tbsp chopped pecans

1. Spread ½ teaspoon of the margarine on 1 side of each slice of bread.

2. Spread the pumpkin on the plain side of 1 slice, line up the chocolate chips in 4 rows of 4, and sprinkle with the nuts. Place the second slice on top with the margarine facing up.

3. Place the sandwich in a hot sandwich toaster or a non-stick frying pan over a medium heat, close the toaster (if using a frying pan, press the sandwich with a spatula), and toast for 2 to 3 minutes (if using a frying pan, turn the sandwich and press again).

Per serving: 261 calories/1,010 kJ, 12 g fat (3 g sat fat), 6 g protein, 38 g carbohydrate, 12 g fibre, 192 mg sodium

VARIATION

Chocolate and Banana Grilled Panini: Use ½ sliced banana instead of the pumpkin and omit the pecans.

Per serving: 258 calories/1,078 kJ, 7 g fat (3 g sat fat), 6 g protein, 51 g carbohydrate, 12 g fibre, 176 mg sodium

DINNERS

Sesame-Soy Chicken

If you use thin slices of breast, this dinner is ready in less than 15 minutes.

SERVES 4

4 boneless, skinless chicken breasts (weighing about 685 g/1½ lb), cut into thin slices
Pinch of salt
2 tsp extra-virgin olive oil
2 tsp grated fresh ginger or garlic
3 tbsp sesame seeds, toasted
4 tbsp low-sodium soy sauce
4 tbsp sherry

1. Rinse the chicken and pat dry. Salt lightly (use no more than ⅛ teaspoon) and set aside.

2. Heat the oil in a non-stick frying pan. Add the ginger and sauté for a few seconds.

3. Add the chicken and cook for 4 to 5 minutes. Turn the chicken, add the sesame seeds, soy sauce and sherry, and cook for 4 to 5 minutes (do not overcook).

Per serving: 275 calories/1,149 kJ, 11 g fat (2 g sat fat), 36 g protein, 5 g carbohydrate, 1 g fibre, 706 mg sodium

Carrot Cider-Glazed Chicken

No one (besides the chef) can ever figure out the secret ingredient in this dish. It's carrot juice, of course, but you don't need to tell! The subtle sweetness of the carrot juice helps you reach the Flavour Point quickly and makes this glaze a favourite for grown-ups and kids alike. Enjoy it to your heart's content – literally.

SERVES 4

4 chicken thighs, skin removed

4 chicken drumsticks, skin removed

3/4 tsp salt

30 g/1 oz light brown flour

2 1/2 tsp extra-virgin olive oil

1 tsp finely chopped fresh ginger

2 garlic cloves, thickly sliced

120 ml/4 fl oz carrot juice

80 ml/3 fl oz cider

120 ml/4 fl oz brown ale

1 tsp ground coriander*

1. Preheat the oven to 190°C/375°F/gas 5. Rinse the chicken and pat dry. Salt lightly (use no more than 1/8 teaspoon of the salt).

2. Place the flour on a flat plate and dredge the chicken pieces, coating both sides.

3. Drizzle 2 teaspoons of the oil into a large non-stick frying pan (it needs to be deep enough to hold 480 ml/16 fl oz of liquid) over a medium-high heat and sauté the chicken on both sides for 4 to 5 minutes, or until slightly browned. (You'll be tempted to add more oil here, but don't. That's all it needs.) Transfer the chicken to a baking dish and set aside.

4. Drizzle the remaining 1/2 teaspoon oil into the frying pan and sauté the ginger for a few seconds. Add the garlic, carrot juice, cider, beer, coriander and

the remaining salt and bring to the boil. Reduce the heat and simmer for 2 to 3 minutes. Pour the liquid over the chicken.

5. Bake for 30 minutes. Turn the pieces and bake for an additional 15 to 20 minutes, or until the chicken almost falls off the bone and the sauce is thick and golden.

Per serving: 271 calories/1,133 kJ, 11 g fat (3 g sat fat), 27 g protein, 11 g carbohydrate, 1 g fibre, 543 mg sodium

*For maximum flavour, grind whole coriander seeds freshly in a coffee grinder.

Chicken with Chocolate Port Wine Sauce

Remember the mouthwatering scene in the movie Chocolat *where everyone gathers around a feast of dishes imbued with chocolate flavour? This luscious sauce could well have been in that scene. It's rich and enticing, with just a hint of chocolate – just enough to make the sauce creamy and velvety (velouté). This recipe is time-consuming but well worth it if you want to indulge in a chocolate day!*

SERVES 4

SAUCE
1 tbsp flaked almonds

2 medium shallots

3 garlic cloves

2 tsp extra-virgin olive oil

1 can (400 g/14 oz) chopped tomatoes, drained

½ tsp salt

Freshly ground black pepper to taste

240 ml/8 fl oz fat-free chicken stock

240 ml/8 fl oz port

30 g/1 oz 60%-cocoa chocolate

2 tsp pink peppercorns

1 tsp cognac

CHICKEN
4 whole boneless, skinless chicken breasts (weighing about 900 g/2 lb), halved

Pinch of salt

Freshly ground black pepper to taste

1. **To make the sauce:** Grind the almonds to a fine powder in a coffee grinder. Finely chop the shallots and garlic in a small food processor.

2. Heat the oil in a heavy frying pan and lightly sauté the almonds, shallots and garlic for 2 to 3 minutes.

3. Add the tomatoes, salt and pepper and cook for 5 to 6 minutes. Add the stock and port and bring to a boil.

4. Reduce the heat and add the chocolate, stirring constantly to blend. Simmer for 15 minutes. Remove from the heat, cover, and let stand for a few minutes.

5. Ladle the mixture into a blender and process until smooth. Strain through a medium sieve into a small saucepan and reserve the liquid, discarding what remains in the sieve.

6. *To make the chicken:* Rinse the chicken and pat dry. Season both sides lightly with salt and pepper.

7. Coat a large cast-iron grill pan with olive oil spray and heat over a medium-high heat. Add the chicken and cook on each side for 8 to 10 minutes, or until cooked through.

8. Return the saucepan to the heat. Rub the peppercorns between your palms to crush them and add to the pan along with the cognac; simmer just until heated through. Serve over the chicken.

Per serving: 403 calories/1,685 kJ, 11 g fat (3 g sat fat), 41 g protein, 19 g carbohydrate, 1 g fibre, 865 mg sodium

Chicken in Creamy Dijon Mushroom Sauce

Your family will never suspect that this wonderful, rich and creamy dish has no added fat. There's no need to add salt since there's enough in the mustard, stock and buttermilk to provide flavour. If you're lucky enough to have leftovers, use them to make a great sandwich for tomorrow's lunch.

SERVES 4

570 g/1¼ lb boneless, skinless chicken breasts or fillets

3 tbsp Dijon mustard

60 ml/2 fl oz fat-free natural yoghurt

60 ml/2 fl oz fat-free chicken stock

120 ml/4 fl oz vermouth

1 tsp extra-virgin olive oil

230 g/8 oz mushrooms, washed, drained and sliced

60 ml/2 fl oz fat-free or low-fat buttermilk

1 tbsp wholegrain mustard

Freshly ground black pepper to taste

1. Preheat the oven to 190°C/375°F/gas 5. Rinse the chicken and pat dry. If using breasts, cut each one in two lengthways.

2. In a small bowl, combine the Dijon mustard and yoghurt. Coat the chicken with the mixture, then cover and refrigerate for at least 15 minutes (this can be done the night before; the chicken will be more tender, and you can assemble the dish quickly).

3. Arrange the chicken in a shallow baking dish that can also be used on the hob. Combine the stock and half the vermouth and pour around the chicken. Bake in the oven for about 10 minutes. Turn the chicken once and bake for a further 10 minutes, or just until cooked (do not overcook).

4. Meanwhile, heat the oil in a non-stick frying pan over a medium heat. Add the mushrooms and sauté until tender. Drain in a colander and set aside.

5. Transfer the chicken to a plate. Place the baking dish over a medium-high heat and add the mushrooms. Bring to the boil and whisk in the buttermilk, mustard, pepper and remaining vermouth. Reduce the heat and cook for a few minutes, stirring constantly, until well blended and creamy.

6. Return the chicken to the baking dish and spoon the sauce over it.

Per serving: 242 calories/1,012 kJ, 5 g fat (1 g sat fat), 32 g protein, 9 g carbohydrate, 1 g fibre, 334 mg sodium

Coconut Thai Chicken

Because coconut is relatively high in saturated fat, the Flavour Point Diet uses it sparingly. It makes for wonderful, slightly exotic flavour, so enjoy.

SERVES 4

570 g/1¼ lb boneless, skinless chicken breasts

¾ tsp salt

120 ml/4 fl oz hot green tea

60 ml/2 fl oz light unsweetened coconut milk

4 tbsp natural peanut butter (no added salt, sugar, or oils)

Juice of 2 limes (about 3 tbsp)

1 tbsp grated fresh ginger

1 tbsp natural honey

2 tbsp low-sodium soy sauce

Chopped fresh coriander to taste

2 tsp extra-virgin olive oil

1. Rinse the chicken and pat dry. Salt lightly (use no more than ⅛ teaspoon of the salt) and cut into 12 equal pieces. Place in a baking dish.

2. In a blender, combine the tea, coconut milk, peanut butter, lime juice, ginger, honey, soy sauce, coriander and remaining salt. Process until smooth.

3. Pour half of the marinade over the chicken and mix to coat well (you can make the marinade ahead of time and refrigerate for more flavour). Reserve the remaining marinade.

4. Heat the oil in a cast-iron grill pan. When the pan is very hot, add the chicken pieces one by one and cook for 4 to 5 minutes on each side (do not overcook).

5. Transfer the chicken to a serving platter and pour the remaining sauce over it.

Per serving: 308 calories/1,287 kJ, 14 g fat (3 g sat fat), 33 g protein, 11 g carbohydrate, 1 g fibre, 848 mg sodium

Pistachio-Crusted Chicken

This dish is deliciously crunchy on the outside and filled with pistachio flavour.

SERVES 4

25 g/1 oz multi- or whole-grain crackers (i.e. Kashi 7-grain or Dr Karg's wholegrain 3-seed)
75 g/2½ oz roasted salted pistachio nuts
455 g/1 lb boneless, skinless chicken breasts, thinly sliced
Pinch of salt
2 tsp extra-virgin olive oil

1. Grind the crackers and pistachios in a coffee grinder or small food processor and place in a shallow bowl.

2. Rinse the chicken and pat dry. Salt lightly (use no more than ⅛ teaspoon).

3. Dredge the chicken in the crumbs, coating both sides.

4. Heat the oil in a large non-stick frying pan. Add the chicken and sear on each side for 4 to 5 minutes.

Per serving: 260 calories/1,087 kJ, 13 g fat (2 g sat fat), 27 g protein, 9 g carbohydrate, 2 g fibre, 232 mg sodium

Roast Chicken with Currant Wine Glaze and Caramelized Onions

This dish always gets high praise. The blend of currants and wine is deliciously sweet. It's quick and easy to prepare, but you need to schedule the time to roast the chicken for about an hour so it's glazed to perfection.

SERVES 4

1 medium roasting chicken

$1/4$ tsp salt

Freshly ground black pepper to taste

2 tsp extra-virgin olive oil

2 onions, thinly sliced

240 ml/8 fl oz red wine

240 ml/8 fl oz fat-free chicken stock

6 tbsp dried currants

2 tbsp rinsed and drained capers

2 tsp crushed dried rosemary

1. Preheat the oven to 190°C/375°F/gas 5. Rinse the chicken and pat dry. Remove all of the bottom skin and as much of the skin on the sides as you can with kitchen scissors, leaving only the skin on top. Lightly salt and pepper the cavity and place the chicken in a roasting tin.

2. Heat the oil in a heavy frying pan. Add the onions and cook for about 5 minutes, or until soft. (Do not add more oil; the onions will 'sweat' perfectly with this amount and don't need to brown at this point. They will caramelize in the oven.)

3. Add the wine, stock, currants, capers and rosemary, bring to the boil, and simmer for 5 to 7 minutes.

4. Pour the liquid over the chicken and roast for 1 hour, or until the sauce thickens and becomes a glaze.

Per serving: 395 calories/1,651 kJ, 9 g fat (2 g sat fat), 51 g protein, 22 g carbohydrate, 2 g fibre, 857 mg sodium

Grilled Chicken with Caramelized Onion on Pitta

This tasty, fun dinner can get messy! Don't even try to stuff it into the pitta, or the pitta will break apart.

SERVES 4

570 g/1¼ lb boneless, skinless chicken breasts
¼ tsp salt
2 tbsp extra-virgin olive oil
2 onions, thinly sliced
90 g/3 oz oil-packed sun-dried tomatoes, drained
Freshly ground black pepper to taste
4 large wholewheat pittas
Mixed greens

1. Rinse the chicken and pat dry. Salt lightly (use no more than ⅛ teaspoon of the salt).

2. Heat the oil in a medium non-stick frying pan over a medium-high heat. Add the onions and the remaining salt. Reduce the heat, cover and cook, stirring occasionally, for 10 minutes.

3. Add the tomatoes and cook for 10 more minutes, or until the onions are soft and golden.

4. Meanwhile, coat a large cast-iron grill pan with olive oil spray and heat over a medium-high heat. Cook the chicken on each side for 6 to 8 minutes and add the pepper. While the chicken is hot, cut into strips with a sharp knife.

5. To serve, place a pitta flat on each of 4 plates and top with equal portions of the greens, chicken and onion mixture.

Per serving: 413 calories/1,726 kJ, 14 g fat (2 g sat fat), 36 g protein, 38 g carbohydrate, 7 g fibre, 360 mg sodium

Grilled Chicken
with White Beans Provençal

If you have the time to open two cans of beans and grill some chicken, you'll have yourself a Chow Now dinner. You just have to be sure to use thinly cut chicken breast and have the vermouth on hand in your cupboard.

SERVES 4

455 g/1 lb chicken breast, cut across the breast into thin 'steaks'
Pinch of salt
4 tsp extra-virgin olive oil
3 garlic cloves, thickly sliced
120 ml/4 fl oz vermouth
240 ml/8 fl oz fat-free chicken stock
2 cans (400 g/14 oz each) cannellini beans, rinsed and drained
2 tsp dried thyme
Freshly ground black pepper to taste

1. Rinse the chicken and pat dry. Salt lightly (use no more than ⅛ teaspoon).

2. Heat 2 teaspoons of the oil in a medium non-stick frying pan over a medium-high heat. Add the garlic and sauté for a few seconds.

3. Add the vermouth and bring to the boil for 1 to 2 minutes. Add the stock and beans and bring to the boil. Reduce the heat, add the thyme and pepper, and simmer for 10 minutes.

4. Meanwhile, heat the remaining oil in a large cast-iron grill pan. When the pan is hot, cook the chicken for 2 to 3 minutes on each side, or until cooked through (do not overcook). Serve the beans over the chicken.

Per serving: 385 calories/1,609 kJ, 8 g fat (1 g sat fat), 33 g protein, 34 g carbohydrate, 8 g fibre, 615 mg sodium

Honey Curry-Glazed Chicken

This dish takes all of 5 minutes to prepare, but it needs a good hour to bake so the juices simmer down to a rich, thick, golden glaze and coat the chicken perfectly (be sure to use only drumsticks, since only they will remain tender and juicy). It's definitely worth the wait. Serve it hot or cold. Make it in advance, refrigerate, and take along on a picnic. The kids will love it because it's sweet, and it's messy fun to eat with their fingers.

SERVES 4

12 chicken drumsticks, skin removed
2 tbsp Dijon mustard
4 tbsp lemon juice
4 tbsp natural honey
$\frac{1}{4}$ tsp mild curry powder
$\frac{1}{2}$ tsp salt

1. Preheat the oven to 190°C/375°F/gas 5. Rinse the chicken and pat dry.

2. In a large bowl, combine the mustard, lemon juice, honey, curry powder and salt. Add the chicken and stir to coat (you can do this ahead of time and refrigerate, covered, overnight if you like).

3. Bake for 1 hour, turning once and basting occasionally, until the chicken almost falls off the bone and the sauce has thickened to a rich golden glaze.

Per serving: 295 calories/1,233 kJ, 7 g fat (2 g sat fat), 38 g protein, 18 g carbohydrate, 0 g fibre, 514 mg sodium

Pecan-Crusted Chicken

The pecan crust on this chicken is out of this world. You finish cooking the chicken breasts in the oven so the nutty crust doesn't burn. If you'd like to cut down on time, slice the chicken breasts more thinly.

SERVES 4

2 boneless, skinless chicken breasts (about 570 g/1¼ lb), halved

¼ tsp salt

30 g/1 oz multi- or whole-grain crackers (i.e. Kashi 7-grain or Dr Karg's wholegrain 3-seed)

2 egg whites

60 g/2 oz pecans, finely chopped

Freshly ground black pepper to taste

2 tsp extra-virgin olive oil

1. Preheat the oven to 200°C/400°F/gas 6. Rinse the chicken and pat dry. Salt lightly (use no more than ⅛ teaspoon of the salt) and set aside.

2. Grind the crackers in a coffee grinder or small food processor.

3. In a wide, shallow dish, whisk the egg whites with a fork. On a flat plate, combine the cracker crumbs, pecans, pepper and the remaining salt.

4. One at a time, dip the chicken pieces first in the egg whites and then in the crumbs, coating both sides well.

5. Heat the oil in a large, non-stick, ovenproof frying pan. Add the chicken and cook over a medium-high heat for 2 to 3 minutes on each side, or until browned. Transfer the pan to the oven for 5 minutes to finish cooking.

Per serving: 291 calories/1,216 kJ, 16 g fat (2 g sat fat), 27 g protein, 9 g carbohydrate, 2 g fibre, 278 mg sodium

Mexican Stuffed Peppers

A complete meal stuffed in a convenient package!

SERVES 4

4 red or yellow peppers (capsicums)*
2 tsp extra-virgin olive oil
1 garlic clove, finely chopped
230 g/8 oz lean ground turkey
1 can (400 g/14 oz) fat-free refried beans†
250 g/9 oz mild salsa
60 g/2 oz bulgur wheat, cooked (page 228)
4 tbsp light mozzarella cheese, grated

1. Preheat the oven to 180°C/350°F/gas 4.

2. Rinse and dry the peppers. Slice off the tops, remove the cores and seeds, and place on a baking tray.

3. Heat the oil in a frying pan. Add the garlic and sauté for a few seconds. Add the ground turkey and cook, stirring, for 5 minutes.

4. Add the beans, salsa and cooked bulgur and cook for 3 to 4 minutes, or until bubbly.

5. Stuff each pepper with ¼ of the stuffing and top with ¼ of the cheese. Bake for 20 to 25 minutes, then grill for 5 minutes, or until the cheese is sizzling and golden.

Per serving: 321 calories/1,342 kJ, 10 g fat (3 g sat fat), 19 g protein, 39 g carbohydrate, 10 g fibre, 763 mg sodium

*Pick short, stout ones that will stand upright.

†If these are unavailable, use canned kidney beans – drain well and lightly mash before adding to the pan along with a good pinch of onion powder and chilli powder.

Satisfaction at the Flavour Point

THE FLAVOUR FACTS

Name: Laura Coppola

Age: 40

Family status: Married

Occupation: Buyer for hospital
   purchasing department

Starting weight: 81 kg/12 st 10 lb

Weight lost: 18.5 kg/19 lb in 12
   weeks

Health stats: Cholesterol dropped
   0.28 points; blood pressure
   dropped 10 points; waist measurement shrank 10 cm/4 in;
   6 per cent decline in body fat

'Since my father died a few years ago,
I ate out of depression and put on a
lot of weight. I tried Weight Watchers
for a while, and it worked, but I didn't
stick to it because it was too much
measuring. I was looking for another
programme, and Dr Katz's plan came
into my life at just the right time.

'Not only was the timing perfect,
but Dr Katz's programme is really
great – I love the recipes, and I'm
learning to shop, cook and eat
healthily. My energy level is much
higher (I can go from 8 in the morning to 11 at night without stopping),
my clothes fit much better, and I feel
like I can breathe.

'I have to admit, when I took a
first glance through the meal plan,
there were some recipes that I was
unsure of because the combinations
of ingredients were strange to me.
But when you put them all together,
they taste really good. You can take
a plain old piece of chicken or fish
and add poppy seeds or something
to it, and it's wonderful. I never
would have thought to do those
things before.

'My favourite breakfast dishes
were the omelettes because they were
both flavoursome and filling; I usu-

ally ate them on the weekends when I had more time to cook. During the week, I ate the wholegrain cereal for breakfast to save time.

'For lunch, I particularly liked the walnut chicken salad and the tuna salad because they were easy to prepare and tasted excellent. I also liked them because I ate them on wholewheat bread, which was a switch from eating all the salads.

'My favourite dinners were Pan-Seared Cod with Lemon Chives and Capers and Prawn Pasta Primavera with Basil Pesto. The pasta primavera was particularly good, and sometimes I would add grilled chicken breast to it for variety. Even better, my husband – a really finicky eater – has been eating a lot of the meals with me.

'Another great thing about Dr Katz's programme is that I never feel hungry or deprived. If I do start to feel a little hungry, it's not until 9 or 10 o'clock, and I just have one of the snacks. If I feel a craving coming on, like for chocolate, I just make something out of the plan with chocolate in it. (I'm a chocolate lover, so it was great that after the first 3 weeks, the programme started to incorporate chocolate.) The chocolate brownies are really good.

'It's also really easy to adjust to the programme if I eat out. My husband and I pick restaurants that offer healthy choices, or we look for a place with a salad bar.

'The best part of the programme is that it works – I look at myself in the mirror and my face looks thinner, I can put on a pair of size 12 shorts (I used to wear a 16), and people at work tell me I look great.

'I really love Dr Katz's programme; I am definitely going to try to stick to it for life. It's so much better than all the fad diets out there.' ■

Apple-Prune Chicken

This is an absolute delight! The apples and prunes make a perfect pair.

SERVES 4

4 chicken breasts (weighing about 900 g/2 lb), skin removed
   and cut in half
³/₄ tsp salt
30 g/1 oz light brown flour
3 tsp extra-virgin olive oil
4 garlic cloves, thickly sliced
1 medium apple, rinsed and sliced
350 ml/12 fl oz 100% apple juice or cider
90 g/3 oz stoned prunes

1. Preheat the oven to 190°C/375°F/gas 5. Rinse the chicken and pat dry. Salt lightly (use no more than ⅛ teaspoon).

2. Place the flour on a flat plate and dredge each chicken piece, coating on both sides.

3. Add 2 teaspoons of the oil to a large baking pan over a medium-high heat and briefly sauté the chicken on both sides for 4 to 5 minutes, or until slightly browned. (You'll be tempted to add more oil, but don't. That's all it needs, really!) Transfer the chicken to a plate and set aside.

4. Add the remaining teaspoon of oil to the pan and sauté the garlic and apple for 1 to 2 minutes.

5. Add the apple juice, prunes and the remaining salt and bring to the boil. Reduce the heat and simmer for 5 to 8 minutes.

6. Return the chicken to the pan and spoon some of the liquid over it. Bake for 30 minutes. Turn the pieces and bake for an additional 10 to 15 minutes, or until the chicken is tender and the sauce is thick and glistening. If you like, crush the prunes so they become part of the sauce.

Per serving: 328 calories/1,371 kJ, 7 g fat (1 g sat fat), 30 g protein, 36 g carbohydrate, 3 g fibre, 654 mg sodium

Cranberry and Sweet Onion Turkey Breast Steaks

This is one of those 'throw-everything-in-the-pan' kinds of dishes
that's very simple and quick to prepare and very satisfying.

SERVES 4

4 turkey breast steaks (weighing about 685 g/1½ lb)
Pinch of salt
1 medium onion, sliced
1 tbsp extra-virgin olive oil
120 ml/4 fl oz fat-free chicken stock
180 ml/6 fl oz 100% cranberry or cranberry-apple juice
115 g/4 oz dried cranberries
6 dried prunes
1 tbsp balsamic vinegar
Freshly ground black pepper to taste

1. Rinse the turkey and pat dry. Salt lightly (use no more than ⅛ teaspoon).

2. In a large frying pan over a medium heat, sauté the onions in the oil for 3 to 5 minutes.

3. Add the turkey and cook, turning once, for 5 to 8 minutes, or until it begins to brown.

4. Add the stock, cranberry juice, cranberries, prunes and vinegar and cook for 10 to 15 minutes, or until the turkey is well done and the sauce is rich and thick. Season with the pepper. If you like, crush the prunes in the pan so they become part of the sauce.

Per serving: 351 calories/1,467 kJ, 5 g fat (<1 g sat fat), 44 g protein, 33 g carbohydrate, 3 g fibre, 398 mg sodium

Peach-Coriander Turkey
with Oven-Roasted Potatoes and Turnips

The sweet flavour of peach blends wonderfully with the slight tartness of the beer, creating a very satisfying and hearty dinner.

SERVES 4

POTATOES AND TURNIPS

4 small red potatoes, scrubbed and halved

4 turnips, scrubbed, peeled and cut into large pieces

2 tsp extra-virgin olive oil

1 tsp garlic granules

¼ tsp salt

Freshly ground black pepper to taste

TURKEY

900 g/2 lb turkey breast crown

¾ tsp salt

Freshly ground black pepper to taste

3 tbsp high-fruit peach jam (no added sugar)

6 dried peaches*

2 tbsp wholegrain mustard

1 tbsp coriander seeds

3 garlic cloves, finely chopped

240 ml/8 fl oz brown ale

2 tsp extra-virgin olive oil

1. **To make the potatoes and turnips:** In a medium bowl, combine the potatoes, turnips, oil, garlic granules, salt and pepper and toss to coat. Set aside.

2. **To make the turkey:** Preheat the oven to 190°C/375°F/gas 5. Coat a baking pan with olive oil spray.

3. Remove the skin from the turkey with kitchen scissors, rinse, and pat dry. Season with salt and pepper (use no more than $\frac{1}{8}$ teaspoon of the salt). Place in the baking pan and set aside.

4. In a small bowl, stir together the jam, peaches, mustard, coriander, garlic, ale, oil and the remaining salt. Pour over the turkey and bake for 35 to 45 minutes until cooked. Add the potatoes and turnips to the pan during the final 20 to 25 minutes of cooking time.

Per serving (turkey): 321 calories/1,342 kJ, 9 g fat (2 g sat fat), 30 g protein, 26 g carbohydrate, 3 g fibre, 664 mg sodium

Per serving (potatoes and turnips): 180 calories/752 kJ, 3 g fat (0 g sat fat), 4 g protein, 35 g carbohydrate, 5 g fibre, 238 mg sodium

* You can use fresh peaches instead of dried: stone 2 large peaches, cut into large segments and fry quickly in olive oil over high heat until lightly browned. Add to the baking pan 5 minutes before serving.

Turkey, Bean and Thyme Pot au Feu

A pot au feu is one of those feel-good comfort stews that simmer slowly in the oven for a long time and fill the whole house with wonderful smells.

SERVES 4

2 tsp extra-virgin olive oil

90 g/3 oz baby carrots, sliced

1 medium onion, chopped

4 garlic cloves, thickly sliced

685 g/1½ lb boneless, skinless turkey breast joint

2 tsp dried thyme

1 bay leaf

Pinch of salt

1 can (400 g/14 oz) chopped tomatoes

480 ml/16 fl oz fat-free chicken stock

180 ml/6 fl oz red table wine

2 cans (400 g/14 oz each) small cannellini beans, rinsed and drained

1. Preheat the oven to 180°C/350°F/gas 4.

2. Heat the oil in a large baking pan. Add the carrots, onion and garlic, and sauté for 2 minutes.

3. Add the turkey, thyme, bay leaf and salt and cook for 8 to 10 minutes. Turn the turkey to brown on the other side.

4. Stir in the tomatoes (with juice), stock and wine, and bring to the boil. Stir in the beans. Transfer to the oven and bake for 1 hour. Remove the bay leaf before serving.

Per serving: 477 calories/1,994 kJ, 5 g fat (<1 g sat fat), 55 g protein, 44 g carbohydrate, 11 g fibre, 857 mg sodium

Almond-Crusted Haddock

This is a great quick and simple dish.

SERVES 4

685 g/1 1/2 lb fresh haddock fillets, skinned
30 g/1 oz multi- or whole-grain crackers (i.e. Kashi 7-grain or Dr
    Karg's wholegrain 3-seed)
2 egg whites
60 g/2 oz almonds, finely chopped
1/4 tsp salt
Freshly ground black pepper to taste
2 tsp extra-virgin olive oil

1. Preheat the oven to 200°C/400°F/gas 6. Rinse the fish, pat dry, and set
   aside.

2. Grind the crackers in a coffee grinder or small food processor.

3. In a wide, shallow dish, whisk the egg whites with a fork. On a flat plate,
   combine the crackers, almonds, salt and pepper.

4. One at a time, dip the fillets first in the egg whites and then in the crumbs,
   coating both sides well.

5. Heat the oil in a large, non-stick frying pan and sear the filets over medium-
   high heat for 2 to 3 minutes on each side.

6. Transfer the fillets to a shallow ovenproof dish and bake in the oven for
   5 minutes.

Per serving: 284 calories/1,187 kJ, 11 g fat (2 g sat fat), 37 g protein, 9 g carbohydrate,
2 g fibre, 283 mg sodium

Baked Monkfish with Tomatoes, Olives and Capers

This is a very tasty way to bake fish with a southern French flavour. All the ingredients for this quick and easy dish are mixed right in the baking dish, so you'll have just one pan to clean.

SERVES 4

685 g/1½ lb monkfish fillet
Pinch of salt
1 can (400 g/14 oz) chopped tomatoes
2 tbsp tomato purée (paste)
2 tbsp water
65 g/2¼ oz kalamata olives
2 tbsp rinsed and drained capers
2 tbsp oil-packed sun-dried tomatoes, drained
1 tbsp extra-virgin olive oil
4 garlic cloves, thickly sliced
Freshly ground black pepper to taste

1. Preheat the oven to 190°C/375°F/gas 5.

2. Rinse the fish, pat dry and cut into large chunks. Salt lightly (use no more than ⅛ teaspoon).

3. In a baking dish, stir together the tomatoes (with their juice), tomato purée, water, olives, capers, sun-dried tomatoes, oil, garlic and pepper.

4. Add the fish to the baking dish and spoon some of the sauce on top. Bake for 30 minutes, basting once or twice.

Per serving: 292 calories/1,221 kJ, 10 g fat (2 g sat fat), 34 g protein, 17 g carbohydrate, 3 g fibre, 928 mg sodium

Pan-Seared Cod with Lemon, Chives and Capers

CN

This cooks very quickly, so it's perfect for Chow Now nights. If you wish, substitute another kind of white fish that has a mild flavour – sea bass would work well.

SERVES 4

Juice of 2 lemons (about 3 tbsp)
1 tbsp fresh chives, snipped
1 tsp rinsed and drained capers
3 tbsp extra-virgin olive oil
685 g/1½ lb fresh cod fillets
Salt
Freshly ground black pepper to taste
30 g/1 oz light brown flour

1. In a small bowl, stir together the lemon juice, chives, capers, dash of salt and 2 tablespoons of the oil. Set aside.

2. Rinse the fish and pat dry. Season with the salt (use no more than ⅛ teaspoon) and pepper. Place the flour on a flat plate and dredge the fish, coating both sides.

3. Heat the remaining oil in a large non-stick frying pan over medium-high heat. Add the fish and cook, turning once, for 7 to 8 minutes, or until tender and browned on both sides.

4. To serve, place a fillet on each of 4 plates and drizzle with the lemon mixture.

Per serving: 261 calories/1,010 kJ, 12 g fat (2 g sat fat), 33 g protein, 6 g carbohydrate, 1 g fibre, 227 mg sodium

Orange Cod

The orange makes this dish very tasty, and it's so quick and easy, you can put it together at the last minute.

SERVES 4

1 tbsp extra-virgin olive oil

2 tbsp rice wine vinegar or cider vinegar

3 tbsp frozen 100% orange juice concentrate, thawed*

2 tbsp orange juice

½ tsp salt

Freshly ground black pepper to taste

570 g/1¼ lb cod fillets

1 orange, peeled and sliced

1 tbsp rinsed and drained capers (optional)

Chopped fresh coriander (optional)

1. Preheat the oven to 200°C/400°F/gas 6.

2. In a medium bowl, stir together the oil, vinegar, orange juice concentrate, orange juice, salt and pepper. Set aside.

3. Rinse the fish and pat dry. Add to the marinade and turn to coat on both sides. Place in a baking dish and pour the remaining marinade over it.

4. Arrange the orange slices on top of the fish and add the capers (if using). Bake for 15 minutes. Garnish with the coriander (if using).

Per serving: 171 calories/715 kJ, 5 g fat (<1 g sat fat), 22 g protein, 10 g carbohydrate, 1 g fibre, 445 mg sodium

* If the concentrate is unavailable, use a total of 4 tbsp of orange juice mixed with 1 tbsp high-fruit orange marmalade.

Orange Grilled Tuna

You can throw this dinner together in just 15 minutes.

SERVES 4

685 g/1½ lb tuna steak (sushi grade)

4 tbsp 100% orange juice concentrate, thawed*

1 tbsp natural honey

1 tbsp Dijon mustard

Pinch of salt

Freshly ground black pepper to taste

1 tsp extra-virgin olive oil

1. Cut the fish into 8 equal pieces and set aside.

2. In a medium bowl, stir together the orange juice concentrate, honey, mustard, salt and pepper. Add the fish and stir to coat.

3. Add the oil to a cast-iron grill pan and place over a high heat. When the pan is very hot, add the fish and cook for 6 to 7 minutes on each side (do not overcook).

Per serving: 239 calories/999 kJ, 3 g fat (<1 g sat fat), 40 g protein, 11 g carbohydrate, 0 g fibre, 185 mg sodium

* If the concentrate is unavailable, use a total of 4 tbsp of orange juice mixed with 1 tbsp high-fruit orange marmalade.

Lemon Salmon with Garlic Spinach

This lemony meal is fast, easy and elegant. And let's face it, when it comes to nutrition, you can hardly do better than salmon and spinach in the same dish!

SERVES 4

4 salmon fillets (about 685 g/1½ lb total; preferably wild)
4 tsp extra-virgin olive oil
4 tbsp lemon juice
Salt and freshly ground black pepper (optional)
2 garlic cloves, chopped
2 bags (340 g/12 oz each) baby spinach, rinsed

1. Preheat the grill. Line a baking sheet with foil.

2. Place the fish on the baking sheet and drizzle each fillet evenly with 2 teaspoons of the oil and 2 tablespoons of the lemon juice. Sprinkle with salt and pepper, if desired. Grill for 10 to 12 minutes, or just until cooked through.

3. Meanwhile, heat the remaining oil in a large non-stick frying pan. Add the garlic and sauté, stirring, for 20 seconds. Add the spinach several handfuls at a time. Using 2 wooden spoons, toss the spinach until it wilts. Continue cooking until all the spinach fits into the frying pan. Stir in the remaining lemon juice.

4. To serve, place a mound of spinach on each of 4 plates and top with a fillet.

Per serving: 357 calories/1,492 kJ, 17 g fat (3 g sat fat), 41 g protein, 10 g carbohydrate, 4 g fibre, 511 mg sodium

Poached Salmon with Cucumber-Dill Sauce

This simple classic recipe is delicious hot or cold.

SERVES 4

350 ml/12 fl oz water

180 ml/6 fl oz vermouth

Juice of 1 lemon

2 tbsp fresh dill or 2 tsp dried

3/4 tsp salt

4 salmon fillets (weighing about 685 g/1 1/2 lb; preferably wild)

350 ml/12 fl oz fat-free natural yoghurt

1/2 large cucumber, peeled, seeded and thinly sliced

1 red onion, finely chopped

3 tbsp coarsely chopped fresh dill

2 tsp rice wine vinegar or cider vinegar

1/4 tsp sugar

Freshly ground black pepper to taste

1. Combine the water, vermouth, lemon juice, dried dill and 1/2 teaspoon of the salt in a pan large enough to hold the salmon. Bring to a gentle simmer and add the salmon. Cook for 5 to 7 minutes, or until cooked through. Transfer the fillets to a plate.

2. Meanwhile, in a medium bowl, stir together the yoghurt, cucumber, onion, fresh dill, vinegar, sugar, pepper and the remaining salt. Serve over the poached salmon.

Per serving: 409 calories/1,710 kJ, 13 g fat (2 g sat fat), 43 g protein, 19 g carbohydrate, 1 g fibre, 583 mg sodium

Poppy Seed-Crusted Salmon

Both simple and delicious, this quick dish cooks even faster if you replace the quinoa on the meal plan with bulgur wheat and any frozen veggie of your choice.

SERVES 4

25 g/1 oz multi- or whole-grain crackers (i.e. Kashi 7-grain or Dr Karg's wholegrain 3-seed)
4 salmon fillets (weighing about 685 g/1½ lb; preferably wild)
¼ tsp salt
2 egg whites
2 tbsp poppy seeds
Freshly ground black pepper to taste
2 tbsp extra-virgin olive oil

1. Grind the crackers in a coffee grinder or small food processor. Rinse the fish and pat dry. Salt lightly (use no more than ⅛ teaspoon of the salt).

2. In a wide, shallow dish, whisk the egg whites with a fork. On a flat plate, combine the cracker crumbs, poppy seeds, pepper and the remaining salt.

3. One at time, dip the fillets first in the egg whites and then in the crumbs, coating both sides well.

4. Heat the oil in a large non-stick frying pan. Add the fish and sear over a medium-high heat for 2 to 3 minutes on each side, or until browned.

Per serving: 393 calories/1,643 kJ, 22 g fat (3 g sat fat), 42 g protein, 6 g carbohydrate, 1 g fibre, 298 mg sodium

Prawn Pasta Primavera with Basil Pesto

This tastes fantastic served cold on a summer day.

SERVES 4

40 frozen large prawns

75 g/2½ oz fresh basil leaves

2 tbsp grated Parmesan or pecorino cheese

3 tbsp pine nuts

2 garlic cloves

¼ tsp salt

4 tbsp extra-virgin olive oil

285 g/10 oz wholewheat pasta spirals*

455 g/1 lb frozen chopped vegetables of your choice

1. Quickly thaw the prawns by rinsing in cold water. Peel, pat dry and set aside.

2. In a food processor, finely chop the basil, cheese, pine nuts, garlic and salt. Scrape down the sides of the bowl and drizzle in 3 tablespoons of the oil with the motor running. Set aside.

3. Cook the pasta according to the directions on the packet. Drain in a colander, rinse with cold water, and transfer to a large bowl.

4. Meanwhile, lightly coat a cast-iron grill pan with olive oil spray and place over a high heat. When the pan is very hot, add the prawns and cook for 2 to 3 minutes on each side (do not overcook). Add to the bowl with the pasta.

5. Add the remaining oil to the pan and sauté the frozen vegetables for a few minutes.

6. Add the vegetables and pesto to the pasta and prawns and stir to blend.

Per serving: 606 calories/2,533 kJ, 30 g fat (4 g sat fat), 29 g protein, 59 g carbohydrate, 12 g fibre, 441 mg sodium

*I use wholewheat pasta with milled flaxseed; if it's available it's worth the extra expense.

Pineapple Prawns

You can throw this great dish together quickly. The only time-consuming step is peeling the prawns. If you prefer and need to cut time, use tuna steak or chicken breast cut into chunks instead.

SERVES 4

40 frozen medium prawns

60 ml/2 fl oz frozen 100% pineapple juice concentrate*, thawed

1 tbsp natural honey

1 tbsp Dijon mustard

Pinch of salt

Freshly ground black pepper to taste

2 tsp extra-virgin olive oil

170 g/6 oz fresh or canned unsweetened pineapple, diced

1. Quickly thaw the prawns by rinsing in cold water. Peel, pat dry and set aside.

2. In a medium bowl, stir together the juice concentrate, honey, mustard, salt and pepper. Add the prawns and stir to coat.

3. Drizzle the oil in a cast-iron grill pan and place over a high heat. When the pan is very hot, add the prawns one by one and cook for 2 to 3 minutes on each side (do not overcook). Serve with the pineapple.

Per serving: 152 calories/635 kJ, 4 g fat (<1 g sat fat), 12 g protein, 18 g carbohydrate, 1 g fibre, 284 mg sodium

* If this is unavailable, use 3 tbsp of pineapple juice mixed with 1 tbsp high-fruit pineapple preserves.

Tossed Garden Salad

Keep these ingredients on hand so you won't hesitate to throw this great salad together with dinner in a flash.

SERVES 4

SALAD

Unlimited mixed greens, baby spinach, or favourite lettuce (not iceberg)

As many raw vegetables as you can pile in a big salad bowl, such as tomatoes, cucumbers, onions, peppers (capsicums), alfalfa sprouts, and so on. (For ease and convenience, use packaged prewashed grated carrots, grated cabbage, etc.)

DRESSING

1 tbsp extra-virgin olive oil

3 tbsp vinegar

Pinch of salt

Freshly ground black pepper to taste

OR

5 tbsp (5 capfuls) Newman's Own Light Italian Dressing

Build your salad any way you like!

Per serving (on average): 96 calories/401 kJ, 4 g fat (<1 g sat fat), 4 g protein, 13 g carbohydrate, 5 g fibre, 116 mg sodium

Cucumber, Tomato, Olive and Red Onion Salad

This classic Mediterranean salad is delicious and reminds us of blue skies and sun.

SERVES 4

1 cucumber, sliced

1 red onion, thinly sliced

2 tomatoes, chopped

65 g/2¼ oz kalamata olives

3 tbsp red wine vinegar

1 tbsp extra-virgin olive oil

Pinch of salt

Freshly ground black pepper to taste

In a medium bowl, combine the cucumber, onion, tomatoes, olives, vinegar, oil, salt and pepper. Toss to mix.

Per serving: 128 calories/535 kJ, 8 g fat (1 g sat fat), 3 g protein, 12 g carbohydrate, 3 g fibre, 305 mg sodium

Lentil and Bean Salad with Coriander

This easy recipe is nutritious and very satisfying.

SERVES 4

340 g/12 oz lentils, cooked (page 219)

170 g/6 oz canned cannellini beans, rinsed and drained

1 medium tomato, chopped

1 spring onion, chopped

Chopped fresh coriander to taste

1 tsp + 1 tbsp extra-virgin olive oil

2 tsp + 3 tbsp balsamic vinegar

Mixed greens

Pinch of salt

Freshly ground black pepper to taste

In a large bowl, combine the lentils, beans, tomato, spring onion, coriander, 1 teaspoon of the oil and 2 teaspoons of the vinegar. Serve over a bed of mixed greens, drizzle with the remaining oil and vinegar, and season with the salt and pepper.

Per serving: 220 calories/920 kJ, 6 g fat (1 g sat fat), 11 g protein, 33g carbohydrate, 8 g fibre, 112 mg sodium

Minty Tabbouleh Salad

The fresh mint infuses this salad with a taste of summer. It tastes even better the next day, when the ingredients have spent some time together.

SERVES 4

285 g/10 oz bulgur wheat, cooked (page 218)

2 medium tomatoes, chopped

1 can (400 g/14 oz) chickpeas, rinsed and drained

3 spring onions, chopped

Juice of 2 lemons

1 tbsp extra-virgin olive oil

Pinch of onion powder

Pinch of garlic granules

$^1/_2$ tsp salt

4 tbsp fresh mint, rinsed, patted dry, and chopped

115–170 g/4–6 oz mixed greens

In a large bowl, combine the bulgur, tomatoes, chickpeas, spring onions, lemon juice, olive oil, onion powder, garlic granules, salt and mint. Refrigerate until ready to serve over the greens.

Per serving: 275 calories/1,149 kJ, 6 g fat (<1 g sat fat), 11 g protein, 49 g carbohydrate, 13 g fibre, 463 mg sodium

Pasta Fagioli with Spinach Marinara Sauce

*This Italian classic features the nutritional goodness of spinach. If you orchestrate
this well, you can make this dish within 15 minutes.*

SERVES 4

1 tbsp extra-virgin olive oil

4 garlic cloves, chopped

340 g/12 oz baby spinach

800 g/1¾ lb tomato passata (no added oil or sugar)

1 can (400 g/14 oz) cannellini beans, rinsed and drained

65 g/2¼ oz kalamata olives

1 bay leaf

1 tsp dried thyme

¼ tsp salt

Freshly ground black pepper to taste

340 g/12 oz organic wholewheat penne (with milled flaxseed,
   if available)

1. Heat the oil in a large frying pan. Add the garlic and sauté for a few
   seconds. Add the spinach one bag at a time and cook for 4 to 5 minutes, or
   until wilted.

2. Add the tomatoes, beans, olives, bay leaf, thyme, salt and pepper and
   simmer for 8 to 10 minutes.

3. Meanwhile, cook the pasta according to the directions on the packet. Drain
   in a colander and transfer to a bowl. Remove the bay leaf from the sauce
   and serve over the pasta.

Per serving: 568 calories/2,374 kJ, 12 g fat (1 g sat fat), 24 g protein, 102 g carbohydrate,
21 g fibre, 971 mg sodium

Pasta with Marinara Sauce

What could be simpler than this classic tomato dinner?

SERVES 4

1 tbsp extra-virgin olive oil

4 garlic cloves, chopped

800 g/1¾ lb tomato passata (no added oil or sugar)

1 tsp dried thyme or oregano

1 bay leaf

¼ tsp salt

Freshly ground black pepper to taste

340 g/12 oz wholewheat spaghetti

2 tbsp grated Parmesan

1. Heat the oil in a deep frying pan. Add the garlic and sauté for a few seconds.

2. Add the tomatoes, thyme, bay leaf, salt and pepper and simmer for 8 to 10 minutes.

3. Meanwhile, cook the pasta according to the directions on the packet. Drain in a colander and transfer to a bowl. Remove the bay leaf from the sauce and serve over the pasta, sprinkled with the cheese.

Per serving: 397 calories/1,659 kJ, 6 g fat (1 g sat fat), 18 g protein, 76 g carbohydrate, 13 g fibre, 469 mg sodium

Apple-Butternut Squash Soup

*This soup is very creamy even though it's very low in fat. The sweet flavour of apple
intensifies if you make it in advance and refrigerate it before puréeing.*

SERVES 4

2 tsp extra-virgin olive oil

1 large onion, finely chopped

2 tsp mild curry powder

$^3/_4$ tsp salt

570 g/1$^1/_4$ lb pounds butternut squash, peeled and chopped

2 medium apples, peeled, cored and cut into large chunks

700 ml/1$^1/_4$ pints fat-free chicken stock

180 ml/6 fl oz cider

350 ml/12 fl oz fat-free or low-fat buttermilk

1. Heat the oil in a large saucepan over a medium heat. Reduce the heat to
   low, add the onion and curry powder, and sauté for 8 to 10 minutes, or
   until tender.

2. When the onion is tender, add the salt, squash, apples and stock and bring
   to the boil. Reduce the heat, add the cider, and simmer for about 20 minutes, until the squash and apples are very tender. Remove from the heat
   and let stand for a few minutes.

3. Pour the soup in batches into a blender or food processor and purée until
   smooth. Return to the saucepan, add the buttermilk, and simmer briefly to
   heat through.

Per serving: 225 calories/943 kJ, 3 g fat (<1 g sat fat), 10 g protein, 42 g carbohydrate,
8 g fibre, 659 mg sodium

Satisfaction at the Flavour Point

THE FLAVOUR FACTS

Name: Jim Butler

Age: 39

Family status: Married with two
children, aged 7 and 8

Occupation: Security, telecom,
safety and facilities supervisor

Starting weight: 148 kg/23 st 3 lb

Weight lost: 14 kg/31 lb in 12 weeks

Health stats: Blood pressure
dropped 0.49 points; blood
sugar dropped 0.82 points; lost
10 cm/4 in from waist; over 5 per
cent decline in body fat

'I was diagnosed with Guillain-Barré syndrome, paralyzed from the waist down, and hospitalized for a week in August 2004. After I was discharged, things went downhill fast. My food consumption went way up, my energy went down, and I gained 4 st 12 lb [31 kg]. I felt like a slug – fat, with no energy. I was eating 7,000-plus calories, including two or three servings of red meat per day. I was the perfect example of how not to eat. I would get out of a meeting at 10.00 pm and stop at McDonald's for two or three double cheeseburgers . . . for a snack. I had to do something!

'Prior to starting this programme, I, as well as my whole family, would eat in order to not feel hungry. I was living to eat rather than eating to live.

'I work full-time and am the local fire chief, so I'm pretty busy. I wasn't sure I'd have the time to follow a meal plan, but I made the commitment to do it. My health was at stake.

'To keep myself going in the beginning, I decided not to weigh myself for the first 2 weeks. When I had to move down a belt hole, I knew it was time to step on the scales. In the first 2 weeks, I lost 21 lb [9.6 kg]. I was very pleased at that point, and I have been ever since.

'I like the flavour themes on Dr Katz's programme, particularly the pineapple and nuts. And the bulgur wheat was by far my best new find. I eat it with everything. For a snack (or even a late-night fix if I need it), the bulgur mixed with yoghurt is great.

'I wish I had changed my eating habits years ago. I have not had red meat in 12 weeks, and I don't miss it at all. When I go to parties or gatherings, I have a salad. My eating habits have changed 100 per cent. Now I eat real food.

'Many people have commented on my weight loss, saying, "You look great!" and asking me how much I've lost. Everyone asks me about the diet I'm on, and I always explain it the same way: it is a serious lifestyle change, and you need to approach it as such. You need to stay focused; if you do, and you combine a little exercise with it, the results are astounding.

'Today, I feel great. I have lots more energy, and I only expect to get more as the weight continues to come off. I don't consider this a diet as much as I do a way to eat well.

'Although I have to admit I was a little sceptical at first, I'm so happy I've stuck with Dr Katz's programme. I was a walking time bomb, and if I had gone on one of those fad diets, I think I would have given up a long time ago. Those are diets; this is a lifestyle change.' ■

Portobello Mushrooms with Walnut Stuffing

This dish requires a little more preparation than most other Flavour Point recipes. You can prepare the mushrooms in advance and refrigerate them so you can just pop them in the oven when you're ready.

SERVES 4

8 medium or 4 large portobello mushroom caps

30 g/1 oz multi- or whole-grain crackers (i.e. Kashi 7-grain or Dr Karg's wholegrain 3-seed)

2 tsp extra-virgin olive oil

1 small onion, chopped

2 garlic cloves, chopped

1 stick celery, chopped

6 baby carrots, chopped

40 g/1¼ oz chopped walnuts

145 g/5 oz bulgur wheat (dry)

480 ml/16 fl oz fat-free chicken stock

1 tsp dried thyme

Pinch of salt

Freshly ground black pepper to taste

4 tbsp grated Parmesan cheese

1 tsp ground paprika

1. Preheat the oven to 190°C/375°F/gas 5. Coat a baking dish with olive oil spray.

2. Rinse the mushrooms, pat dry, and trim the stems (there's no need to hollow out the caps). Set aside.

3. Grind the crackers in a coffee grinder or small food processor. Set aside.

4. Heat the oil in a non-stick frying pan over a medium heat. Add the onion, garlic, celery and carrots, and sauté for 2 to 3 minutes.

5. Add the bulgur and cook, stirring, for a few seconds. Add the stock and cook until the bulgur is tender and all the liquid is absorbed. Remove from the heat and stir in the thyme, cracker crumbs, walnuts, salt and pepper.

6. Place the mushrooms in the baking dish and use an ice cream scoop to fill them with the stuffing mixture, packing it down slightly (they'll be over-stuffed, but that's okay).

7. Sprinkle the tops with the cheese and paprika and coat lightly with olive oil spray. Bake for 15 to 20 minutes.

Per serving: 341 calories/1,425 kJ, 13 g fat (2 g sat fat), 15 g protein, 43 g carbohydrate, 8 g fibre, 381 mg sodium

Mint, Sweet Pea and Spinach Soup

Catherine adapted this recipe from an old-time favourite from The Silver Palate Cookbook. *She was sceptical when she first discovered it years ago but was won over by the delicious blend of flavours, so here it is with a few healthy changes that preserve its creaminess. It's quick and easy to put together, as long as you have a blender.*

SERVES 4

2 tbsp extra-virgin olive oil

230 g/8 oz onion, finely chopped

570 g/1¼ lb frozen chopped spinach, thawed

570 g/1¼ lb frozen peas, thawed

1 litre/1¾ pints fat-free chicken stock

75 g/2½ oz fresh mint

¾ tsp salt

Freshly ground black pepper to taste

400 ml/14 fl oz fat-free or low-fat buttermilk

1. Heat the oil in a large saucepan. Add the onions and sauté for about 5 minutes, or until soft.

2. Add the spinach, peas and stock and bring to the boil. Reduce the heat and simmer for 10 to 12 minutes. Add the mint, salt and pepper, remove from the heat, and let stand for a few minutes.

3. Pour the soup in batches into a food processor or blender and process until smooth. Return to the pan, add the buttermilk, and simmer briefly, stirring, to heat through.

Per serving: 315 calories/1,317 kJ, 8 g fat (1 g sat fat), 23 g protein, 40 g carbohydrate, 13 g fibre, 972 mg sodium

Pumpkin Soup

This soup takes 8 minutes to make from opening the cans to putting it on the table.
It's so creamy and satisfying you could swear it was made with pure cream.
It's perfect on an autumn evening.

SERVES 4

2 tsp extra-virgin olive oil

1 tsp finely chopped fresh ginger or garlic

4 cans (425 g/15 oz each) pumpkin (no added salt or sugar)

700 ml/1¼ pints fat-free vegetable or chicken stock

480 ml/16 fl oz fat-free or low-fat buttermilk

½ tsp salt

60 ml/2 fl oz light unsweetened coconut milk

1. Heat the oil in a large saucepan over a medium heat. Add the ginger or garlic and sauté for 1 minute.

2. Add the pumpkin, stock, buttermilk and salt and stir. Simmer for 5 to 7 minutes, or until hot.

3. To serve, ladle the soup into 4 bowls and drizzle a swirl of coconut milk on top of each.

Per serving: 242 calories/1,012 kJ, 4 g fat (2 g sat fat), 14 g protein, 41 g carbohydrate, 12 g fibre, 553 mg sodium

Dill Potatoes

Fresh dill is the perfect complement to steamed potatoes. Used frequently in potato salads, dill lets you avoid the calories and saturated fat that come with potato's other customary partners – butter and soured cream.

SERVES 4

3 medium red potatoes, cut into chunks
2 tsp extra-virgin olive oil
1 tbsp fresh dill
Pinch of salt

1. Steam the potatoes until tender.

2. In a small bowl, combine the oil, dill and salt.

3. Place the potatoes in a serving bowl and drizzle with the oil.

Per serving: 137 calories/573 kJ, 3g fat (0 g sat fat), 3 g protein, 26 g carbohydrate, 2 g fibre, 156 mg sodium

Sautéed Spaghetti Squash

This squash can also be served as is right out of the microwave,
drizzled with olive oil.

SERVES 4

1 medium spaghetti squash
2 tsp extra-virgin olive oil
Pinch of salt
Freshly ground black pepper to taste

1. Pierce the rind of the squash with a fork and microwave on high for 10 to 12 minutes (or 5 to 6 minutes per 455 g/1 lb) until the skin feels soft. Cut in half and remove the seeds. Twist out the strands with a fork.

2. Heat the oil in a non-stick frying pan. Add the squash and sauté until heated through. Season with the salt and pepper.

Per serving: 84 calories/351 kJ, 3 g fat (<1 g sat fat), 2 g protein, 15 g carbohydrate, 3 g fibre, 115 mg sodium

Roasted Asparagus with Pecans and Sun-Dried Tomatoes

Along with rich, enticing flavour, pecans add healthy unsaturated oils and vitamin E to this dish.

SERVES 4

455 g/1 lb asparagus
1 tbsp chopped pecans
3 tbsp oil-packed julienned sun-dried tomatoes, drained
1 tsp extra-virgin olive oil
¼ tsp salt

1. Preheat the oven to 190°C/375°F/gas 5. Cut 1 cm/½ in off the ends of the asparagus. Rinse the spears and pat dry.

2. In a small baking dish, drizzle the asparagus, pecans and tomatoes with the oil and sprinkle with the salt. Stir to mix.

3. Bake for 8 to 10 minutes, or until the asparagus is crisp-tender.

Per serving: 65 calories/271 kJ, 3 g fat (0 g sat fat), 3 g protein, 6 g carbohydrate, 3 g fibre, 159 mg sodium

Wholemeal Garlic Bread

Yes, you can even eat garlic bread on the Flavour Point Diet, as long as you make it with wholemeal bread.

SERVES 4

1 loaf (455 g/1 lb) wholemeal Italian-style bread
2 tsp extra-virgin olive oil
1 garlic clove, crushed

Cut the bread in half lengthways, then drizzle one half with the olive oil and top with the garlic (freeze the other half for another day). Bake at 190°C/375°F/gas 5 until browned, then cut into 4 slices.

Per serving: 122 calories/510 kJ, 3 g fat (0 g sat fat), 3 g protein, 24 g carbohydrate, 8 g fibre, 134 mg sodium

COOKED WHOLE GRAINS AND LENTILS

Brown Rice

*More flavoursome than white rice, brown rice is also much more nutritious;
in particular, it's an excellent source of fibre.*

MAKES ABOUT 685 g/1½ lb

1.2 litres/2 pints water
300 g/10½ oz brown rice

Bring the water to the boil in a large saucepan. Add the rice and cook for about
15 minutes, or until tender.

**Per serving: 258 calories/1,078 kJ, 2 g fat (0 g sat fat), 5 g protein, 54 g carbohydrate,
2 g fibre, 9 mg sodium**

Bulgur Wheat

*Bulgur wheat has no fat and is relatively low in calories and high in fibre and protein. It
takes all of 5 minutes to make (much less time than pasta or rice), never clumps, and is
always 'forgiving' if you boil it in a little too much water. On top of that, kids love it. The
rule of thumb is simple: use almost twice as much water (but not quite: it's a 1:1¾ ratio)
as dry bulgur.*

MAKES ABOUT 455 g/1 lb

700 ml/1¼ pints water
285 g/10 oz bulgur wheat

Bring the water to the boil in a medium saucepan. Add the bulgur and cook for
5 minutes. Let cool, then refrigerate in an airtight container for up to 1 week.

**Per serving: 180 calories/524 kJ, <1 g fat (0 g sat fat), 6 g protein, 40 g carbohydrate,
10 g fibre, 14 mg sodium**

Lentils

Lentils are so good for everyone's health that having them already cooked in the fridge may encourage the rest of your family to eat them more often.

MAKES 650 g/1 lb 6 oz

340 g/12 oz dry lentils
1.2 litres/2 pints water

1. Rinse and drain the lentils.

2. Bring the water to the boil in a large saucepan. Add the lentils and cook for 10 to 15 minutes, or until tender but not mushy. Drain in a colander and rinse with cold water. Refrigerate in an airtight container for up to 1 week.

Per serving: 243 calories/1,016 kJ, 0 g fat (0 g sat fat), 20 g protein, 41 g carbohydrate, 22 g fibre, 7 mg sodium

Quinoa

This nutritious, delicious grain keeps well in the fridge, precooked, and won't clump even when reheated in the microwave. It's great as a side dish alone or can be mixed with bulgur wheat. It takes roughly 10 minutes longer to cook than bulgur.

MAKES ABOUT 500 g/1 lb 2 oz

1.1 litres/36 fl oz water
285 g/10 oz quinoa

Bring the water to the boil in a large saucepan. Add the quinoa and cook for 12 to 15 minutes, or until tender. Drain if necessary. Let cool, then refrigerate in an airtight container for up to 1 week.

Per serving: 238 calories/995 kJ, 4 g fat (0 g sat fat), 8 g protein, 44 g carbohydrate, 4 g fibre, 13 mg sodium

DESSERTS

Baked Bananas with Rum-Pecan Topping

This quick and easy dessert features the buttery taste of pecans.

SERVES 4

30 g/1 oz pecans

1 tbsp rum

1 tbsp water

1 tbsp dark brown sugar

2 ripe bananas, halved lengthways*

1. Preheat the oven to 180°C/350°F/gas 4. Coarsely grind the pecans in a small food processor.

2. In a small bowl, combine the rum, water, brown sugar and pecans. Drizzle over each banana half.

3. Bake for 5 to 7 minutes, then grill for 1 minute, or until the top is sizzling.

Per serving: 129 calories/539 kJ, 6 g fat (<1 g sat fat), 1 g protein, 18 g carbohydrate, 2 g fibre, 2 mg sodium

*Keep the skin on so you can serve it right from its 'shell'.

Baked Cinnamon Apples

This dessert is as heartwarming as it is delicious.

SERVES 4

2 apples, halved and cored

2 tbsp cider

2 tsp dark brown sugar

Pinch of ground cinnamon

1. Preheat the oven to 180°C/350°F/gas 4. Line a baking sheet with foil and place the apples on the tray, core side up.

2. Combine the cider, brown sugar and cinnamon. Drizzle over the apples.

3. Bake for 10 to 12 minutes, then grill for 1 minute, or until the top is sizzling.

Per serving: 53 calories/222 kJ, 0 g fat (0 g sat fat), 0 g protein, 14 g carbohydrate, 2 g fibre, 2 mg sodium

VARIATIONS

Baked Cinnamon-Almond Apples: Add 30 g/1 oz chopped almonds in step 2.

Per serving: 88 calories/368 kJ, 3 g fat (0 g sat fat), 1 g protein, 15 g carbohydrate, 3 g fibre, 2 mg sodium

Baked Cinnamon-Walnut Apples: Add 30 g/1 oz chopped walnuts in step 2.

Per serving: 86 calories/359 kJ, 4 g fat (0 g sat fat), 1 g protein, 14 g carbohydrate, 2 g fibre, 2 mg sodium

Chocolate Brownies

These moist little brownies taste as rich and chewy as they sound, yet they contain no added butter or oil. Tofu is the magic ingredient, but your family will never know it's there. Be sure to cut them into exactly 24 squares and have only 1 per person. (Freeze the rest for another indulgence day!)

MAKES 24 BROWNIES (5-CM/2-IN SQUARES)

50 g/1¾ oz almonds

120 ml/4 fl oz skimmed milk

115 g/4 oz 60%-cocoa chocolate

125 g/4½ oz soft silken tofu, extra water discarded

3 eggs

8 tbsp non-fat dried milk

2 tbsp unsweetened cocoa

65 g/2¼ oz dark brown sugar

30 g/1 oz light brown flour

½ tsp baking powder

30 g/1 oz good-quality chocolate chips

1–2 tsp icing sugar, sifted (optional)

1. Preheat the oven to 170°C/325°F/gas 3.

2. Bring the skimmed milk to the boil in a small saucepan, then remove from the heat. Break up the chocolate, add to the milk, and stir until creamy. Set aside.

3. Place the tofu, eggs, dried milk, cocoa and brown sugar in the bowl of an electric mixer and beat until well blended.

4. Grind the almonds in a coffee grinder or small food processor. Set aside.

5. Add the melted chocolate to the tofu mixture and beat until blended. Add the ground almonds, flour and baking powder, and beat until well blended. Stir in the chocolate chips.

6. Pour the batter into an ungreased 30 × 20 × 3 cm/12$\frac{1}{4}$ × 8$\frac{1}{4}$ × 1$\frac{1}{4}$ in cake tin (foil trays work well) and bake for 15 to 20 minutes. When cool, sift the icing sugar (if using) on top and cut into 24 squares.

Per brownie: 98 calories/410 kJ, 5 g fat (2 g sat fat), 3 g protein, 12 g carbohydrate, 1 g fibre, 30 mg sodium

Strawberries Dipped in Dark Chocolate

Although it tastes decadently delicious, this is in fact a very nutritious treat!

SERVES 1

30 g/1 oz dark chocolate (unsweetened)
4 large strawberries
4 tsp skimmed milk

1. Break up the chocolate. Rinse and dry the strawberries.

2. In a small microwaveable bowl, microwave the chocolate and milk on medium-high for 25 seconds, or until melted. Stir until creamy and let cool for a few minutes before dipping the strawberries.

Per serving: 198 calories/828 kJ, 10 g fat (6 g sat fat), 3 g protein, 25 g carbohydrate, 5 g fibre, 13 mg sodium

Caramelized Pineapple Rings

This simple, quick and delicious dish provides a perfect ending to Pineapple Day.

SERVES 4

8 fresh or canned unsweetened pineapple rings

4 tsp brown sugar

1. Spread the pineapple in a single layer on a baking sheet and sprinkle the brown sugar evenly over the top.

2. Grill for 3 to 5 minutes, or until caramelized.

Per serving: 77 calories/322 kJ, 0 g fat (0 g sat fat), 0 g protein, 20 g carbohydrate, 1 g fibre, 12 mg sodium

Peach Flat Cake

This cake is similar to the luscious, buttery galettes from Brittany in the north of France, except, of course, it has no butter! Its dense flat batter topped with fresh peaches rises slightly as it bakes to embrace the fruit, so it's not only delicious, it's also beautiful. Surprisingly, it's quick and simple to make. Freeze any leftovers and save for another Peach Day.

SERVES 6

$\frac{1}{2}$ tsp + 60 g/2 oz Benecol margarine

4 tbsp non-fat dried milk

60 g/2 oz granulated sugar

1 tbsp flaked almonds

2 eggs

30 g/1 oz light brown flour

$\frac{1}{4}$ tsp baking powder

2 medium ripe peaches, peeled and thinly sliced,
    or 1 can 230 g/8 oz juice-packed sliced peaches, drained

1. Preheat the oven to 180°C/350°F/gas 4. Grease the bottom of a round cake tin with $\frac{1}{2}$ teaspoon of the spread.

2. Place the dried milk, sugar, almonds and the remaining spread in the bowl of an electric mixer and beat on medium speed until creamy. Add the eggs and beat for a few minutes, or until the batter is 'airy'. Add the flour and baking powder and mix again until well blended.

3. Pour batter into the tin and lay the peaches in a circle on top. Bake for 20 minutes, or until golden.

Per serving: 151 calories/631 kJ, 9 g fat (2 g sat fat), 4 g protein, 16 g carbohydrate, 1 g fibre, 118 mg sodium

Satisfaction at the Flavour Point

THE FLAVOUR FACTS

Name: Jonathan Link

Age: 33

Family status: Single

Occupation: Software engineer

Starting weight: 81 kg/12 st 10 lb

Weight lost: 6.8 kg/15 lb in 12 weeks

Health stats: Cholesterol dropped 1.86 points; waist measurement shrank 12 cm/4½ in; 7 per cent decline in body fat

'Before starting Dr Katz's programme, I could not hold myself to a reasonable portion size. I would empty a whole box of cereal into a container that looked like a trough, and that was my breakfast. Throughout my life, I had always been pretty thin – fluctuating between 11 and 11½ st [70 and 72.5 kg]. Once I hit my thirties, however, I started working first shift instead of third and started eating more and exercising less. It caught up with me.

'When I first saw how much cereal I really should be eating, I was like, 'Get out of here – that's it?' I thought I'd be hungry on the programme all the time. I was wrong. In fact, I never felt hungry. After week 2, I couldn't eat everything. I only made three of the desserts throughout the entire programme – two fruit salads and a peach flatbread as I was too full to eat them.

'I'm a pretty eclectic eater (I eat everything except internal organs), so I had tried most of the foods on the programme before. The food was excellent. I remember a grilled pumpkin and chocolate panini I had for lunch one day. It was to die for. I thought, 'There is no possible way this is good for me – it's too delicious and decadent.'

'I also loved the way Catherine Katz incorporated so many different textures into the dishes, like nuts and cranberries sprinkled on a salad. It goes along with my philosophy that eating should really be a whole experience; food can't just taste good – it has to look good and feel good in your mouth, too. Otherwise everything would just be like apple sauce.

'Although all the recipes were really good, I think I enjoyed the chicken ones the best. I was surprised at some of the ingredients in the dishes. When I looked over the meal plan, I thought there was no way these things would taste good together. Again, I was wrong. The combinations were consistently delicious.

'I also learned how to make a bunch of simple sauces. When I used to cook for myself, I'd skip the sauce because I thought it would take forever. Now that I've learned how to and got in the habit of doing it, I know all I have to do is take whatever I cooked with and work with it for a few more seconds to make a great sauce – one that tastes as delicious as something I would eat at a restaurant.

'I also learned many great new tricks that I will definitely use for the rest of my life. For instance, when it came to salad dressings, I always liked them creamy. When I saw that I had to squeeze an orange on my chicken salad, I thought, 'This isn't going to be good', but it tasted great. Now, I figure there's no sense in buying salad dressings if I can make my own. I used to be a mayonnaise freak. When I tried the fat-free yoghurt in chicken salad instead of mayonnaise, it was awesome. I loved it. I'll probably never eat mayo again because the yoghurt is so much healthier and it tastes just as good.

'When I eat out, I have to admit, I've become one of those people I used to hate – I order the plain chicken and the salad with the dressing on the side – because you know what? I'm paying for it, and I should be able to have it the way I want it. I used to be able to eat a whole fast-food value meal and still be hungry for something else, and now I eat one veggie burger and I can't even eat the fries.

'I'm definitely going to stay on Dr Katz's programme, and I will advertise it like it's going out of style – I'm a walking advertisement for it! If you stick with it, you can't fail. There is no way for you to follow these recipes and not lose weight and feel great about yourself in the process. It's a can't-fail plan.' ■

Piña Colada Frozen Dessert

This fun, easy tropical dessert will make you feel as if you are relaxing on a sunny island.

SERVES 4

120 ml/4 fl oz light unsweetened coconut milk
340 g/12 oz crushed pineapple in its own juice (preferably fresh)
2 tbsp dark rum
240 ml/8 fl oz crushed ice

Place the coconut milk, pineapple, rum and ice in a blender and process until smooth. Pour into 4 individual bowls or glasses and place in the freezer for at least 15 minutes before serving.

Per serving: 110 calories/460 kJ, 2 g fat (1 g sat fat), <1 g protein, 21 g carbohydrate, 1 g fibre, 9 mg sodium

Peanut Katz Flax Crisps

These no-bake cookies are a healthy and nutritious alternative to conventional Rice Krispies treats, which typically contain no fibre, lots of saturated and hydrogenated fat, and marshmallow sugar goo. Instead, these little squares are filled with the healthy omega-3 fatty acids found in flaxseed and, with the peanut butter and organic crispy brown rice cereal, are a great source of dietary fibre. They freeze well, so keep them handy, and remember to stick to 1 square per person.

MAKES 30 SQUARES

340 g/12 oz natural honey
230 g/8 oz natural peanut butter
115 g/4 oz dark flaxseed*
230–250 g/8–9 oz crispy brown rice cereal†
15 g/½ oz good-quality chocolate chips

1. Heat the honey in a pan over a low heat for 2 to 3 minutes, or until warm and slightly liquefied. Remove from the heat and stir in the peanut butter until melted and smooth.

2. Finely grind the flaxseed in two batches in a coffee grinder. Place in a large bowl with 170 g/6 oz of the cereal and mix gently with clean hands.

3. Add the warm peanut butter-honey mixture and stir well with a spoon. Add the remaining cereal, a third at a time (if it gets too hard to stir at the end, you may leave out a third). Stir in the chocolate chips while still warm.

4. Pour into an ungreased 30 × 20 × 3 cm/12 × 8 × 1¼ in cake tin (foil trays work well) and press down to flatten with slightly damp, clean hands until nicely compact and flat throughout. Refrigerate for 15 minutes, then cut into 30 squares.

Per serving: 146 calories/610 kJ, 7 g fat (1 g sat fat), 3 g protein, 19 g carbohydrate, 2 g fibre, 61 mg sodium

*To fully benefit from the healthy nutritional value of the omega-3s in flaxseed, it's best to grind it fresh, but it's fine to use ground flax meal.

†This is often found in the 'healthy eating' or 'free from' section of supermarkets, not in the cereals aisle.

Raisin-Muesli Parfait

Refrigerate this dessert for at least 30 minutes after assembling and before serving, as each layer becomes infused with the other. Be sure to follow the amounts speci-fied in the recipe and not get carried away with the raisins and the muesli!

SERVES 4

125 g/4½ oz low-fat fruit-free muesli
4 tbsp raisins or currants
240 ml/8 fl oz fat-free vanilla yoghurt
240 ml/8 fl oz fat-free natural yoghurt

1. Grind the muesli in a coffee grinder, then grind the raisins or currants or finely chop.

2. In a small bowl, stir together the vanilla and natural yoghurt until creamy.

3. Line up 4 tall, thin glasses. Spoon 1 tablespoon of the yoghurt into each glass, then add a sprinkle of muesli and a sprinkle of raisins. Continue alternating layers, ending with the muesli. Use a total of 120 ml/4 fl oz of yoghurt for each glass. Refrigerate for at least 30 minutes before serving (you can also freeze it if you prefer).

Per serving: 187 calories/782 kJ, 1 g fat (0 g sat fat), 8 g protein, 39 g carbohydrate, 2 g fibre, 131 mg sodium

Warm Apple Crisp

A classic quick and simple dessert.

SERVES 4

60 g/2 oz fruit-free nutty muesli

2 tsp Benecol margarine

3 apples, rinsed, cored and thickly sliced

80 ml/2½ fl oz cider

1 tbsp chopped almonds

1 tbsp brown sugar

Pinch of cinnamon

1. Preheat the oven to 180°C/350°F/gas 4.

2. Finely grind the muesli in a coffee grinder or small food processor.

3. Spread the margarine in the bottom of a shallow baking dish and arrange the apples in a single layer.

4. Pour the cider over the apples and sprinkle with the muesli, almonds, brown sugar and cinnamon.

5. Bake for 15 to 20 minutes, or until the apples are tender.

Per serving: 163 calories/681 kJ, 4 g fat (<1 g sat fat), 2 g protein, 33 g carbohydrate, 4 g fibre, 52 mg sodium

Mint Chocolate Chip Shake

So minty, delicious and satisfying, you'll forget you're on a diet.

SERVES 4

350 ml/12 fl oz low-fat vanilla frozen yoghurt

240 ml/8 fl oz skimmed milk

1 tbsp good-quality chocolate chips

Drop of peppermint extract

In a blender, process the yoghurt, milk, chocolate chips and peppermint until smooth.

Per serving: 118 calories/493 kJ, 1 g fat (<1 g sat fat), 6 g protein, 21 g carbohydrate, 0 g fibre, 84 mg sodium

Cranberry-Vanilla Soft Ice Cream

Deliciously tart, this dessert provides a perfect ending to Cranberry Day.

SERVES 4

480 ml/16 fl oz fat-free vanilla ice cream or frozen yoghurt

80 ml/3 fl oz skimmed milk

2 tbsp fresh or frozen cranberries

In a blender, process the ice cream, milk and cranberries until smooth.

Per serving: 97 calories/405 kJ, 0 g fat (0 g sat fat), 5 g protein, 19 g carbohydrate, 0 g fibre, 64 mg sodium

Pumpkin Soft Ice Cream

If you love pumpkin pie, you'll love this tasty ice cream dessert.

SERVES 4

480 ml/16 fl oz fat-free vanilla ice cream

2 tbsp canned puréed pumpkin (no added salt or sugar)

4 tbsp skimmed milk

Pinch of allspice

In a blender, process the ice cream, pumpkin, milk and allspice until smooth.

Per serving: 98 calories/410 kJ, 0 g fat (0 g sat fat), 4 g protein, 20 g carbohydrate, 1 g fibre, 74 mg sodium

6

STAYING ON POINT
FOR LIFE

You've graduated from the school of flavour themes.
You no longer need them as long as you adhere to
the Flavour Point principles.

Learning to lower your Flavour Point is similar to learning to ride a bike. In the beginning, you needed stabilizers – in the form of flavour themes – to guide your eating and balance your appetite. Now, after spending 6 weeks using the Flavour Point Meal Plan, you're ready to dispose of the stabilizers as you continue to pedal towards your weight-loss goal.

How do you avoid falling? How do you permanently maintain the Flavour Point benefits without flavour themes? Without necessarily even realizing it, you have *already* learned all the principles you need to balance at the Flavour Point – permanently. Here's a quick recap of how you travelled from point A to point B.

In Phase 1 of the meal plan, you followed daylong flavour themes to subdue your appetite.

During this phase, you also began eating meals and snacks that were wholesome, minimally processed and free of unnecessary flavours. As you gained mastery over Flavour Point principles – learning to choose Flavour Point-approved foods and cook Flavour Point–worthy meals – you were able to decrease your dependence on the flavour themes. That's why, in Phase 2 of the plan, you ate a greater variety of flavours over the course of each day, limiting your flavour themes to individual meals. Thus, you learned how to have variety *over time* without having too much variety *at any one time*.

That is a crucial Flavour Point principle that you must stick with for a lifetime in order to reach and maintain your goal. Over time, you can have all the variety you want. Savoury foods, salty foods, sweet foods and spicy foods are all fine; you just can't eat them all at once. Go ahead and enjoy slightly sweetened wholegrain cereal for breakfast along with sweet fruit. Have a savoury bean salad at lunch with flavour-neutral wholemeal bread. At dinner, eat a slightly spicy, herb-encrusted fish fillet or chicken breast with a flavour-neutral salad. That's variety over time.

On the other hand, don't eat a breakfast that consists of salted eggs with sweet jam on toast. Don't have a savoury cheese or meat sandwich with salty potato crisps and a sweet fizzy drink at lunch. Don't snack on sweet fruit *and* salted nuts. These are all examples of too much variety at any one time.

To adhere to this principle, distribute flavours over the course of each day according to the following guidelines.

Breakfast. Combine a flavour-neutral food with either a sweet or salty food. For example, try grains with sweet fruit (see day 1 of the meal plan on page 72 for an example) or salted eggs with flavour-neutral wholemeal bread *without* sweet jam (see day 18 on page 93).

Midmorning snack. Have sweet fruit with a dairy product (see day 36 on page 114) and don't have savoury or salty items.

Lunch. Eat either savoury and/or salty foods, but not sweet ones. For example, you can have a turkey sandwich on wholemeal bread with lettuce, tomato and mustard (see day 21 on page 96).

Midafternoon snack. Snack on items with savoury and/or salty flavours, but don't have sweet items. For example, lightly salted nuts are a great snack (see day 19 on page 94).

Dinner. Use the same simple sauce or dressing on your main course as you do on your side dish (see day 4 on page 75).

Dessert. If you have dessert, keep it simple. Try a bit of plain dark chocolate or a fruit salad. Consider having a flavour for dessert that you had at dinner, such as orange sorbet following a dinner that used orange in a sauce (see day 17 on page 92).

In addition to being aware of how you combine the flavours in your meals and snacks, you must also pay attention to the individual brands and products that you eat. As you've learned, many packaged foods have too many conflicting flavours. After using the meal plan for 6 weeks, you should have developed the habit of choosing wholesome, conveniently available products and brands that do not contain excess flavours.

REDIRECTING RECIPES TO THE FLAVOUR POINT

You can also apply Flavour Point strategies to the preparation of your favourite recipes, improving their nutritional value and cutting out unnecessary flavour additions while preserving their taste and appearance. The following suggestions provide guidance, though you will need to experiment with this process as it involves some trial and error.

REDUCING SUGAR IN BAKED GOODS

Use the following substitutions for some of the sugar in your recipes.

Non-fat dried milk. The natural sugar (lactose) found in milk sweetens baked goods, although less so than sugar. Replace one-third to one-half of the sugar in your recipes with non-fat dried milk.

Ground almonds. You can use roughly-ground almonds to reduce some of the sugar needed in recipes. The slight richness of nuts enhances both the taste and texture of baked goods.

Unsweetened apple sauce. Although apple sauce is generally used to replace butter in baked goods, it also reduces the amount of sugar needed in those recipes. This is because apples contain natural fruit sugar, or fructose. It also provides nutrients and soluble fibre not found in sugar.

Satisfaction at the Flavour Point

THE FLAVOUR FACTS

Name: Donna Durmazlar

Age: 38

Family status: Married with two
children, aged 15 and 21

Occupation: Nursing staff
coordinator

Starting weight: 94 kg/14 st 11 lb

Weight lost: 4.5 kg/10 lb in 12
weeks

Health stats: Blood pressure
dropped 17 points; lost
1 cm/ ½ in off waist

'I grew up in a household where you could never find biscuits or ice cream, and we only had fizzy drinks on the holidays. My mother made us finish our vegetables before we could eat any other part of our dinner. It was good for me at the time, but it really made me rebel. For the past 25 years, I've eaten whatever I wanted, and it usually wasn't vegetables.

'As a result, I gained 3½ st [22 kg] with my first pregnancy (way back in 1989), and then during the past 3 years, I gained another 20 lb

[9 kg]. I tried Weight Watchers in 1998 and lost about 35 lb [15.5 kg], but I got lazy, didn't stick with it, and gained it all back. I started to get really sick of being overweight, so I decided to try Dr Katz's programme.

'When I first began the programme and Dr. Katz said, "Don't think of this as a diet but as a way of eating," I didn't quite get it. Now I truly understand what he meant and have adopted his philosophy.

'I have to admit, the first week was an adjustment, but after that, I was fine. My biggest temptation is chocolate, and when I got to Chocolate Day, I was beside myself – I was like, "Oh, my God . . . you can have chocolate on this diet?" Better yet, I always feel satisfied. I haven't made many of the desserts called for on the meal plan because I'm usually too full. And my tastes have changed – I *want* more wholesome foods.

'Not only are the foods and recipes delicious, they're also healthy. I never knew there were so many foods out there that are good for you and still have so much flavour. I never would have thought to cook with fruit before, but it makes everything so sweet; it's pretty much a substitute for sugar. Catherine Katz definitely put a lot of thought and creativity into the programme to make the recipes tasty. Overall, I have to say the Pistachio-Crusted Chicken is my favourite.

'Schedule-wise, I'm pretty busy, so I follow the flavour-friendly options for breakfast and lunch. For breakfast, I have cereal or fruit, and for lunch, I have a salad with chicken or tuna. If I go out to eat, I always find something that fits in the diet. It's a really flexible programme. It's simple to substitute other dishes – all you have to do is stay within the flavour theme. So if I loved what I ate the night before, I'll just make it again the next night.

'For the most part, my family did the programme with me, especially the dinners. My older child likes almost all of the recipes, and my younger one (who's a little more finicky) liked some of them. My husband also has lost some weight on the plan.

'People have definitely noticed my weight loss. My stomach is my problem area, and they tell me it's getting smaller and that my clothes look looser.

'But my absolute favourite thing about the programme is the way I feel. I have so much more energy. The sleepy midafternoon feeling has gone away, I have more energy to do things on the weekends, and I find myself staying up later without feeling tired in the morning.

'I would tell anyone to do Dr Katz's Flavour Point programme. The foods are healthy, and you don't sacrifice flavour. And I'm only human. Sometimes I crave something, and I have it. Dr. Katz says, "If you really, really want something, eat it; otherwise you'll try to make up for the craving in other ways, and it's going to be worse." I'm definitely going to stick with the programme for life.' ■

REDUCING FAT IN MOST COOKED DISHES

Use the following substitutions in place of saturated fat.

Olive oil. In all your cooked savoury dishes, replace all of the butter called for with olive oil. Add a spout to your olive oil bottle to easily control the amount you pour.

Fat-free dairy products. In all cooking or baking, use skimmed milk or fat-free natural yoghurt in place of the standard versions.

Skinless poultry. Use only skinless poultry and white-meat chicken or turkey except when a long cooking time would dry it out. In those cases, use thighs or drumsticks with the skin removed.

Water. Add about 1 tablespoon of water for every 2 teaspoons of olive oil in salad dressing. This will increase the volume of the dressing so it coats the salad with less fat.

REDUCING FAT IN BAKED GOODS

Use these substitutions for butter.

Trans-fat-free spread. To eliminate the saturated fat found in butter or the trans fat found in most margarines, replace the amount of either ingredient called for in a recipe with the same amount of non-hydrogenated margarine, such as Benecol.

Ground almonds. Finely ground almonds can be used to replace fat as well as some of the sugar in baked goods. They create the richness of butter while adding healthy unsaturated fat in place of saturated fat, and, unlike other nuts, they have a mild flavour that can enhance a recipe without overpowering it.

Unsweetened apple sauce. When making baked goods, you can use apple sauce to replace not only some of the sugar but some of the fat, without losing the moisture that fat usually provides.

REDUCING FAT IN SAUCES AND GLAZES

Use the following substitutions.

Fat-free or low-fat buttermilk. Replace double cream or soured cream with low-fat buttermilk in creamy soups and sauces.

Dried fruit or natural fruit preserves. As long as they have no added sugar, you can simmer dried fruit or preserves with a fat-free stock or 100% fruit juice and/or wine or dark beer to create a luscious, rich glaze.

Honey mixed with mustard. You can use this as a marinade to coat prawns, tuna or chicken for the grill. Use just enough honey to make the marinade sticky but not enough to overpower the flavour of the dish.

ADDITIONAL ADVICE FOR A LIFETIME OF HEALTHY EATING

To maintain the Flavour Point lifestyle, keep the following advice front and centre at all times.

- Always aim for variety over time, not variety all the time. Limit the variety of flavours in any given meal or snack, and never cruise from snack to snack.

- Use daily food patterns as a lifelong adaptation of flavour themes. For example, limit your morning food choices on most days to cereal grains, fruits and dairy foods, and don't mix in meats, cheese or salty items. Do the opposite for lunch and afternoon snacks: have salty and savoury items, such as vegetables, lean meats, beans and nuts, but no sweets. For a sense of closure, end lunch with a hot beverage rather than dessert. At dinner, use a single sauce, spread or dressing, or variations on a single theme, such as citrus marinade for fish and citrus vinaigrette on salad.

- Don't add salt to sweet baked goods. We're all used to putting salt into items such as home-made biscuits, brownies, cakes and muffins, if only out of habit. You know what? Brownies, biscuits, cakes and muffins do not need salt. Some may need baking powder in order to rise, but most do not need bicarbonate of soda, which is high in sodium. Break yourself of these habits, and you'll reach the Flavour Point more easily.

- Don't add sugar to salty foods. This is less of a problem in home cooking than in processed foods, but many recipes call for unnecessary sugar. Try your recipes without it and see if they work. If a dish is supposed to be fruity, use either dried, fresh or concentrated fruit and/or 100% fruit juice. This way, even when you add sugar, you're adding it in its unprocessed natural state in the company of appetite-suppressing fibre.

- In your home, keep nutritious foods (such as fresh fruit) on display all the time. Keep any addictive foods concealed.

- Always serve less of any dish on a plate than you think you (or family members) will want. Keep more available, but keep it out of sight and serve it only upon request.

- Invest in small plates, bowls, cups and glasses. When you place a normal portion of food on a huge plate, it tricks your brain into thinking you're eating a small amount, which makes you want more.

- On any given day, serve only one kind of dessert. You may break that rule 3 days a year, but no more.

- Serve soups, stews, fizz beverages (120 ml/4 fl oz of 100% fruit juice mixed with 180 ml/6 fl oz of fizzy mineral water) and smoothies (see pages 140–143) whenever possible to get the benefit of relatively few calories distributed in a large, filling volume.

- Don't buy products that contain trans fat (partially hydrogenated oil).

- Don't buy products that contain high-fructose corn syrup (added sugar).

- Choose products with short ingredient lists.

- Avoid all-you-can-eat buffets.

- Drink water instead of fizzy drinks and minimize your consumption of artificial sweeteners.

- Don't use more than one sauce, dressing or spread at any given meal, if possible, and *never* exceed two. In other words, if your pasta sauce has olive oil in it, use olive oil and not butter on your bread. If your chicken has a marinade, use the same marinade with the accompanying grains and vegetables.

- Always start your dinner with a mixed green salad. Salads are nutritious, filling and low in calories. Use a simple vinaigrette or a dressing that resembles the sauce used for the main course. For example, squeeze a little lemon in your dressing if you're having a lemon-flavoured main course or add chopped fresh basil to the salad if your meal includes basil.

BON APPÉTIT

Eating well – for good health and permanent weight control – is, to say the least, challenging in the modern world. You can do it with the right approach and the right knowledge, skills and strategies. Now you have all of those tools. I believe in you! I hope that by now, you believe in yourself, too.

You have learned how appetite has been controlling you, and you have learned how to control appetite at its source. You have learned how the food industry has been manipulating you into eating more than you should, and you have learned how to choose foods so that you feel fully satisfied with less. You have learned to master the Flavour Point.

With this knowledge, you don't need me any more. You don't need those stabilizers, but if you don't think you're quite ready for solo cruising, that's fine. Back up a bit. Repeat some or all of the meal plan.

You can keep the stabilizers for as long as you want, but when you feel confident, take them off and pedal away. I want you to have the kind of relationship with food that my patients, the testers of the Flavour Point Diet, and my family and I have. When we sit down to dinner, we feel relaxed. We take pleasure in the unique flavours of the meal, and we feel fulfilled at the meal's end. I want you to apply the Flavour Point principles for the rest of your life so you never need to worry about your weight again. You can cruise past the challenges of confusing food labels, misleading advertisements and fast-food bargains. You can reconcile the pleasure of good food with the deep gratification of good health.

I wish you and your family a lifetime of good health and good times. *Bon appétit!*

SELECTED BIBLIOGRAPHY

Almiron-Roig E, Chen Y, Drewnowski A. 2003. 'Liquid calories and the failure of satiety: How good is the evidence?' *Obes Rev* 4:201–12.

American College of Preventive Medicine Position Statement. *'Diet in the prevention and control of obesity, insulin resistance, and type II diabetes'*. www.acpm.org/2002-057(F).htm.

Anderson GH, Moore SE. 2004. 'Dietary proteins in the regulation of food intake and body weight in humans'. *J Nutr* 134:974S–79S.

Ball SD, Keller KR, Moyer-Mileur LJ, Ding YW, Donaldson D, Jackson WD. 2003. 'Prolongation of satiety after low versus moderately high glycemic index meals in obese adolescents'. *Pediatrics* 111:488–94.

Baschetti R. 'Paleolithic nutrition'. 1997. *Eur J Clin Nutr* 51:715–16.

Bell EA, Roe LS, Rolls BJ. 2003. 'Sensory-specific satiety is affected more by volume than by energy content of a liquid food'. *Physiol Behav* 78:593–600.

Bellisle F. 2003. 'Why should we study human food intake behaviour?' *Nutr Metab Cardiovasc Dis* 13:189–93.

Berthoud HR. 2004. 'Mind versus metabolism in the control of food intake and energy balance'. *Physiol Behav* 81:781–93.

Bjorck I, Elmstahl HL. 2003. 'The glycaemic index: Importance of dietary fibre and other food properties'. *Proc Nutr Soc* 62:201–6.

Blass EM. 2003. 'Biological and environmental determinants of childhood obesity'. *Nutr Clin Care* 6:13–19.

Blundell JE, Burley VJ, Cotton JR, Lawton CL. 1993. 'Dietary fat and the control of energy intake: Evaluating the effects of fat on meal size and postmeal satiety'. *Am J Clin Nutr* 57(5 Suppl):772S–77S.

Blundell JE, Lawton CL, Cotton JR, Macdiarmid JI. 1996. 'Control of human appetite: Implications for the intake of dietary fat'. *Annu Rev Nutr* 16:285–319.

Blundell JE, MacDiarmid JI. 1997. 'Fat as a risk factor for overconsumption: Satiation, satiety, and patterns of eating'. *J Am Diet Assoc* 97(7 Suppl):S63–69.

Blundell JE, Stubbs RJ. 1999. 'High and low carbohydrate and fat intakes: Limits imposed by appetite and palatability and their implications for energy balance'. *Eur J Clin Nutr* 53 Suppl 1:S148–65.

Brand-Miller JC, Holt SH, Pawlak DB, McMillan J. 2002. 'Glycemic index and obesity'. *Am J Clin Nutr* 76:281S–85S.

Bray GA. 2000. 'Afferent signals regulating food intake'. *Proc Nutr Soc* 59:373–84.

Critchley HD, Rolls ET. 1996. 'Responses of primate taste cortex neurons to the astringent tastant tannic acid'. *Chem Senses* 21(2):135–45.

Crovetti R, Porrini M, Santangelo A, Testolin G. 1998. 'The influence of thermic effect of food on satiety'. *Eur J Clin Nutr* 52:482–88.

Dallman MF, La Fleur SE, Pecoraro NC, Gomez F, Houshyar H, Akana SF. 2004. 'Minireview: Glucocorticoids—food intake, abdominal obesity, and wealthy nations in 2004'. *Endocrinology* 145:2633–38.

De Araujo IE, Rolls ET, Kringelbach ML, McGlone F, Phillips N. 2003. 'Taste-olfactory convergence, and the representation of the pleasantness of flavour, in the human brain'. *Eur J Neurosci* 18(7):2059–68.

De Graaf C, Blom WA, Smeets PA, Stafleu A, Hendriks HF. 2004. 'Biomarkers of satiation and satiety'. *Am J Clin Nutr* 79:946–61.

De Graaf C, De Jong LS, Lambers AC. 1999. 'Palatability affects satiation but not satiety'. *Physiol Behav* 66:681–88.

De Graaf C, Schreurs A, Blauw YH. 1993. 'Short-term effects of different amounts of sweet and nonsweet carbohydrates on satiety and energy intake'. *Physiol Behav* 54:833–43.

DeLorgeril M, Salen P, Martin JL, Monjaud I, Delaye J, Mamelle N. 1999. 'Mediterranean diet, traditional risk factors, and the rate of cardiovascular complications after myocardial infarction: Final report of the Lyon Diet Heart Study'. *Circulation* 99:779–85.

Drewnowski A. 1998. 'Energy density, palatability, and satiety: Implications for weight control'. *Nutr Rev* 56:347–53.

———. 2003. 'The role of energy density'. *Lipids* 38:109–15.

———. 2000. 'Sensory control of energy density at different life stages'. *Proc Nutr Soc* 59:239–44.

Druce M, Bloom SR. 2003. 'Central regulators of food intake'. *Curr Opin Clin Nutr Metab Care* 6:361.

Eaton SB, Eaton SB III. 2000. 'Paleolithic vs. modern diets—selected pathophysiological implications'. *Eur J Nutr* 39:67–70.

Eaton SB, Eaton SB III, Konner M. 1997. 'Paleolithic nutrition revisited: A twelve-year retrospective on its nature and implications'. *Eur J Clin Nutr* 51:207-16.

Eaton SB, Eaton SB III, Konner M, Shostak M. 1996. 'An evolutionary perspective enhances understanding of human nutritional requirements'. *J Nutr* 126:1732–40.

Eaton SB, Strassman BI, Nesse RM, Neel JV, Ewald PW, et al. 2002. 'Evolutionary health promotion'. *Prev Med* 34:109–18.

Ebbeling CB, Leidig MM, Sinclair KB, Hangen JP, Ludwig DS. 'A reduced-glycemic load diet in the treatment of adolescent obesity'. 2003. *Arch Pediatr Adolesc Med* 157: 773–79.

Flatt JP. 2000. 'Macronutrient composition and food selection'. *Obes Res* 9 (November) Suppl 4:256S–62S.

Food and Nutrition Board, Institute of Medicine, National Academies of Science. 2002. *Dietary reference intakes for energy, carbohydrate, fiber, fat, fatty acids, cholesterol, protein, and amino acids (macronutrients)*. Washington, D.C.: National Academy Press.

French SA. 2003. 'Pricing effects on food choices'. *J Nutr* 133:841S–43S.

Gerstein DE, Woodward-Lopez G, Evans AE, Kelsey K, Drewnowski A. 2004. 'Clarifying concepts about macronutrients' effects on satiation and satiety'. *J Am Diet Assoc* 104:1151–53.

Ginsberg HN, Karmally W, Siddiqui M, Holleran S, Tall AR, Rumsey SC, Deckelbaum RJ, Blaner WS, Ramakrishnan R. 1994. 'A dose-response study of the effects of dietary cholesterol on fasting and postprandial lipid and lipoprotein metabolism in healthy young men'. *Arterioscler Thromb* 14:576–86.

Golay A, Bobbioni E. 1997. 'The role of dietary fat in obesity'. *Int J Obes Relat Metab Disord* 21 Suppl 3:S2–11.

Gray RW, French SJ, Robinson TM, Yeomans MR. 2003. 'Increasing preload volume with water reduces rated appetite but not food intake in healthy men even with minimum delay between preload and test meal'. *Nutr Neurosci* 6:29–37.

Green SM, Blundell JE. 1996. 'Effect of fat- and sucrose-containing foods on the size of eating episodes and energy intake in lean dietary restrained and unrestrained females: Potential for causing overconsumption'. *Eur J Clin Nutr* 50:625–35.

Green SM, Burley VJ, Blundell JE. 1994. 'Effect of fat- and sucrose-containing foods on the size of eating episodes and energy intake in lean males: Potential for causing over-consumption'. *Eur J Clin Nutr* 48:547–55.

Green SM, Wales JK, Lawton CL, Blundell JE. 2000. 'Comparison of high-fat and high-carbohydrate foods in a meal or snack on short-term fat and energy intakes in obese women'. *Br J Nutr* 84:521–30.

Guinard JX, Brun P. 1998. 'Sensory-specific satiety: Comparison of taste and texture effects'. *Appetite* 31:141–57.

He W, Yasumatsu K, Varadarajan V, Yamada A, Lem J, Ninomiya Y, Margolskee RF, Damak S. 2004. 'Umami taste responses are mediated by alpha-transducin and alpha-gustducin'. *J Neurosci* 24(35):7674–80.

Hellstrom PM, Geliebter A, Naslund E, Schmidt PT, Yahav EK, Hashim SA, Yeomans MR. 2004. 'Peripheral and central signals in the control of eating in normal, obese and binge-eating human subjects'. *Br J Nutr* 92 Suppl 1:S47–57.

Hetherington MM. 2002. 'The physiological-psychological dichotomy in the study of food intake'. *Proc Nutr Soc* 61:497–507.

Holt S, Brand J, Soveny C, Hansky J. 1992. 'Relationship of satiety to postprandial glycaemic, insulin and cholecystokinin responses'. *Appetite* 18:129–41.

Holt SH, Brand-Miller JC, Petocz P. 1996. 'Interrelationships among postprandial satiety, glucose and insulin responses and changes in subsequent food intake'. *Eur J Clin Nutr* 50:788–97.

Holt SH, Brand-Miller JC, Stitt PA. 2001. 'The effects of equal-energy portions of different breads on blood glucose levels, feelings of fullness and subsequent food intake'. *J Am Diet Assoc* 101:767–73.

Holt SH, Miller JC, Petocz P, Farmakalidis E. 1995. 'A satiety index of common foods'. *Eur J Clin Nutr* 49:675–90.

Howarth NC, Saltzman E, Roberts SB. 'Dietary fiber and weight regulation'. 2001. *Nutr Rev* 59:129–39.

Hu FB. 2003. 'Plant-based foods and prevention of cardiovascular disease: An overview'. *Am J Clin Nutr* 78:544S–51S.

Hu FB, Manson JE, Willett WC. 2001. 'Types of dietary fat and risk of coronary heart disease: A critical review'. *J Am Coll Nutr* 20:5–19.

Hu FB, Stampfer MJ, Rimm EB, Manson JE, Ascherio A, Colditz GA, Rosner BA, Spiegelman D, Speizer FE, Sacks FM, Hennekens CH, Willett WC. 1999. 'A prospective study of egg consumption and risk of cardiovascular disease in men and women'. *JAMA* 281:1387–94.

Hu FB, Willett WC. 2002. 'Optimal diets for prevention of coronary heart disease'. *JAMA* 288:2569–78.

Hung T, Sievenpiper JL, Marchie A, Kendall CW, Jenkins DJ. 2003. 'Fat versus carbohydrate in insulin resistance, obesity, diabetes and cardiovascular disease'. *Curr Opin Clin Nutr Metab Care* 6:165–76.

Jequier E. 2002. 'Pathways to obesity'. *Int J Obes Relat Metab Disord* 26 Suppl 2:S12–17.

Johnson J, Vickers Z. 1992. 'Factors influencing sensory-specific satiety'. *Appetite* 19:15–31.

Katz DL. 2005. 'Competing dietary claims for weight loss: Finding the forest through truculent trees'. *Annu Rev Public Health* 26:61–88.

———. 'Diet, sleep-wake cycles, and mood'. In Katz DL. 2001. *Nutrition in clinical practice*. Philadelphia: Lippincott Williams & Wilkins. 243–47.

———. 'Dietary recommendations for health promotion and disease prevention'. In Katz DL. *Nutrition in clinical practice*. Philadelphia: Lippincott Williams & Wilkins. 291–98.

———. 'Evolutionary biology, culture, and determinants of dietary behavior'. In Katz DL. 2001. *Nutrition in clinical practice*. Philadelphia: Lippincott Williams & Wilkins. 279–90.

———. 'Hunger, appetite, taste, and satiety'. In Katz DL. 2001. *Nutrition in clinical practice*. Philadelphia: Lippincott Williams & Wilkins. 260–67.

———. 2001. *Nutrition in clinical practice*. Philadelphia: Lippincott Williams & Wilkins.

Katz DL, Evans MA, Nawaz H, Njike VY, Chan W, Comerford BP, Hoxley ML. 2005. 'Egg consumption and endothelial function: A randomized controlled crossover trial'. *Int J Cardiol* 99:65–70.

Kennedy E. 2004. 'Dietary diversity, diet quality, and body weight regulation'. *Nutr Rev* 62(7 Pt 2):S78–81.

Kennedy ET, Bowman SA, Spence JT, Freedman M, King J. 2001. 'Popular diets: Correlation to health, nutrition, and obesity'. *J Am Diet Assoc* 101:411–20.

Key TJ, Schatzkin A, Willett WC, Allen NE, Spencer EA, Travis RC. 2004. 'Diet, nutrition and the prevention of cancer'. *Public Health Nutr* 7:187–200.

Knopp RH, Retzlaff BM, Walden CE, Dowdy AA, Tsunehara CH, Austin MA, Nguyen T. 1997. 'A double-blind, randomized, controlled trial of the effects of two eggs per day in moderately hypercholesterolemic and combined hyperlipidemic subjects taught the NCEP step I diet'. *J Am Coll Nutr* 16:551–61.

Knowler WC, Barrett-Connor E, Fowler SE, Hamman RF, Lachin JM, et al. 2002. 'Reduction in the incidence of type 2 diabetes with lifestyle intervention or metformin'. *N Engl J Med* 346:393–403.

Kritchevsky SB. 2004. 'A review of scientific research and recommendations regarding eggs'. *J Am Coll Nutr* 23(6 Suppl):596S–600S.

Kritchevsky SB, Kritchevsky D. 2000. 'Egg consumption and coronary heart disease: An epidemiologic overview'. *J Am Coll Nutr* 19(5 Suppl):549S–555S.

Lang V, Bellisle F, Oppert JM, Craplet C, Bornet FR, Slama G, Guy-Grand B. 1998. 'Satiating effect of proteins in healthy subjects: A comparison of egg albumin, casein, gelatin, soy protein, pea protein, and wheat gluten'. *Am J Clin Nutr* 67:1197–204.

Leibowitz SF, Alexander JT. 1998. 'Hypothalamic serotonin in control of eating behavior, meal size, and body weight'. *Biol Psychiat* 44:851–64.

Liu S, Willett WC, Manson JE, Hu FB, Rosner B, Colditz G. 2003. 'Relation between changes in intakes of dietary fiber and grain products and changes in weight and development of obesity among middle-aged women'. *Am J Clin Nutr* 78:920–27.

Macht M, Simons G. 2000. 'Emotions and eating in everyday life'. *Appetite* 35:65–71.

Mann NJ. 2004. 'Paleolithic nutrition: What can we learn from the past?' *Asia Pac J Clin Nutr* 13(Suppl):S17.

Marmonier C, Chapelot D, Louis-Sylvestre J. 2000. 'Effects of macronutrient content and energy density of snacks consumed in a satiety state on the onset of the next meal'. *Appetite* 34:161–68.

Mathers JC. 2003. 'Nutrition and cancer prevention: Diet-gene interactions'. *Proc Nutr Soc* 62:605–10.

McCrory MA, Fuss PJ, McCallum JE, Yao M, Vinken AG, Hays NP, Roberts SB. 1999. 'Dietary variety within food groups: Association with energy intake and body fatness in men and women'. *Am J Clin Nutr* 69:440–47.

McCrory MA, Suen VM, Roberts SB. 2002. 'Biobehavioral influences on energy intake and adult weight gain'. *J Nutr* 132:3830S–34S.

McDonald BE. 2004. 'The Canadian experience: Why Canada decided against an upper limit for cholesterol'. *J Am Coll Nutr* 23(6 Suppl):616S–20S.

McNamara DJ. 2000. 'The impact of egg limitations on coronary heart disease risk: Do the numbers add up?' *J Am Coll Nutr* 19(5 Suppl):540S–48S.

Meier U, Gressner AM. 2004. 'Endocrine regulation of energy metabolism: Review of pathobiochemical and clinical chemical aspects of leptin, ghrelin, adiponectin, and resistin'. *Clin Chem* 50:1511–25.

National Institutes of Health, National Heart, Lung, and Blood Institute, and the North American Association for the Study of Obesity. 'The practical guide to identification, evaluation, and treatment of overweight and obesity in adults'. www.nhlbi.nih.gov/guidelines/obesity/prctgd_b.pdf

Nestle M, Wing R, Birch L, DiSogra L, Drewnowski A, Middleton S, Sigman-Grant M, Sobal J, Winston M, Economos C. 1998. 'Behavioral and social influences on food choice'. *Nutr Rev* 56(5 Pt 2):S50–64; discussion S64–74.

O'Keefe JH Jr, Cordain L. 2004. 'Cardiovascular disease resulting from a diet and lifestyle at odds with our paleolithic genome: How to become a 21st-century hunter-gatherer'. *Mayo Clin Proc* 79:101–8.

Ornish D, Scherwitz LW, Billings JH, Brown SE, Gould KL, et al. 1998. 'Intensive lifestyle changes for reversal of coronary heart disease'. *JAMA* 280:2001–7.

Phillips SM, Bandini LG, Naumova EN, Cyr H, Colclough S, Dietz WH, Must A. 2004. 'Energy-dense snack food intake in adolescence: Longitudinal relationship to weight and fatness'. *Obes Res* 12:461–72.

Poppitt SD, McCormack D, Buffenstein R. 1998. 'Short-term effects of macronutrient preloads on appetite and energy intake in lean women'. *Physiol Behav* 64:279–85.

Poppitt SD, Prentice AM. 1996. 'Energy density and its role in the control of food intake: Evidence from metabolic and community studies'. *Appetite* 26:153–74.

Porrini M, Crovetti R, Riso P, Santangelo A, Testolin G. 1995. 'Effects of physical and chemical characteristics of food on specific and general satiety'. *Physiol Behav* 57:461–8.

Prentice AM, Jebb SA. 2003. 'Fast foods, energy density and obesity: A possible mechanistic link'. *Obes Rev.* 4:187–94.

Raben A, Agerholm-Larsen L, Flint A, Holst JJ, Astrup A. 2003. 'Meals with similar energy densities but rich in protein, fat, carbohydrate, or alcohol have different effects on energy expenditure and substrate metabolism but not on appetite and energy intake'. *Am J Clin Nutr* 77:91–100.

Raynor HA, Epstein LH. 2001. 'Dietary variety, energy regulation, and obesity'. *Psychol Bull* 127:325–41.

Reddy KS, Katan MB. 2004. 'Diet, nutrition and the prevention of hypertension and cardiovascular diseases'. *Pub Health Nutr* 7:167–86.

Rolls BJ. 1995. 'Carbohydrates, fats, and satiety'. *Am J Clin Nutr* 61(4 Suppl):960S–67S.

———. 2000. 'The role of energy density in the overconsumption of fat'. *J Nutr* 130(2S Suppl):268S–71S.

Rolls BJ, Bell EA. 1999. 'Intake of fat and carbohydrate: Role of energy density'. *Eur J Clin Nutr* 53 Suppl 1:S166–73.

Rolls BJ, Bell EA, Castellanos VH, Chow M, Pelkman CL, Thorwart ML. 1999. 'Energy density but not fat content of foods affected energy intake in lean and obese women'. *Am J Clin Nutr* 69:863–71.

Rolls BJ, Bell EA, Thorwart ML. 1999. 'Water incorporated into a food but not served with a food decreases energy intake in lean women'. *Am J Clin Nutr* 70:448–55.

Rolls BJ, Bell EA, Waugh BA. 2000. 'Increasing the volume of a food by incorporating air affects satiety in men'. *Am J Clin Nutr* 72:361–68.

Rolls BJ, Castellanos VH, Halford JC, Kilara A, Panyam D, Pelkman CL, Smith GP, Thorwart ML. 1998. 'Volume of food consumed affects satiety in men'. *Am J Clin Nutr* 67:1170–77.

Rolls BJ, Hetherington M, Burley VJ. 1998. 'Sensory stimulation and energy density in the development of satiety'. *Physiol Behav* 44:727–33.

Rolls BJ, Miller DL. 1997. 'Is the low-fat message giving people a license to eat more?' *J Am Coll Nutr* 16:535–43.

Rolls ET. 2004. 'Convergence of sensory systems in the orbitofrontal cortex in primates and brain design for emotion'. *Anat Rec A Discov Mol Cell Evol Biol.* 281(1):1212–25.

———. 2000. 'The representation of umami taste in the taste cortex'. *J Nutr* 130(4S Suppl):960S–65S.

———. 2004. 'Smell, taste, texture, and temperature multimodal representations in the brain, and their relevance to the control of appetite'. *Nutr Rev* 62(11 Pt 2):S193–204; discussion S224–41.

———. 1997. 'Taste and olfactory processing in the brain and its relation to the control of eating'. *Crit Rev Neurobiol* 11(4):263–87.

Rolls ET, Critchley HD, Browning A, Hernadi I. 1998. 'The neurophysiology of taste and olfaction in primates, and umami flavor'. *Ann NY Acad Sci* 855(November 30):426–37.

Romon M, Lebel P, Velly C, Marecaux N, Fruchart JC, Dallongeville J. 1999. 'Leptin response to carbohydrate or fat meal and association with subsequent satiety and energy intake'. *Am J Physiol* 277(5 Pt 1):E855–61.

Sacks FM, Svetkey LP, Vollmer WM, Appel LJ, Bray GA, et al. 2001. 'Effects on blood pressure of reduced dietary sodium and the Dietary Approaches to Stop Hypertension (DASH) diet'. *N Engl J Med* 344:3–10.

Saris WH. 2003. 'Sugars, energy metabolism, and body weight control'. *Am J Clin Nutr* 78:850S–57S.

Shepherd R. 1999. 'Social determinants of food choice'. *Proc Nutr Soc* 58:807–12.

Small CJ, Bloom SR. 2004. 'Gut hormones and the control of appetite'. *Trends Endoc Metab* 15(6):259–63.

Snoek HM, Huntjens L, Van Gemert LJ, De Graaf C, Weenen H. 2004. 'Sensory-specific satiety in obese and normal-weight women'. *Am J Clin Nutr* 80:823–31.

Sorensen LB, Moller P, Flint A, Martens M, Raben A. 2003. 'Effect of sensory perception of foods on appetite and food intake: A review of studies on humans'. *Int J Obes Relat Metab Disord* 27:1152–66.

Stubbs J, Ferres S, Horgan G. 'Energy density of foods: Effects on energy intake'. 2000. *Crit Rev Food Sci Nutr* 40:481–515.

Stubbs RJ, Johnstone AM, Mazlan N, Mbaiwa SE, Ferris S. 2001. 'Effect of altering the variety of sensorially distinct foods, of the same macronutrient content, on food intake and body weight in men'. *Eur J Clin Nutr* 55:19–28.

Stubbs RJ, Whybrow S. 2004. 'Energy density, diet composition and palatability: Influences on overall food energy intake in humans'. *Physiol Behav* 81:755–64.

U.S. Preventive Services Task Force. 'Healthy diet counseling'. www.ahrq.gov/clinic/uspstf/uspsdiet.htm; accessed March 2005.

Vickers Z. 1999. 'Long-term acceptability of limited diets'. *Life Support Biosph Sci* 6:29–33.

Vozzo R, Wittert G, Cocchiaro C, Tan WC, Mudge J, Fraser R, Chapman I. 2003. 'Similar effects of foods high in protein, carbohydrate and fat on subsequent spontaneous food intake in healthy individuals'. *Appetite* 40:101–7.

Wansink B. 2004. 'Environmental factors that increase the food intake and consumption volume of unknowing consumers'. *Annu Rev Nutr* 24:455–79.

Wardle J. 1987. 'Hunger and satiety: A multidimensional assessment of responses to caloric loads'. *Physiol Behav* 40:577–82.

Weggemans RM, Zock PL, Katan MB. 2001. 'Dietary cholesterol from eggs increases the ratio of total cholesterol to high-density lipoprotein cholesterol in humans: A meta-analysis'. *Am J Clin Nutr* 73:885–91.

Westerterp-Plantenga MS. 2001. 'Analysis of energy density of food in relation to energy intake regulation in human subjects'. *Br J Nutr* 85:351–61.

Westerterp-Plantenga MS, IJedema MJ, Wijckmans-Duijsens NE. 1996. 'The role of macronutrient selection in determining patterns of food intake in obese and non-obese women'. *Eur J Clin Nutr* 50:580–91.

Westerterp-Plantenga MS, Lejeune MP, Nijs I, Van Ooijen M, Kovacs EM. 2004. 'High protein intake sustains weight maintenance after body weight loss in humans'. *Int J Obes Relat Metab Disord* 28:57–64.

Westerterp-Plantenga MS, Rolland V, Wilson SA, Westerterp KR. 1999. 'Satiety related to 24-hour diet-induced thermogenesis during high protein/carbohydrate vs high fat diets measured in a respiration chamber'. *Eur J Clin Nutr* 53:495–502.

Willet WC. 2001. *Eat, drink, and be healthy.* New York: Simon & Schuster Source.

Wylie-Rosett J, Segal-Isaacson CJ, Segal-Isaacson A. 2004. 'Carbohydrates and increases in obesity: Does the type of carbohydrate make a difference?' *Obes Res* 12 Suppl 2:124S–29S.

Wynne K, Stanley S, Bloom S. 2004. 'The gut and regulation of body weight'. *J Clin Endoc Metab* 89:2576–82.

Zhang Y, Hoon MA, Chandrashekar J, Mueller KL, Cook B, Wu D, Zuker CS, Ryba NJ. 2003. 'Coding of sweet, bitter, and umami tastes: Different receptor cells sharing similar signaling pathways'. *Cell* 2003 112(3):283–84.

INDEX

Underscored page references indicate boxed text.

ABOUT THE AUTHORS

David L. Katz, MD, MPH, FACPM, FACP, is an associate professor of public health at the Yale University School of Medicine. He is the director and co-founder of Yale's Prevention Research Center, associate director of nutrition science at the Rudd Center for Food Policy and Obesity at Yale University, and the founder and director of a holistic clinical facility at the Integrative Medicine Center in Derby, Connecticut.

In addition to more than 80 scientific papers and innumerable columns, essays, op-eds, chapters, essays and newsletters, Dr Katz has published eight previous books. Among these are several textbooks for health professionals, including *Nutrition in Clinical Practice,* a nutrition textbook that is widely used in medical education, including at the Harvard Medical School.

Dr Katz lectures on nutrition, health promotion and disease prevention throughout the United States and abroad and has consulted on these topics to the US Department of Health and Human Services, the US Food and Drug Administration, and the National Governors Association.

Dr Katz is a medical contributor for *ABC News*, the nutrition columnist for *O: The Oprah Magazine,* and the author of a syndicated health/nutrition column for the *New York Times*. His expert opinion has been featured in *Business Week, Glamour, Good Housekeeping, Health, Time* magazine, *U.S. News & World Report, Wall Street Journal,* the *Washington Post,* among dozens of other publications.

Catherine S. Katz, PhD, was raised in the south of France and learned the fine art of southern French and North African cooking from her mother and aunt. She moved to the United States at age 14, and promptly gained about 25 lb (11.3 kg) from her sudden immersion in the 'toxic nutritional environment' of the United States. It took her several years to learn all the strategies necessary to compensate for the challenges of that environment and stabilize her weight permanently.

Catherine is a neuroscientist by training, earning her PhD from Princeton University. She has made significant scientific contributions in the area of olfaction (sense of smell) and its links to memory and learning. During recent years, her talents have been devoted to the raising of her five children and raising the standards of gourmet nutrition. Catherine's cooking talents have been featured in *O: The Oprah Magazine, Child, Men's Health, Women's Health & Fitness, Nick Jr.* and several books, as well as in cooking classes for both adults and children at the Silo Cooking School in New Milford, Connecticut, where, among others, Jacques Pepin is an instructor.

Drs David and Catherine Katz live in Connecticut with their five children: Rebecca, Corinda, Valerie, Natalia and Gabriel.

OTHER RODALE BOOKS
AVAILABLE FROM PAN MACMILLAN

1-4050-7771-9	The Great American Detox Diet	*Alex Jamieson*	£10.99
1-4050-8808-7 978-1-4050-8808-4	The Greek Doctor's Diet	*Dr Fedon Alexander Lindberg*	£6.99
1-4050-9548-2 978-1-4050-9548-8	Beyond GI: Understanding Glycaemic Load	*Dr Fedon Alexander Lindberg*	£4.99
1-4050-9346-3 978-1-4050-9346-0	The Genesis Breast Cancer Prevention Diet	*Dr Michelle Harvie*	£9.99
1-4050-9338-2 978-1-4050-9338-5	Outsmart Diabetes	*Prevention*	£9.99
1-4050-9324-2 978-1-4050-9324-8	The Abs Diet Get Fit Stay Fit Plan	*David Zinczenko*	£12.99

All Rodale/Pan Macmillan titles can be ordered from the website, *www.panmacmillan.com*, or from your local bookshop and are also available by post from:

Bookpost, PO Box 29, Douglas, Isle of Man IM99 1BQ
Tel: 01624 677237; fax: 01624 670923; e-mail: *bookshop@enterprise.net*; or
visit: *www.bookpost.co.uk*. Credit cards accepted. Free postage and packing in the
United Kingdom

Prices shown above were correct at time of going to press.
Pan Macmillan reserve the right to show new retail prices on covers which may differ from
those previously advertised in the text or elsewhere.

For information about buying Rodale titles in **Australia**, contact Pan Macmillan Australia. Tel:
1300 135 113; fax: 1300 135 103; e-mail:
customer.service@macmillan.com.au; or visit: *www.panmacmillan.com.au*

For information about buying Rodale titles in **New Zealand**, contact Macmillan Publishers
New Zealand Limited. Tel: (09) 414 0356; fax: (09) 414 0352; e-mail:
lyn@macmillan.co.nz; or visit: *www.macmillan.co.nz*

For information about buying Rodale titles in **South Africa**, contact Pan Macmillan South
Africa. Tel: (011) 325 5220; fax: (011) 325 5225; e-mail:
marketing@panmacmillan.co.za